THE
KENNEDY MEN

THE
KENNEDY MEN:
THREE GENERATIONS OF
SEX, SCANDAL AND SECRETS

NELLIE BLY

KENSINGTON BOOKS

KENSINGTON BOOKS are published by

Kensington Publishing Corp.
850 Third Avenue
New York, NY 10022

Kensington and the K logo Reg. U.S. Pat. & TM Off.

Library of Congress Card Catalog Number: 95-081479
ISBN 1-57566-015-6

First Printing: March, 1996

Printed in the United States of America

For my father,
JOSEPH PAUL GALLICK

ACKNOWLEDGMENTS

The author owes an enormous debt to Janet Kronstadt for her invaluable research.

My gratitude is due Denise Little, Hilary Sales Lefferts and Stephanie Finnegan for their editorial attention, and to Amy Garvey for her unstinting assistance.

Thanks also to my publisher Walter Zacharius, who suggested a book about the Kennedys.

CONTENTS

Introduction

It was all very careless and confused. They were careless people. . . . They smashed up things and creatures and then retreated back into their money or their vast carelessness, or whatever it was that kept them together, and let other people clean up the mess they had made.

—F. Scott Fitzgerald,
The Great Gatsby

It all began with obsession. Joseph Patrick Kennedy wanted Rose Fitzgerald and he was willing to do anything to get her. He would wait six years for her father's approval. He would put up with Rose's religiosity and her old man's notoriety for as long as it took. As in so many other things he strived for, he refused to consider failure. But once he had her, he would lose interest and move on to new conquests, setting a pattern that still prevails among Kennedy men to this day.

Together Joe and Rose would raise nine children, born during a span of almost fifteen years. So great was the age difference between the older children, Rosemary, Joe, Jr., Kathleen and John, and the younger ones, Eunice, Patricia, Robert, Jean and Edward, that they form almost two separate generations, with Eunice on the cusp of both. The older generation was the golden one. Except for poor Rosemary, they were gifted with everything: good looks, charm and serious intelligence. They were achievers who benefited from their parents' time and attention. As the younger children grew up, they received less attention. Their parents were distracted by travel, business and the glorious debacle that was Joe's stint as U.S. Ambassador to the Court of St. James.

Joe and Rose shared a philosophy about child-rearing: Raise the oldest ones right and they'll take care of the younger ones. In Joe's master plan it was entirely possible that once he had installed his oldest son Joe, Jr., in the White House, the others—quiet, studious Jack, devoutly religious Bobby, and fatheaded baby brother Teddy—would follow. In Joe's rigorous training schools at Palm Beach and Hyannis Port, the boys learned they could trust only the family; winning was everything; and Kennedys were a special breed endowed by God and Joe Kennedy to someday rule America.

But the boys also learned something else: The rules of responsibility, fidelity and honesty did not apply to Kennedy men. Their confidence that they were above the ordinary rules of man bred in Joe's sons a pattern which would ultimately destroy them. The recklessness of the Kennedy men had many facets: a disregard for their own safety, a thirst for dangerous liaisons with unlikely women, and an unwillingness to delay their personal gratification, even when it could have life-threatening consequences. This quality still characterizes the Kennedy men, even into the third generation, and has already led to the fatal drug overdose of David Kennedy, the crippling of his young female friend and, of course, the Good Friday rape scandal in Palm Beach.

Joseph P. Kennedy, Jr.'s, family-bred love of the limelight and competitiveness with a younger brother who suddenly threatened to overshadow him sent the young naval commander on the wartime mission that killed him. John F. Kennedy's conviction that Kennedys were above consequences encouraged the President to maintain an Oval Office affair with the mistress of a Mafia capo, to encourage an invasion of Cuba, and even to disregard safety advice and ride in a topless limousine through downtown Dallas, making himself an easy target for his assassin.

It was similar recklessness that led Robert F. Kennedy into a disastrous affair with his brother's discarded mistress Marilyn Monroe. It also spurred him to follow his brother on the campaign trail, with fatal results.

And, of course, only an inherited sense of invincibility could have sent Senator Edward M. Kennedy on the wild ride off Chappaquiddick bridge that left a young woman dead under murky circumstances that have never been adequately explained.

This brings us to the second sad legacy of the founding father, and that is the family's conviction that media is a tool to be con-

trolled and manipulated. The Kennedy men can certainly be forgiven for this belief. Starting with Joe, Kennedys have had a special relationship with the press (which more than accommodated
Joe in building a dazzling public image for his family). Joe virtually owned the esteemed columnist Arthur Krock, his man at the
New York Times, and he managed simultaneously close friendships
with two very different press lords: Henry Luce and William Randolph Hearst.

Joe put all of this to good use to promote the public image of his
sons, beginning with Joe, Jr., and after his death, Jack. When Jack
was a U.S. senator, he grew particularly close to the brilliant
manic-depressive publisher of the *Washington Post,* Phil Graham,
even sharing women with him. But when that relationship started
to go wrong, and Graham wanted thanks for his help getting Jack
elected president, Jack turned his back on him. A furious Graham
exploded at a newspaperman's conference and started to tell the
crowd about the President's affair with the troubled ex-wife of a
CIA officer. Before the sun set that day, Graham was on his way
back to Washington in a straitjacket, never to return to his desk at
the *Post.* He would die from suicide less than a year later. No wonder other journalists gave the Kennedy brothers a free pass when
it came to philandering.

Unfortunately, this only encouraged the Kennedy spirit of invincibility. When Teddy's irresponsible actions led to the drowning death of a young woman, most of the press accepted his
version of the story, discrepancies and all. Their philosophy
seemed to be that since Teddy and his family had already suffered
so much, no one should question his behavior too closely.

Encouraged by this attitude, Teddy proceeded to revel in two
decades of womanizing, barroom escapades and drug-taking, all
the time protected by the press. It was therefore a great shock to
him when he interrupted his revel long enough to declare for the
presidency in 1980, only to be ambushed in an interview with
trusted journalist Roger Mudd, who had been chosen for the
honor of interviewing Teddy mainly because he was perceived as
one of the family's "pocket people." It turned out that Mudd was
not in the Kennedy pocket after all. Poor Teddy was exposed to
the world as a bumbling, incoherent fellow who was less than
forthright about topics like his unconventional marriage and the
events at Chappaquiddick.

This interview signaled a turning point for the Kennedys. The world had changed and the Kennedy men had failed to change with it. A new generation of women was uncomfortable with the conflict between Teddy's public position on women's rights and his notorious private behavior. His friends in the media had always assured Teddy that the presidency was his for the asking, but when he actually put his name on primary ballots, he discovered that the American voter was no pushover for family legend. He failed to win a single primary and slouched to the 1980 convention a figure of defeat, beloved but not electable.

The Senator has made it clear in years since that he will not run for president again, but he has left a clear field for Kennedy men of the next generation: his sons, Ted, Jr., and Patrick, a congressman from Rhode Island; his nephews, Joe II, a congressman from Massachusetts, and Robert, Jr., an environmental activist; Mark Kennedy Shriver, a recently elected member of the Maryland House of Delegates; and of course John F. Kennedy, Jr. At least one Kennedy daughter, Kathleen Kennedy Townsend, Bobby's oldest child, has demonstrated political ambitions and was elected lieutenant governor of Maryland in 1994. But in spite of the fact that she had a far more illustrious private and public record than any of the men of her generation, she got there with virtually no support from her family. During that election they were all up in Massachusetts, helping Uncle Ted in a squeaker.

Unfortunately, the message has still not gotten through to the Kennedy men. The scandals, arrests and tragedies compiled by the third generation of Kennedys may be the worst yet. Yet, when the Good Friday rape story broke in 1991, much of the media fell into line; accepting the Kennedy version; ignoring the senator's lying, disingenuous responses to police investigating the woman's charges; even feeding pro-Kennedy stories to a complacent *New York Times*. In spite of all the efforts of the mighty Team Kennedy however, the case stirred up something deeply disturbing that could no longer be ignored.

With the 1994 death of Jacqueline Kennedy Onassis, perhaps the only woman who survived the Kennedy experience and went on to make a rewarding life on her own terms, and the 1995 death of matriarch Rose Fitzgerald Kennedy, it seems that a chapter in our nation's history has come to a close. The Palm Beach mansion, full of the ghosts of three generations of dynastic dreams, has been sold and will be turned into a museum. Today the family is scattered and seldom comes together except for weddings and funerals and, of course, political campaigns.

Yet the name Kennedy is still magic. It is still closely tied with fifty years of our country's history. The family has moved into American legend.

But how much of that legend is true?

Let's take a look at the record. . . .

PART ONE

AN AMERICAN GOTHIC

Where else but in Gothic fiction, where else among real people, could one encounter such triumphs and tragedies, such beauty and charm and ambition and pride and human wreckage, such dedication to the best and lapses into the mire of life; such vulgar, noble, driven, generous, self-centered, loving, suspicious, devious, honorable, vulnerable, indomitable people. . . . No wonder the American public, their audience—for that matter much of the world—has been fascinated by them.

—Clare Boothe Luce

CHAPTER ONE
THE MARRIAGE OF
JOE AND ROSE

The Kennedy family myth about JFK is that he was this kind of glorious person produced by this wonderful set of parents whose whole purpose was to bring up clean-living, honest children dedicated to public service. That is baloney. The Kennedy household was an emotional wasteland.

—Nigel Hamilton

Joseph P. Kennedy, the self-described "youngest banker in America," and Rose Elizabeth Fitzgerald could not have known what lay ahead as they stood in the private chapel of William Cardinal O'Connell on October 7, 1914, and said their marriage vows. All they knew was that they were young and in love, and shared the promise of a golden future.

It was a low-key, modest ceremony because Rose's father, John F. Fitzgerald, the recently retired mayor of Boston, was under a cloud of scandal. In the years to come, Joe and Rose would found a dynasty that would change the course of American history, but they would also create an almost century-long epic marked by more tragedy and violence than a Greek play.

Joe's father, Patrick Joseph, known as P.J., was an East Boston saloonkeeper and ward boss. By 1900 the sons of the once-despised Irish Catholic immigrants had come to dominate the city's politics. P.J. was a master at behind the scenes deal making, dispensing patronage, arbitrating feuds. And he taught his son Joe everything he knew.

Born in Boston on September 6, 1888, while P.J. was serving in the Massachusetts House of Representatives, one of Joe's earliest memories was the day that two of his father's constituents arrived at the Kennedy house with the good news that each had cast 128 votes that day.

With an eye to the future, P.J. and his wife, the former Mary Hickey, removed thirteen-year-old Joe from the East Boston Catholic school system and placed him in Boston Latin School. From then on, Joe's education would be strictly secular and first class.

Boston Latin was one of the finest schools in the country. Its alumni included Cotton Mather, Benjamin Franklin and John Quincy Adams, and it was also a bastion of the Protestant establishment, the Boston Brahmins.

When it was time for college, Harvard was the obvious choice. One of Mary Hickey's brothers had already gone to Harvard Medical School. At Harvard, Joe, handsome, red-haired and athletic, participated in sports and an active social life, but was ignored by the prestigious clubs, Porcellian, A.D. and Fly. (His later ally Franklin D. Roosevelt didn't make Porcellian, either.) Joe was chosen for Hasty Pudding, a significant accomplishment for a Boston Irish Catholic at that time. He graduated with the class of 1912.

The classic story told about Joe at Harvard concerns a baseball game. Joe was determined to win his letter in baseball his senior year, but he had not been permitted to play in a single game, having been beaten out at first base by Charles McLaughlin. During the ninth inning of the final game of the season, against Yale, with Harvard leading four to one, "Chick" McLaughlin, who was now pitcher and captain of the team, suddenly asked his coach to put Kennedy in for the final play, thus assuring Joe of the varsity letter he coveted.

Tradition dictated that McLaughlin, as captain, should get the winning ball, but Joe refused to hand it over.

Long after the game, when McLaughlin was asked why he ever put Joe Kennedy in for the final play, he confessed that a few days before the game, some of P.J. Kennedy's wardheelers had spoken privately to him. They were aware that Chick wanted to apply for a city license to operate a movie theater after he graduated from

Harvard. Either he played ball by putting Joe in the game, or he would be out of the theatre business before he began.

And the message that stayed with Joe was that anyone and anything can be bought, even a Harvard letter. It was the beginning of sportsmanship, Kennedy style.

Rose Elizabeth Fitzgerald was born in Boston on July 22, 1890, the first of six children, three of them girls.

Rose's mother, the former Josephine Hannon, shunned the limelight, and Rose, as outgoing and vivacious as Honey Fitz, became her father's companion. Together, Rose and her father toured Europe, traveled to Washington and Palm Beach, and Rose threw out the first ball at Fenway Park. When Rose, at fifteen, graduated second in her class from Dorchester High School—and was presented with her diploma by her father the mayor—it was front-page news in Boston.

Rose's lavish coming-out party was attended by more than 450 guests including the governor of Massachusetts, but she was ignored by the elite WASP women's clubs. Resilient Rose founded her own, the Ace of Clubs, limited to young women like herself who had studied abroad and spoke fluent French.

The great disappointment of Rose's young life was that she was not allowed to attend Wellesley College, where she had been accepted. At the last minute her father, influenced by the cardinal and concerned with his Irish Catholic power base, rejected her choice of a secular college and insisted she attend a convent school. Although not given to bitterness, she would return to that disappointment again and again in later years. Yet, strangely, she did not encourage any of her daughters to pursue a secular education and sent them to the same Sacred Heart convent schools she had attended.

Joe and Rose knew each other well, having spent summers since Rose was five years old in Old Orchard Beach, Maine, the crowded beach community favored by prosperous Boston Irish Catholics. Their romance began in earnest the summer of 1906. Full of confidence and ambition, Joe had, according to Rose, "the most wonderful smile that seemed to light up his entire face from within and made an instant impression on everyone he met."

Rose discovered that she and Joe shared an ambition to live life to its fullest. Together they dismissed the commonplace. Each had grown up the favored child of the family. Indulged, encouraged, nurtured, they had known only appreciation and success and they had every reason to expect to conquer the world.

They both valued family. Her father, Honey Fitz, relied so much on his six brothers, most of whom visited him at City Hall daily, that the Fitzgeralds were dubbed "the royal family" and "the Fitzgerald dynasty." Responding to charges of nepotism, Honey Fitz said, "If I were to be without their assistance tomorrow, I would not think of running for public office ever again."

After Joe graduated from Harvard, P.J. arranged a job for him as a state bank examiner, and for the next year and a half Joe traveled eastern Massachusetts reviewing bank records. When Columbia Trust, in which P.J. had a substantial interest, was threatened with a hostile takeover, young Joe managed to rally enough support and hard cash to save it. He then informed the directors, including P.J., that he wanted to be president of the bank. They proceeded to vote him in, and at twenty-six he could claim to be the youngest bank president in the country. Actually, it was more accurate to call him the youngest bank president in Massachusetts, but that phrase was not as impressive.

On Joe and Rose's wedding day only the immediate families of the bride and groom were present. The early-morning nuptial mass was followed by a wedding breakfast for seventy-five guests at the Fitzgerald mansion.

After the reception the couple left for a two-week honeymoon at the Greenbrier in White Sulphur Springs, West Virginia.

On their return young Mr. and Mrs. Joseph P. Kennedy would set up house in a modest nine-room wood-frame house at 83 Beals Street in the wealthy suburb of Brookline. Rose played her piano, a wedding gift from her Fitzgerald uncles, while Joe set out to make his fortune with a brilliant and imaginative combination of stock speculation, mortgage foreclosure and war profiteering.

For Joe and Rose, a key element in the master plan was the press. When Rose gave birth to their first child, Joseph P. Kennedy, Jr., on July 25, 1915, Honey Fitz immediately telephoned the *Boston Post* with the news. "I'm sure he's going to make a good man on the platform one day," Honey Fitz announced. "Is he going into politics? Well, of course, he is going to be president of the United States."

By the time their second son, John Fitzgerald Kennedy, arrived on May 29, 1917, the United States was in the middle of the First World War. While many of Joe's contemporaries enlisted in the so-called "war to end wars," Joe set about turning this global tragedy to his advantage.

Joe was hired by Charles Schwab, head of Bethlehem Steel Corporation and a friend of Honey Fitz, to work at the Fore River Shipyard in Quincy, Massachusetts, where ships were being built for the Navy. Joe immediately clashed with the labor unions, and the resulting strike paralyzed the yard. It took Franklin Delano Roosevelt, assistant secretary of the Navy, to smooth out the situation, and Joe was demoted and relieved of supervisory duties until the end of the war, when he returned to private enterprise.

The transition from debutante to suburban matron was difficult for Rose. For a while things looked up when Honey Fitz considered making a comeback. Fitz, full of confidence, was unaware that the city, and especially political circles, were abuzz with talk of his latest protégée, a blond cigarette girl known as "Toodles" Ryan. He made it clear that he planned to challenge the incumbent, his longtime rival, James Michael Curley. But suddenly Curley made an announcement:

"I am preparing three addresses which, if necessary, I shall deliver in the fall, and which, if a certain individual had the right to restrict free speech, I would not be permitted to deliver.

"One of the addresses is entitled: 'Graft, Ancient and Modern,' another: 'Great Lovers from Cleopatra to Toodles,' and last, but not least interesting, 'Libertines, from Henry VIII to the Present Day.' "

Taking the hint, Honey Fitz announced the next day that he would not be a candidate for mayor after all.

Gone was the glory of life as the mayor's daughter. And the joy of a bride was soon gone, too, as Rose discovered she was married to a money-mad workaholic, who was away from home for months at a time.

But she still had her children and the only thing she ever really shared with Joe: her dream of a dynasty.

ROSE: "THE KENNEDYS ARE A SELF-CONTAINED UNIT."

"Years ago, we decided that our children were going to be our best friends and that we never could see too much of them," she told an interviewer in the late thirties. "Since we couldn't do both, it was better to bring up our family than go out to dinners. The Kennedys are a self-contained unit. If any of us wants to sail or play golf or go walking or just talk, there's always a Kennedy eager to join in." It was this tight-knit closeness that would be the political strength of the Kennedy men. Ultimately, it would also be their undoing.

On September 13, 1918, Rose gave birth to her first daughter, Rose Marie, who would always be known as Rosemary and who would become the most troubled and tragic of the Kennedys.

In years to come, Rose Kennedy would be held up as an example of a devoted, selfless mother buoyed by her profound religious faith. The truth is that Rose suffered all the exhaustion, depression and conflicts of any mother, especially one who bore a child almost every eighteen months for seventeen years, and got little emotional support from her husband. Even with a household staff and a generous budget, the loneliness, responsibilities of motherhood and social obscurity were finally too much for Rose. In January 1920, eight-months pregnant with her fourth child, she packed her bags and moved in with her parents, leaving her three young children behind with Joe and the servants.

The catalyst for Rose's daring move was Joe's philandering. Almost from the beginning of the marriage, Joe had romanced other women, mostly glamorous chorus girls, not unlike his father-in-law's onetime favorite Toodles Ryan. Among his conquests was the beautiful blond star of silent films, Betty Compson, whom he wooed with diamonds and furs on his frequent trips to New York.

Rose found little welcome in her old home. Honey Fitz pressured his daughter to resume her duties. And after three weeks, informed that two-and-a-half-year-old Jack was ill with scarlet fever, Rose reluctantly returned to Beals Street in time to give birth to a second daughter, Kathleen, on February 20.

Materially, Rose wanted for nothing. Just before her fifth child, Eunice, was born on July 10, 1921, the family moved to a larger house at 131 Naples in Brookline. Because of Joe's increasingly risky activities, the house was put in Rose's name.

Rose's theory of child-rearing was simple: "I always felt that if the older children are brought up right, the younger ones will follow their lead."

As the first son, Joe, Jr., took precedence. Rose explained: "It was easy for all of the children to look up to Joe, Jr., because he was a good scholar, a good athlete, and popular with girls as well as men in every neighborhood where we lived."

Rose chose to ignore young Joe's bullying, immortalized in a 1921 family photo posing young Joe, Jr., and Jack together, where it is clear that Joe, Jr., is squeezing Jack's hand so hard Jack is grimacing.

In Brookline in the early 1920s Joe was considered a hell-raiser, the kind of boy who "couldn't pass a hat without squashing it or leave an unprotected shin unkicked. He was cracked on the head by the Sisters with a catechism book so often, it was a wonder the top of his head wasn't flatter than a pancake."

According to psychohistorian Nancy Gager Clinch, author of The Kennedy Neurosis: "Joe's constant attempts to dominate his younger brother and his apparently insatiable need for stardom strongly suggest a deep-seated ego lack, a need for public reaffirmation, identity and aplause. Such a probable lack is not hard to understand in view of the constant parental pressures, the ceaseless criticism (although tempered with praise), and the example of a father who established that ruthless activity is the sure route to success."

Eunice recalled her big brother: ". . . he was very good, but he had quite a strong temper and would be cross as a billy goat and would blame somebody else when he didn't win."

FRANK COSTELLO: "I HELPED JOE KENNEDY GET RICH!"

At thirty-one Joe went to work for Galen Stone of Hayden, Stone. Here he was exposed to the inside information that informed his stock market speculation and established him as a plunger. Joe made his real money in ethically questionable stock pools, inflating cheap stocks through rumors and erratic but well publicized buying and selling. The "action" was calculated to impress naive investors. When the price of the stock was inflated sufficiently, the pool would sell short for huge profits. The humble investor would be left holding the bag when the stocks went down.

The cash that fueled Joe's speculating came from bootlegging. The Eighteenth Amendment—prohibition—had passed in 1919 and since then Joe had been actively involved in illegally importing liquor. He formed alliances with crime bosses in major markets, among them Boston, New York, Chicago and New Orleans. These would come in handy years later when his son was running for national office. Among his mob associates was Frank Costello, former boss of the Luciano crime family, who bragged, "I helped Joe Kennedy get rich." Sam Giancana, who would later figure prominently in Jack's presidency, called Joe "one of the biggest crooks who ever lived."

The bootlegging business called for guts and nerves of steel, which Joe had in spades. But his hot temper brought him into a nearly fatal scrape with Detroit's Purple Gang. Joe had moved bootleg rum through their territory without their permission. Fearing for his life, Joe had to turn to Diamond Joe Esposito of Chicago to intervene.

Joe's access to bootleg whiskey made him a popular guy in other circles, too. It was Joe who supplied all the liquor for his Harvard class's tenth reunion in 1922. "It came ashore the way the pilgrims did," one classmate recalled.

In spite of her burgeoning family, Rose refused to be tied down and continued to travel widely, sometimes to the distress of the children. Perhaps it was a way of striking back at Joe for his own frequent absences from the hearth. One famous episode demonstrating Rose's wanderlust occurred right after Easter Sunday, 1923, as Rose prepared to leave with her sister Agnes for a three-week trip to California. It was Jack who protested: "Gee, you're a great mother to go away and leave your children alone." But Rose left anyway.

Jack, the more sensitive of her two older sons, later told his roommate Lem Billings that he cried every time she packed her bags, until he realized it did no good. "Better to take it in stride," he concluded.

In 1923, at thirty-five, while still maintaining his affiliation with Hayden, Stone, Joe set up his own office as "Joseph P. Kennedy, Banker." By the mid-1920s, he had built a fortune estimated at two million dollars.

As a businessman and investor, Joe liked to bet on sure things. He bought and sold stock as an insider, profiting from friendships and knowledge to plunge into Wall Street pools and manipulate such stocks as Chicago Yellow Cab and Libbey-Owens-Ford Glass.

Joe also took steps to properly educate his two oldest sons. It was one of the few areas in which he seriously disagreed with Rose. His own people had embraced the mainstream, sending him to the nonsectarian Boston Latin, while Rose's remained almost tribal in their attachment to their Irish Catholic roots. Joe once exploded when a Boston paper referred to him as Irish-American. "How long do you have to live in this country before you become an American? We've been here for two generations. Isn't that enough?"

Joe let Rose send the girls to convent schools, but he insisted that Joe, Jr., and Jack join the mainstream, which to him meant the Protestant establishment. In the fall of 1924 he enrolled his two oldest sons in the prestigious Dexter School, where they were the only two Catholics.

Joe was much less involved with the girls. When Rose gave birth to their fourth daughter, Patricia, on May 6, 1924, in Boston, Joe was miles away in a suite at the Waldorf-Astoria Hotel in New York, where he was attempting a takeover of the Yellow Cab company. "I woke up one morning exhausted, and I realized that I hadn't been out of that hotel room in seven weeks," he recalled. "My baby, Pat, had been born and was almost a month old, and I hadn't even seen her."

By the time Joe's third son, Robert Francis, was born on November 20, 1925, in Brookline, Joe was making plans to move his entire family from Boston to New York.

CHAPTER TWO
JOE HEADS FOR
HOLLYWOOD—ALONE

The Kennedy men were never celebrated for faithfulness to their wives, but their wives found it worthwhile to continue as wives and mothers.

—Pearl Buck

After making his fortune on and off Wall Street, Joe was one of the first Eastern businessmen to grasp the potential of the movie business. In February 1926 he acquired the Film Booking Offices of America (FBO), sight unseen, from its British owners. The small movie company specialized in melodramas and low-budget Westerns featuring stars like Evelyn Brent and Strongheart the Dog. FBO was barely in the same business as MGM, Paramount and Fox. But the industry was about to undergo major changes. The following year, the Warner Brothers would rock the world when they released *The Jazz Singer*, and in the fallout Joe Kennedy would end up controlling the destiny of a filmdom superstar.

At the same time that he plunged into movies, Joe took steps to protect his fortune and the future of his children. He moved to establish the first of a series of trust funds that would eventually make all his children financially independent.

Joe arranged that each of his seven children (Jean and Teddy were not yet born) would begin receiving an income from a trust fund at age twenty-one. At age forty-five, one half of the principal of the trust fund would be divided equally among all his surviving children. As Joe's wealth grew, significant additions to the fund would be made, and in 1936 and 1949 additional funds would be created. These trust funds would eventually guarantee each of his eight surviving children, and their mother, over twenty million dollars apiece. Joe encouraged the idea that he did this to make his children independent, but Jack himself dismissed this. "He was speculating," he said. "It was a very risky business. He was speculating pretty hard and his health was not good at the time, and that was the reason he did it. There was no other reason for it."

In 1927 Joe moved his family out of Boston. On September 15 they traveled by private railroad car to a thirteen-room mansion on five wooded acres in Riverdale, New York, overlooking the Hudson River. Joe claimed that he moved his brood because his daughters would never be invited to join the exclusive clubs in Boston. It was also a fact that more and more of his work was centered in New York.

JOE TEACHES HIS SONS HOW TO ENTERTAIN YOUR MISTRESS IN THE BOSOM OF YOUR FAMILY

While Joe was building his fortune, he also found time to play, contracting a soon-to-be notorious liaison with the superstar Gloria Swanson.

They met for the first time in the Renaissance Room of the Savoy Plaza Hotel on Fifth Avenue and Fifty-ninth Street on November 11, 1927. The meeting had been set up by First National's Robert Kane. Swanson had turned down a million-dollar salary with Famous-Players-Lasky to set up her own producing company under the banner of United Artists. Now she was in serious financial trouble. Kane believed that with proper handling, and by concentrating on her art, not business, she could still be a superstar.

With her glamour, international fame, financial independence and three previous marriages, Gloria Swanson was unlike any other woman Joe had ever met. She was still married to her third husband, Henri de la Falaise de la Coudraye, a French marquis, and she certainly enjoyed being the Marquise de la Falaise. But at this point, through high spending, bad business decisions and clashes with studio heads, Gloria Swanson was almost broke. The attraction between Joe and Gloria was immediate and each realized the potential of the other. But they did not get together professionally or physically at this point.

Joe left to join his family for Christmas in Riverdale, while Gloria and the Marquis headed west for California. Immediately after the holidays, he was on the phone inviting them to join him in Palm Beach. Swanson, the marquis and her seventeen pieces of luggage arrived by train, and Gloria knew immediately that she and Joe were going to become lovers soon.

A day later, they were consummating the affair in the Royal Poinciana Hotel while Joe's right-hand man, Eddie Moore, took the star's husband deep-sea fishing.

In her memoir Swanson recalled the magic moment when Joe arrived at her hotel and stood in her doorway, staring at her for more than a minute before he entered the hotel room and closed the door.

"He moved so quickly," Swanson recalled, "that his mouth was on mine before either of us could speak. With one hand he held the back of my head, with the other he stroked my body and pulled at my kimono. He kept insisting in a drawn-out moan, 'No longer, no longer. Now.' He was like a roped horse, rough, arduous, racing to be free. After a hasty climax he lay beside me, stroking my hair. Apart from his guilty, passionate mutterings, he had still said nothing cogent."

Swanson was by no means Joe's first extramarital adventure, but she was his first real affair. She was the perfect trophy to symbolize the great worldly success he had achieved.

Rose, pregnant with their eighth child, had returned to Boston to be treated by her regular obstetrician. On February 20, 1928, she gave birth to a fifth daughter, Jean Ann. Joe, too busy to visit, sent her a beautiful diamond bracelet. Swanson sent a telegram of congratulations and flowers. Rose spent a month resting in Boston while the faithful Eddie Moore and his wife, Mary, looked after the other children in Riverdale.

That March, Swanson and Joe met with director Erich von Stroheim about the possibility of the three of them working together. Stroheim was an acknowledged genius. He was also a spendthrift, egotist and megalomaniac. Joe was convinced he could handle him. After extensive negotiations contracts were signed that May for the project to be called *Queen Kelly*.

Set in Europe in the days before World War I, *Queen Kelly* is the story of a German kingdom, a mad queen, a dashing prince and an innocent convent girl.

Filming of the European sequences began at the FBO studios in Hollywood in the first week of November. A farsighted Joe managed to get Stroheim to introduce sound into some of the picture. According to the director, Joe told him "Von, the lousiest sound film will be better than the best silent film."

Although Joe was meeting success on the New York stock exchange and Hollywood soundstages and boudoirs, he was still shut out of the Protestant establishment, which was the only bastion of power that meant anything to him. In 1928 he was deeply disappointed when he was not elected to Harvard's Board of Overseers. Friends pointed out that the voters were mainly older alumni, while he was a relatively recent graduate from the class of 1912, but to Joe it was just another example of the Brahmin prejudice that had kept him out of the best clubs when he was a mere commuting student. They were happy to drink his bootleg whiskey at his class reunion, but they still considered him an outsider.

Rose, too, felt the sting of this kind of exclusion. A few years later, when Jack was at Harvard, she asked a friend of his, a member of the Brahmin class, "Tell me, when are the nice people of Boston going to accept us?"

In the fall of 1929 Joe sent Joe, Jr., to Choate, one of the finest prep schools in the country. He was immediately nicknamed "Rat Face," and subjected to the same kind of hazing and bullying by upperclassmen that he doled out to his younger siblings at home. But he survived and adjusted, and by senior year he won the school's Harvard Trophy, awarded to the graduate who best combined scholarship and sportsmanship.

The same year, Joe acquired the fifteen-room, nine-bathroom Hyannis Port house that they had rented on Nantucket Sound for the last three summers and immediately had a screening room installed.

At Hyannis Port the children became known as strong competitors who stuck together. "No matter what anyone else had done, the Kennedy children always praised each other's accomplishments to the skies. While it was amusing and touching for a time, it got to be rather tiresome after a while," one companion recalled. They were particularly poor sports and graceless losers. "There would be hell to pay if they didn't win every race," another witness recalled.

Sometimes corners were cut to win. The discovery that Joe, Jr., once used a mainsail larger than allowed by class regulations in a race did not endear them to neighbors.

As Joe spent months at a time in Hollywood, Rose must have come to feel like a minor colonial official, stationed in a deadend post of the Empire, with no one to talk to but ungrateful subordinates and unruly natives.

By spring, production on *Queen Kelly* was shut down and Joe reluctantly fired Stroheim. The energy seemed to go out of the project. Joe decided to cut his losses and killed the production entirely. Years later, a patched-together version of *Queen Kelly* would be released in Europe and South America, but Stroheim was able to prevent its release in the United States.

As the romance between Joe and Gloria heated up, the star and her daughter visited the Kennedy family at Hyannis Port that summer.

Joe took this opportunity to demonstrate to his sons how it was possible to fully entertain your mistress in the presence of your wife and children. Such lessons did not always come easy, but this was, after all, a man who laid out pornographic magazines on Jack's bed when he was fourteen.

One afternoon Joe took Gloria sailing on the *Rose Elizabeth*. They were supposed to be alone, to discuss important movie business, but young Jack, then twelve years old and perhaps also curious about the movie business, sneaked up and surprised them. Whatever he saw so shocked him that he leaped overboard and his father had to rescue him.

Afterward Joe briefed his son in what to say on their return to shore. The next day Gloria Swanson left Hyannis Port.

The lesson was learned. "A father's sexual ethics can exert a powerful influence on his son's attitude toward women," says John E. Schowalter, a professor of child psychiatry at the Yale Child Study Center in New Haven. "While in some instances a son will react to his father's philandering by vowing never to subject his own wife to the indignities that his mother has suffered, in many cases, sons of blatantly womanizing fathers use their parents as role models.

"Watching their fathers, seeing what they do, sets the stage for their own actions. Simply put, they feel, 'If Dad does it, it must be all right because he wouldn't do anything that was wrong.' "

This was a lesson that all the Kennedy men would take to heart.

Back in Hollywood, Joe hired Edmund Goulding to direct Gloria in her first talkie, in which she played a poor working girl, *The Trespasser.*

Filled with enthusiasm for the completed picture, Joe decided that he and Rose would accompany Gloria to *The Trespasser's* European premieres in Paris and London. Joe booked passage on the *Île de France.*

In her memoir Swanson claimed that she and her friend Virginia sailed with Joe and Rose to Europe. But historian Doris Kearns Goodwin has discovered that this notorious ocean trip never happened. Swanson describes it in detail in her memoir, but according to Goodwin, records reveal that when the Kennedys left New York on August 20, 1929, Gloria and Virginia had already departed, ten days earlier, on a different ship, the *Olympic.* They did all return together and Swanson may have needed their support, for in Paris, through the accidental misdirection of a letter, she had discovered that her cuckolded husband was in fact having an affair of his own, with her rival star, Constance Bennett. Naturally, Swanson was devastated.

Despite her grief, Gloria took the time to introduce Rose to Lucien Lelong, a leading couturier. This marked the beginning of an interest in clothes that would eventually find Rose a place on the best-dressed lists.

It was only after they all returned to the States that there was any hint that Rose understood what was going on between Gloria Swanson and her husband.

According to Swanson, Cardinal O'Connell of Boston called on her in New York, that October, making it clear that Joe would not divorce the mother of his eight children. But divorce was never what Joe had in mind. He merely sought to live apart from Rose and pursue his own life, much like his friend, the press lord William Randolph Hearst. The cardinal explained to Swanson that such a thing was impossible. Here, too, historian Goodwin is skeptical. There is no evidence that Boston's cardinal was even in New York at this time.

For years to follow, rumors circulated that Joe had fathered Gloria's son Joseph P. While it made for a juicy story, the fact is that Swanson adopted her son as an infant in 1922, and named him for her father, years before she met Joe.

In fact, after ending his affair with Swanson, Joe renewed his commitment to Rose and the family, moving them to a twenty-room, $250,000 brick Georgian mansion on nearly six acres of landscaped grounds in Bronxville.

By the fall of 1929, Joe's romance with Gloria Swanson was fast fading. They would make one more movie together, *What a Widow*. He would have other romances, most notably with star Constance Bennett, who was under contract to him at Pathe Studios, and Nancy Carroll, but he was losing interest in Hollywood. He began to liquidate his holdings and made plans to get out of the stock market.

Gloria was left with a pile of debts from *Queen Kelly* and no husband. She eventually learned that her dressing room had been wired so that Joe could monitor her activities, that he had charged the fur coat to *her* account, and even charged her for her bungalow on the set.

HOW JOE FRAMED AN INNOCENT MAN

Hollywood was also the scene of one of the darkest episodes in Joe's career: his role in the Pantages scandal, which was brilliantly recounted by the distinguished director and Hollywood historian Kenneth Anger in his book, *Hollywood Babylon II*. Alexander Pantages was a Greek immigrant who had made millions from a chain of theaters on the West Coast.

It was in Pantages's flagship theater, the Beaux Arts in downtown Los Angeles, on August 9, that an hysterical lady in red emerged from the janitor's broom closet on the mezzanine. Her screams could be heard above the musical score of the feature film.

Collapsing in the arms of a theater employee, she screamed: "There he is, the Beast! The Great God Pan! Don't let him get at me!" She pointed to silver-haired Alexander Pantages in the office next to the broom closet. Pantages insisted he was being framed.

The girl, Eunice Pringle of Garden Grove, California, told police that she had come to Pantages looking for work as a dancer. Instead of offering her a job, he pushed her into the broom closet, wrenched her underwear loose and raped her.

Pantages insisted the young woman had torn and ripped her own clothing.

Poor Pantages was convicted and sentenced to fifty years, but the verdict was overturned on appeal, on the basis that it was prejudicial to Pantages to exclude testimony about the morals of the plaintiff. The court found her testimony "so improbable as to challenge credulity."

Highlights of Pantages's second trial included his lawyer, the famed Jerry Geisler, reenacting the alleged rape with an associate to prove that it could not have happened in the broom closet.

According to Kenneth Anger, Eunice Pringle confessed on her deathbed that Joe Kennedy had masterminded the whole thing, framing Pantages so that he could take over the Pantages theater circuit.

In the end Joe would be remembered in Hollywood for three things: his affair with Gloria Swanson; his acquisitions of FBO and, later, the Keith-Albee-Orpheum theatre chain and their subsequent consolidation into RCA to create the giant Radio-Keith-Orpheum (RKO) holding company; and his anti-Semitism, which would become a greater problem in years to come.

His Hollywood experience soured Joe on the entertainment business. More seriously, the stock market crash that fall shattered the faith of many Americans in their economy and their system of government.

Kennedy could see that America needed a savior, and like millions of Americans he found that savior in Franklin D. Roosevelt.

CHAPTER THREE
JOE FINDS A HERO
IN FRANKLIN D. ROOSEVELT

I'll take any job you want me to and even work for nothing at it so long as it's interesting. I never want to be bored.

—Joseph P. Kennedy to Franklin Delano Roosevelt, 1936

By 1930 Joe was at the peak of his health, handsome, copper-haired, with plenty to smile about. He had seen the Depression coming, and weeks before the stock market crash of 1929 he had taken himself out of the game, and he was now estimated to be worth $100 million. Ever restless, endlessly ambitious, he was ready for new challenges. That year, Henry Morgenthau, Jr., took him to Albany to meet Governor Franklin Delano Roosevelt who had the patrician bloodlines and deft political touch that Joe yearned for. He decided to place his bets on Roosevelt the way he'd been placing his bets on stocks.

"I wanted him in the White House for my own security and the security of our kids," he later said of FDR, "and I was willing to do anything to help elect him."

Joe and Roosevelt had first crossed paths during the war when Joe was assistant manager of the Bethlehem Steel Fore River Ship-yard at Quincy and Roosevelt was assistant secretary of the Navy. Kennedy was immediately impressed and remained so. When FDR declared that he would run for president, Kennedy threw himself into the campaign.

Jack joined his brother Joe at Choate in the fall of 1931 after a difficult year at Canterbury Prep, a Catholic school in Rhode Island, from which illness had forced him to withdraw before the end of the term.

As a sophomore, going out for the Choate yearbook, he met Kirk Le Moyne Billings, a big, unkempt blond boy, and would form, according to Billings, "the closest friendship either of us ever knew." Lem Billings was descended from *Mayflower* aristocrats and his early life had been privileged until his wealthy father lost everything in the 1929 crash. Billings, Sr., a Pittsburgh physician, had died shortly before Lem met Jack, and he was attending Choate on a scholarship.

"I was immediately captivated by Jack," Lem recalled. "He had the best sense of humor of anybody I had ever met and in his company I had more fun than I had ever had in my whole life. No matter where we went he knew how to make the outing a special occasion: If we were at a show together, he'd somehow manage to sneak backstage to see the leading singer; if we were eating out, he'd be so charming to the waitress that we'd end up with an extra dessert. He enjoyed things with such intensity that he made you feel that whatever you were doing was absolutely the most wonderful thing you could possibly be doing."

At seventeen Lem and Jack even lost their virginity together, traveling to Harlem in full evening dress one night so that they could share the same prostitute. The woman charged each of them three dollars. It was part of the Kennedy tradition of sharing women.

Since his affair with Swanson, Joe had returned to Rose in every sense of the word, and on February 22, 1932, she gave birth to her ninth and final child. Young Jack, who asked to be the baby's godfather, wanted to name him George Washington Kennedy. But he was overruled and the baby was christened Edward Moore Kennedy, for Joe's faithful right-hand man. The family the future Senator Teddy was born into was very different from that in which Joe, Jr., and Jack had spent their formative years. The older children were off most of the time at boarding school, Rose was traveling and Joe was more and more involved in the world of presidential politics.

Rose, burdened with supervising nine children and acting as

chatelaine for her hyperactive husband, coped with a kind of awesome self-absorption later expressed in her autobiography. She attempted to run her family like a business, as conscientious as any employee of her husband's. And when it got to be too much for her, she would take a trip. Between 1929 and 1937, while most of the United States was mired in the Great Depression, Rose traveled to Europe seventeen times. When in New York City, which was more and more their real home base, Joe stayed at his personal suite at the Waldorf-Astoria while Rose kept a large apartment of her own at the Plaza.

The children recognized that their parents led separate lives. Barbara Gibson, Rose's last secretary, recalls being in the swimming pool with Rose and Jean Kennedy Smith when Jean commented, "You were the first promoter of women's lib, Mother. You stayed in one hotel and Daddy was in another." She explained to Gibson: "My friends at school were always amazed at how my parents didn't live in the same apartment in New York."

By 1932 Joe was part of FDR's inner circle. At the Democratic convention that year, he demonstrated his usefulness by convincing William Randolph Hearst to throw the California delegation's votes to Roosevelt, thereby breaking a deadlock and assuring FDR the nomination.

Joe also gave Roosevelt $25,000 and lent the Democratic National Committee another $50,000, efforts that won him a position on the campaign finance committee. Soon he was traveling in a private railroad car along with other key FDR aides.

After the election, however, Joe waited in vain for an appointment, the way he had waited to be chosen for one of the important clubs at Harvard. Not until Joe threatened to call in all his loans to the Democratic party did Roosevelt even invite him to the White House. Joe came away from that meeting committed to biding his time and remaining on the sidelines.

MAYBE JIMMY ROOSEVELT THOUGHT HE AND JOE WERE GOING TO BE PARTNERS—BUT HE FOUND OUT JOE DOESN'T HAVE PARTNERS

And if Joe didn't have his presidential appointment, he at least had access, and it never hurt to remind people of that fact. With that in mind, in September 1933, Joe invited the President's son, James Roosevelt, and his wife, Betsy, to join himself and Rose on a trip to England. The states had begun repealing prohibition, and with his usual foresight, Joe could see that it was only a matter of time before the Eighteenth Amendment was repealed and liquor flowed freely again.

Joe used young Roosevelt to get access to those who controlled Scotland's distilleries. Returning with distribution rights to brands such as Haig & Haig, and Dewar's scotch, and Gordon's gin, Joe proceeded to build Somerset Importers into a force in the liquor business.

If Jimmy Roosevelt had expected to be rewarded with a part of the business, he was disappointed. "Maybe Jimmy thought he and Joe were going to be partners," said a friend of both men. "If so, he soon found out that when Joe Kennedy is starting a business he doesn't have partners."

On December 5 the noble experiment was repealed and the forward-thinking Kennedy was ready. As mobsters like Frank Costello, Lucky Luciano and Meyer Lansky moved from bootlegging to also distributing legitimate liquor, the existing clashes with Kennedy heated up.

1933 was also the year that Joe acquired a six-bedroom mansion in Palm Beach. The house had been built for Rodman Wanamaker, a member of the Philadelphia department store family, by celebrated architect Addison Mizner, whose vision would define Palm Beach architecture. Wanamaker had dubbed it "La Guerida," Spanish for "the bounty of war," which seems an appropriate name for the home of a buccaneer like Joe. He acquired the house from the financially pressed Wanamaker for $120,000, and in years to come he would install a swimming pool and tennis courts on the two-acre site.

In spite of Joe's busy schedule and constant travel, he closely monitored each child's activities. According to Doris Kearns Goodwin, he would respond by return mail to each letter from every child. Ironically, Rose, concerned with time management, wrote one letter and made nine carbons for her children.

Yet, for all Joe's correspondence with his children, historian Goodwin notes that the only thing close to moral teaching in any of these letters was his repeated reminder to respect their mother. Not once in more than two hundred letters did he put forward any ultimate moral principles for his children to contemplate. On the contrary, Joe stressed to his children the importance of winning at any cost and the pleasure of coming in first.

In the Kennedy hierarchy, after the parents came Joe, Jr. When they were away on their many trips, Joe, Jr., ruled the children like a benevolent dictator.

To an outsider, turning over the reins of child-rearing to a young man like Joe, Jr., encouraged bullying. Joe, Jr., in a fit of anger, once tossed six-year-old Teddy off a sailboat when he failed to obey an order to pull in the jib.

According to psychohistorian Nancy Gager Clinch, author of the groundbreaking *The Kennedy Neurosis*, Joe, Jr.'s, hair-trigger temper and violent actions were a part of his personality too often overlooked after his heroic death in the war. She states: "Unless we try to understand this less praiseworthy and smoldering side of Joe, Jr., we will fail to understand the emotional conflicts that drove the Kennedys to their extraordinary successes and may well have helped drive young Joe to his death."

But these were not issues that concerned Joe, Sr. Determined to raise a future president, he consulted luminaries in all fields, among them Harvard law professor Felix Frankfurter, who advised him to send young Joe to study with England's leading Socialist, Harold Laski, at the London School of Economics. Laski was a friend of FDR and New Deal leaders, and Frankfurter considered him "the greatest teacher in the world."

Tall, handsome, argumentative and very bright, Joe, Jr., made his goal clear. "He has often sat in my study and submitted with that smile that was pure magic to relentless teasing about his determination to be nothing less than President of the United States," Laski recalled.

Jack accepted his father's preference for Joe because he believed his father always treated him fairly, and because he valued the space and obscurity that his status as the younger brother provided. But about his mother he was ambivalent. According to Lem Billings, Rose was "a tough, minute disciplinarian with a fetish for neatness and order and decorum. This went against Jack's natural temperament—informal, tardy, forgetful, and often downright sloppy—so there was friction, and, on his part, resentment." Resentment was putting it mildly. To others, Jack said, "My mother's a nothing."

To Joe, Sr., his oldest son's only fault may have been smoking cigars. Although he was the son of a saloon keeper and had made a fortune in bootlegging Joe never approved of drinking. He was equally opposed to smoking (his pipe didn't count) and he offered a thousand dollars to any son who finished college without using alcohol or tobacco. Bobby would be the only one to collect. As psychohistorian Clinch points out, "What the father failed to see was that smoking cigars can allow an immature young man to feel more masculine and virile. Later on, Jack, Bobby and Teddy would all take up cigar smoking, the Freudian symbol of potency and power."

FDR finally came through with an important post. Joe stepped into his new position as chairman of the SEC on July 2, 1934. Many were outraged at this appointment because of Joe's shady reputation as a stock speculator and ruthless businessman. It was a lot like putting the fox to guard the chickens. To counter the angry reaction, Roosevelt arranged for Arthur Krock, the *New York Times'* Washington bureau chief, to interview Joe. Krock filed a story summarizing Joe's career exactly the way Joe gave it to him, stressing the Horatio Alger aspects and defending his recent financial practices. The two men took to each other immediately and began a long and profitable relationship that would benefit not only Joe himself, but all his sons.

Joe made the most of his new position. He rented Marwood, a twenty-five-room estate in Maryland, and lavishly entertained key members of the press there. He cultivated relationships with

Henry Luce, who would order up two cover stories on Joe in *Time* and a lengthy feature in *Fortune*, even allowing him to see the draft and make minor corrections.

Fresh from his year at the London School of Economics, Joe, Jr., entered Harvard that fall. He drove a yellow Ford and played football and rugby, scoring a winning goal against Yale. He managed to make Dean's List sophomore year and the prestigious Tercentary Celebration Committee. He skied, swam, sailed, and played golf, basketball and intramural squash.

In junior year Joe was elected to Hasty Pudding and the Spee Club. By then he had developed a reputation for poaching other men's dates on college weekends, thus avoiding paying for the girls' transportation.

Joe, Jr., and his fellow jocks were also fond of visiting in East Boston saloons on Saturday nights and getting into brawls with drunken steelworkers.

Recalling Joe, Jr., in later years, Jack wrote: "I suppose I knew Joe as well as anyone and yet I sometimes wonder if I ever really knew him. He was very human and most certainly had his faults: a hot temper, intolerance for the slower pace in lesser men, and a way of looking—with a somewhat sardonic half smile—which could cut and prod more sharply than words. But these defects— if defects they were—were becoming smoothed with the passage of time."

Joe resigned from the SEC in triumph in the summer of 1935, and that September he and Rose, with Jack and Kathleen, sailed on the *Île de France* to Europe, traveling first to France, to install Kick in a convent school.

Following the course set by Joe, Jr., Jack was enrolled in the London School of Economics under Harold Laski. But soon Jack fell ill with jaundice and by October 21 his parents had withdrawn him and were taking him home.

Jack entered Princeton in late October, six weeks after fall term had officially begun. He chose Princeton over Harvard, because he could join his beloved Lem Billings who was already there.

Princeton admissions policy did not permit entry after the beginning of the school year, but Joe, Sr., got in touch with another media friend, Herbert Bayard Swope, then editor-in-chief of the *New York World*, who in turn pressed the dean of admissions to bend the rules for young Jack. Unfortunately, Jack was still not up to the work. A few weeks after Thanksgiving he withdrew from Princeton and would spend nearly two months in Peter Bent Brigham Hospital in Boston, before Arthur Krock arranged for him to go to the Jay 6 Ranch in Arizona. There the sunny and dry climate restored him to temporary good health.

For years, none of these details appeared in any of Jack's campaign biographies. The official story was that he had studied with Harold Laski the entire year 1935–36. Even after his death, Kennedy image makers continued to paint Jack as a robust, healthy young president.

Jack joined Joe at Harvard in 1936 and both brothers lived at Winthrop House, the jock dorm. They dined together daily, but the old rivalry was not forgotten. Once Joe moved in on a beautiful young singer Jack was escorting, and the flattered starlet found herself with two escorts. Another time, in New York, Joe spotted Jack with a glamorous date at the Stork Club, lured Jack to the phone and pirated his girl.

JOE: "I HAVE NO POLITICAL AMBITIONS FOR MYSELF OR FOR MY CHILDREN."

As 1936 opened, FDR prepared to campaign for a second term. He encouraged Joe to write a book rallying the business community, which had become deeply disenchanted with the New Deal programs. Joe hired Arthur Krock to be his ghostwriter at $1,000 a week. The tycoon and the journalist worked from January to June. When they were finished, *I'm for Roosevelt* was rushed into August publication so it would be widely available before the November election.

Always hungry for praise and recognition, Joe sent the manuscript to FDR who, after much prodding from his aide, Missy Le Hand, came forth with a letter:

"Dear Joe,
I'm for Kennedy. The book is grand. I am delighted with it.
Yours sincerely,
Franklin"

In the book Joe made his position clear: FDR had saved the capitalist system and he chided ungrateful businessmen who did not appreciate that. The book included Joe's declaration that "I have no political ambitions for myself or for my children, and I put down these few thoughts as a father, for the future of his family and my anxiety as a citizen that the facts about the President's philosophy be not lost in a fog of unworthy emotion."

Although the book helped reelect Roosevelt, Kennedy still didn't get the cabinet post he yearned for. In the spring of 1937 Roosevelt finally came through with a relatively minor appointment: running the newly created Maritime Commission. Joe had never been any good at managing people, especially not laborers. He resigned after several fractious months of clashing with radical unions and reactionary shipowners. "This was the toughest thing I ever did in my life," he said.

There was another disappointment for Joe that year. He still yearned for the approval of the Protestant establishment that snubbed him at Harvard. This time he ran for a seat on the board of governors, finishing tenth in a field of twelve, and angrily attributing his defeat to anti-Catholic bias. It would be another victory that he would experience someday through Jack.

Jack spent every Harvard summer abroad, but the summer of 1937 was especially memorable because he toured Europe with Lem Billings. On June 30 twenty-year-old Jack and Lem sailed on the *George Washington* for Le Havre for a two-month tour of the Continent. They even brought along Jack's Ford sedan convertible. They drove through the Loire Valley but at the Spanish border were turned back by guards. Fascist Francisco Franco was now in charge. They attended a bullfight in Biarritz, visited the shrine at Lourdes, and gambled in Monte Carlo. In Italy they had a private audience with Cardinal Pacelli and attended a rally for Mussolini. They moved on to Munich and Nuremberg, where they narrowly missed seeing Adolf Hitler. Returning via Amsterdam and Brussels, they arrived for a three-day stopover in London with a dachshund they had bought in Germany, but Jack became so severely asthmatic—running a fever, breaking out in hives, and swelling up until his eyes closed—that they had to get rid of the dog.

Back in Washington, Joe was confiding to Jimmy Roosevelt that he would like very much to be the first Irishman to represent the United States at the Court of St. James. According to Jimmy, when he relayed this desire to his father, FDR "laughed so hard he almost toppled from his wheelchair."

In time FDR became intrigued with the idea, and in a mischievous moment he offered the appointment to Joe who immediately accepted. Almost at once FDR tried to renege. He sent Jimmy to see if Joe would consider an appointment as secretary of commerce instead. Arthur Krock, who noted the episode in his memoir, said Joe was irate and refused to consider any other appointment. On December 9 Krock reported the news that Joe would be appointed ambassador in the *New York Times.*

Another FDR aide, Secretary of the Treasury Henry Morgenthau, wrote in his diary that FDR "considered Kennedy a very dangerous man and he was going to send him to England as Ambassador with the distinct understanding that the appointment was only good for six months and that, furthermore, by giving him this appointment, any obligation that he had to Kennedy was paid for."

FDR had no illusions about Joe's loyalty. He assured Morgenthau, "I have made arrangements to have Joe Kennedy watched hourly and the first time he opens his mouth and criticizes me, I will fire him."

CHAPTER FOUR
THE KENNEDYS AT THE COURT OF ST. JAMES

Joe thinks like a king, and kings aren't always nice guys.

—A friend of Ambassador Joseph P. Kennedy, circa 1946

When Joe arrived in England in March 1938 to take up his new post, he was alone except for longtime aide Eddie Moore and Harold Hinton, his personal relations man, whom Joe had hired on the recommendation of Arthur Krock. It was unusual, unprecedented for a government official to have his own press agent, but indicates how sensitive Joe was to spinning the media and, moreover, to the potential in this new job. He had already managed to get front-page headlines for his sons' rugby scores and sailing tournaments, think of the possibilities in an ambassadorship!

Joe intended to use his post to lay the groundwork for his own presidential bid. With Hinton at work planting more stories on Joe Kennedy and his family than any previous diplomat could have imagined, the Ambassador became known as a bit of a publicity hound, or, as the president of the Bank of England put it, "a man permanently on the make."

The Nazi specter was looming over Europe, but even more ominously, just eleven days after Joe arrived, the Nazis pushed into Austria. It seemed strange to some that, at a time when the United States should have sent its most skilled diplomat to Great Britain, FDR sent instead a self-made millionaire, untrained in diplomacy, inept at politics, who loved publicity and who was suspected of harboring hopes of becoming the first Catholic president of the United States. But FDR had a whole secret agenda that poor Joe had yet to discover.

Joe installed himself in the embassy at 9 Prince's Gate and immediately began cultivating the British press as doggedly as he had the American, holding his first news conference at his embassy office, feet propped up on his desk and hands clasped behind his head, warning journalists that they must not expect him to develop into a statesman overnight.

Rose arrived in late March, bringing the children except Joe, Jr., and Jack, who were both at Harvard; Rosemary, who was in a special school in New York; and Eunice, who was to escort Rosemary to London after the term was over.

Servants included Luella Hennessey, a registered nurse hired in 1936 to supervise the children, who remained with the family for a half century. In years to come, Mrs. Hennessey would become an unofficial spokesperson for the family, someone the press and the family could rely on for a sweet anecdote that would emphasize the charm, character and intelligence of whatever Kennedy was running for office that year.

Rose was soon busy planning for Kick and Rosemary's formal presentation at court. The three of them went to Paris to select gowns for the event: white net dresses for the girls, and gold-and-silver embroidered lace over a white satin foundation for Rose. Kick found hers at Lelong; Rose and Rosemary were dressed by Molyneux. That May, when the girls were presented at Buckingham Palace, Rose wore the gown with a tiara of rubies and diamonds borrowed from Lady Bessborough.

A few weeks later Rose held a coming-out party for the girls, receiving more than three hundred guests. Rosemary, shy and not very bright, managed not to behave awkwardly, but she was nowhere near the social sensation that Kick was.

Robert and Teddy attended an English prep school. Rosemary was enrolled in a Montessori school in Hertfordshire while Eunice, Pat and Jean were enrolled in the Sacred Heart Convent in Roehampton.

By the late spring of 1938 Joe's two great aims of furthering his career and preventing war did not seem incompatible. He was seriously considering a run for the presidency himself. The election was two years away and no one could imagine that FDR would seek an unprecedented third term. On June 15 he returned to America to fan a small boomlet encouraging him to run, and to attend Joe, Jr.'s, Harvard graduation in June.

Joe's personal minstrel Arthur Krock celebrated his return in the *New York Times:* "Here is Kennedy back again, the rage of London, the best copy in the British press, his counsel steadily sought by statesmen of the country to which he is accredited, his influence manifest and powerful in all matters in which the United States has an interest in Great Britain. . . . Here he is back again, undazzled by such a taking up socially and officially as no American perhaps has known abroad since Franklin's day."

Still smarting from his rejection for a seat on Harvard's Board of Governors two years earlier, Joe was now angling for an honorary degree from his alma mater. When he heard that the degree committee had decided that the ambassadorship was not sufficient distinction for such an honor, he tried to save face by refusing the degree in advance, as if it were some kind of political offer. He did not even attend Joe, Jr.'s, commencement exercises, giving out a public statement that he wanted to stay near his son Jack who was ill.

Joe never learned from failure. His heavy-handed approach also cost Joe, Jr., the football letter he yearned for. Joe, Sr.'s, pressures on head coach Dick Harlow had backfired, and in the big game the previous November Joe, Jr., had not even played. Joe, Jr., did win a letter in sailing and graduated from Harvard cum laude.

When Joe, Jr., scored a winning goal in a Harvard-Yale rugby game, his father saw to it that it made headlines in the New York papers. In June 1938 the McMillan Cup sailing contest was held at Joe's own Wianno Yacht Club in Hyannis Port. For three days Joe, Jr., and Jack raced in the familiar waters of Nantucket Sound, but they did surprisingly poorly. Neither scored on either the first or third days; on the second day Jack was next to last in the fourth race; neither placed in the fifth; in the sixth race Jack scored second and Joe fourth. But their combined points in the sixth race caused distorted headlines to credit the Kennedy boys with giving Harvard its victory over Williams College. Actually, other Harvard men had scored more points, one man winning two victories, though this was barely mentioned. What did the facts matter? With the help of an adoring press, Joe was building an image for the Kennedy men.

The Ambassador returned to England in late June with Joe, Jr., and Jack, sailing on the *Normandie*. In London, Joe, Jr., became an embassy aide and man-about-town. For the next year he would criss cross Europe. His father arranged a temporary post at the U.S. Embassy in Paris. From Prague to Warsaw, Leningrad to Madrid, young Joe got an education in current affairs. But the lights were going out all over the continent, and all the Kennedys would be affected.

Although his daughter Rosemary was mentally limited, Joe had every reason to be proud of the way Joe, Jr., Jack and Kick were turning out. Young Joe and Jack were following in his footsteps as Harvard men, with all the advantages, including a high media profile, that he could give them. And their convent-bred sister Kick was a high-spirited, party-loving beauty who charmed everyone she met.

That July, at the annual garden party given by the king and queen in the beautiful gardens of Buckingham Palace, a high point of the social season, Kick was introduced to William Cavendish, the marquess of Hartington. Known to all as Billy, he was the heir to the duke of Devonshire, one of the wealthiest, most powerful men in England. And he was a Protestant. Because of the difference in their backgrounds and religions, any romantic relationship was unthinkable. They became the most compatible of friends. And as the friendship warmed, Kick realized that she was falling in love. If she were to allow the relationship to go any further, she would be challenging all the rules that her parents had so vigorously instilled in her.

That August, Kick had to do some serious thinking when the family took a house in Cannes on the French Riviera for the month.

Returning to London that fall, Ambassador Kennedy encouraged Prime Minister Neville Chamberlain of Britain to give in to all of Adolf Hitler's demands, so on September 28 Chamberlain could assure the British public of "peace in our time" and "peace with honor."

But the following day, September 29, an outraged Winston Churchill stood on the floor of the House of Commons and insisted: "We have sustained a total, unmitigated defeat."

Even after Britain went to war, Joe maintained his anti-British, antiwar position, much to the disgust of British leaders.

Yet, shrewd and cynical as Joe was, he remained unaware for a long time that FDR was ignoring him and going behind his back, using Col. William "Wild Bill" Donovan as a secret and sympathetic emisary to Churchill. FDR was shrewdly betting on Churchill to succeed Chamberlain.

In late November, Joe came back to Washington to meet with FDR and assured the President that Germany and Russia would win the war, and that the end of the world was at hand.

JOE PURSUES A MILLION-DOLLAR BABY

On March 15, 1939, Hitler marched into Czechoslovakia. Still, Joe continued to advocate political and financial appeasement of Germany. But in spite of his ambassadorial duties and his family responsibilities, he could always find time to chase a pretty debutante around his desk. Barbara Hutton, the Woolworth heiress, experienced just such caring attention from Joe that summer.

In mid-June, Hutton arrived in England with her young son Lance Reventlow. She immediately learned that the American embassy was advising all United States citizens that there was a strong possibility of war and urging them to return to the States. Hutton was in an awkward position since she had recently renounced her citizenship.

Hutton received a phone call from the office of Ambassador Kennedy, who wanted to see her in person. His secretary arranged an appointment. She considered him an old family friend and was delighted to call on him at the embassy on Grosvenor Square.

Joe informed her that he had called her in because of the urgent political situation. He had gallantly taken the liberty of conferring with the State Department and they had agreed that she could reenter the country on the strength of her Danish passport. She would have to make arrangements to leave as soon as possible.

As they continued to talk, Barbara sensed that the Ambassador had more on his mind than diplomacy. As his intentions grew more obvious and his flirtatious remarks more direct, the debutante grew more distressed. She was anxious to escape without insulting the powerful man who had rescued her and her son. She finally did make a getaway, but not before the Ambassador chased her around his desk.

Another prominent woman who attracted Joe's attention was the young Pamela Digby, who had come out the same year as Kick and Rosemary.

As usual, the Kennedy family gathered in Cannes that August. Also vacationing at Cap d'Antibes were the film star Marlene Dietrich and her daughter Maria Riva. Dietrich danced at the Eden Roc with both young Jack and the Ambassador, whom she tried to dissuade from his appeasement policies while simultaneously trying to interest him in financing a French film.

In later years Dietrich confided to her distinguished biographer Charles Higham that she had bedded Joe, Sr., Joe, Jr., and Jack.

The Hitler-Stalin pact allowed Germany to attack Poland without fear of fighting an Eastern Front war against the Soviet Union. Britain and France had guaranteed Poland's independence. When Hitler invaded Poland on September 1, Britain had no choice but to declare war. Two days later, on Sunday, September 3, Chamberlain was forced to stand before Britain's House of Commons and announce that "this country is at war with Germany."

Days after the declaration of war, the British liner *Athenia*, on its way to the United States with three hundred Americans aboard, was torpedoed west of the Hebrides. After cabling FDR, the Ambassador sent Jack to Scotland to help the survivors and find out details of what had happened. He ordered Joe, Jr., to book space on other ships for survivors. In response to the flood of queries from anxious relatives, Ambassador Kennedy sent out hundreds of personal telegrams, paying for them out of his own pocket because government funds were unavailable for this purpose. He also made arrangements to send his own family back home.

By September 15 Rose, Kick, Eunice and Bobby were gone. Kick begged to stay with her father, but he was adamant, alarmed almost as much by her relationship with Billy Cavendish, as by the international situation. In the end Kick sailed with the others on the S. S. *Washington*.

Joe, Jr., was next, then Pat, Jean and Teddy, and finally Jack, who flew home on a Pan American clipper at the end of September.

Rosemary had been making so much progress in a convent training school for Montessori teachers in rural Hertfordshire that it was decided to let her stay.

With the declaration of war, Britain mobilized. Streetlights were extinguished, and blackout rules took effect. Railings from the front of Buckingham Palace, Brooks's Club and other buildings were removed to be melted down into arms. Hundreds of thousands of Londoners moved to the country to avoid bombing raids.

Back in the States, Joe, Jr., began his first year at Harvard Law School; Jack, his last year at Harvard. The children still at home lined up each Sunday to speak to their father on the one weekly transatlantic call he was allowed.

The Ambassador returned to the States at Christmas, arriving in New York on December 6, met by reporters and Rose. They joined the rest of the family in Palm Beach. After the holidays he delayed returning to London. It was clear that the Ambassador, for whatever reasons, was unwilling to take up his post again.

One reason Joe delayed leaving the States was that he was still considering running for president. Even FDR's biggest boosters were uncomfortable with the idea of the President seeking an unprecedented third term. Many others agreed with the Ambassador's isolationist stance. But if Joe was gaining popularity in the States, he had lost much of it in England. When he finally returned to London on February 28, 1940, he was met by a chilly reception. His long absence was regarded by many Englishmen as cowardice. After all, the king and queen had made it a point to stay put, even as bombs began to drop on Buckingham Palace. The Ambassador, however, had been sunning himself in Palm Beach and telling anyone who would listen that Great Britain did not have a chance against the Nazis.

In May, after the Germans invaded Norway, Chamberlain's government fell. On the day Churchill replaced him, the Nazis overran France's Maginot Line. It was time for Churchill's finest hour, and the Ambassador was now regarded as a pariah.

Restless, trapped in political limbo, Joe wrote Krock that in London he was nothing more than "a $75-a-week errand boy" and tried to get his friend to do something to get him home. Krock dutifully sent up a trial balloon suggesting that the Ambassador was a good candidate for chairman of the Democratic National Committee, but nothing came of it.

Roosevelt ignored Joe's pleas to come home, seeking to keep him out of the presidential campaign. On October 16 Joe finally sent a cablegram to the President insisting that he be allowed to come home, then telephoned Undersecretary of State Sumner Welles to say that he had deposited with Eddie Moore in New York a document containing a full expression of his views, with instructions that it was to be released to the press if he was not back by a certain date. Finally word came back from the State Department that he was to return for consultation. On October 23 he boarded a plane and left London for good.

If Joe's own political career seemed headed for failure, he could take heart that his oldest son's was shaping up just as he had planned. That spring, Joe, Jr., took his first steps toward a political career.

Young Joe was elected a Massachusetts delegate to the Democratic convention in Chicago that summer. When Joe, Jr., arrived at the convention in July, he was pledged to Postmaster James Farley, not FDR. Nevertheless, the convention nominated FDR for a third term.

Returning to Harvard for his second year of law school, young Joe also registered for the draft, and as a loyal Democrat, he campaigned for FDR, presenting him to a Boston crowd where Roosevelt promised, "You boys are not going to be sent into any foreign wars."

ANN GARGAN: "ROSEMARY WAS THE MOST BEAUTIFUL OF ALL THE KENNEDYS."

At this time the Ambassador was also very concerned with the continuing Rosemary problem. In the eighteen months since Rosemary's return from England, she had deteriorated greatly, giving way to tantrums, rages and violent behavior. According to Lem Billings, at twenty-one Rosemary was beginning to understand that she would never measure up to her closest siblings, the brilliant Joe and the charismatic Jack and Kick. The resulting frustration led to physical fights and, worse, long absences at night when she would be wandering the streets.

"She was the most beautiful of all the Kennedys," her cousin Ann Gargan recalls. "She had the body of a 21-year-old yearning for fulfillment with the mentality of a four-year-old. She was in a convent in Washington at the time, and many nights the school would call to say she was missing, only to find her out walking the streets at 2 a.m."

At Harvard, Jack decided to base his senior thesis on Munich. The Ambassador pitched in, arranging interviews and offering memoranda for background.

The thesis earned Jack a cum laude, and some of his professors thought it might be publishable. The Ambassador asked Arthur Krock to get his agent to handle it. But when Krock offered to write a foreword, Joe said that he wanted someone better known and persuaded Henry Luce to do it. *Why England Slept* was rushed to press that summer and by August it was climbing the best-seller lists.

Only Joe, Jr., seemed less than impressed with his younger brother's efforts, writing to his father: "It seemed to represent a lot of work but didn't prove anything."

After graduation Jack let loose, collecting a case of gonorrhea along the way.

Returning to the States on October 27, Joe was met by Rose and their four daughters. He immediately telephoned FDR, who urged him to come to the White House that night for "a little family dinner."

With the election only ten days away, FDR could not risk letting Joe throw his support to his Republican rival, Wendell Willkie.

Years later Jack would claim that Roosevelt had assured his father that Joe, Sr., himself, would have FDR's endorsement as Democratic candidate for the presidency in 1944. In return for this, Joe agreed to endorse FDR's third term.

JOE: "IF YOU CAN'T BE CAPTAIN, DON'T PLAY!"

Back on board, on October 29, Joe spoke to the country on a special coast-to-coast radio hookup he paid for himself, endorsing FDR's precedent-breaking third term. He assured his nationwide audience that "this country must and will stay out of war," and he vigorously defended Roosevelt: "Unfortunately, during this political campaign there has arisen the charge that the President of the United States is trying to involve this country in the world war. Such a charge is false." He insisted that Roosevelt had no "secret commitment" with Great Britain to "lead us into war." He knew that none of this was true because it was the very reason for his near-split with the President in the first place. He concluded: "My wife and I have given nine hostages to fortune. Our children and your children are more important than anything else in the world. The kind of America that they and their children will inherit is of grave concern to us all. In the light of these considerations, I believe that Franklin Delano Roosevelt should be reelected President of the United States."

FDR was so pleased that he wired immediately: "I have just listened to a great speech. Congratulations." *Life* magazine lauded it, too: "As a vote-getting speech, it was probably the most effective of the campaign. For more than anything else it allayed fear that Mr. Roosevelt would 'take this country into war.' "

There's no doubt that Joe's vocal support helped seal the narrow margin that clinched Roosevelt's election.

In the week following the election, Joe visited the White House to deliver his letter of resignation. Traditionally, leading appointees volunteer their resignations at the start of each new presidential term, but by calling on Roosevelt personally, Joe made it clear that he wanted out. He wanted Roosevelt to announce his resignation immediately, but FDR asked him to keep the title until he had time to choose a successor. Joe agreed.

But his reasons for resigning remained the same: he intended to work privately to oppose U.S. entry into the war. While making plans for a trip to Los Angeles to discuss his plans with William Randolph Hearst, he agreed to see three old friends from the press at the Ritz-Carlton Hotel in Boston on November 9. He understood their meeting to be off-the-record, what we today would call "a backgrounder." Among the trio was Louis Lyons, a distinguished reporter for the *Boston Globe*.

When Lyons story appeared in the *Globe* two days later, its consequences were disastrous. Joe had freely voiced his opinion that "democracy is finished in England," and equally negative thoughts on United States' foreign policy and the President's wife Eleanor. When it was published it was the end of his diplomatic career.

The President summoned Joe to Hyde Park. After scarcely ten minutes alone, a furious FDR sought out Eleanor and told her, "I never want to see that son of a bitch as long as I live. Take his resignation and get him out of here!" When Eleanor reminded her husband that the next train did not leave for hours, he said, "I don't give a goddamn. You drive him around Hyde Park, give him a sandwich and put him on that train."

Joe had been undone in the end by his own ambition, and a politician more ruthless than himself.

He did not take defeat gracefully. He first demanded a retraction, and when the *Globe* stood by its reporter, he decided to get even. He withdrew all of Somerset's liquor advertising. The *Globe* remained cut off from that revenue until he sold the firm in 1946.

It is usually accepted that the *Globe* interview cost Joe Kennedy the ambassadorship. In truth, he had already resigned. But the story ended any hope he had of a dignified exit or any continuing influence he might have had on the White House.

CHAPTER FIVE

THE KENNEDYS GO TO WAR

I wish I hadn't acquired respectability. I'd be out selling the market short.

—Joseph P. Kennedy, 1945

Although the family gathered at Hyannis Port for the summer of 1941, they were already being taken in different directions by the coming war. This would be the last time they were all together.

On June 24 Joe, Jr., enlisted in the Naval Reserve and was assigned as a seaman second class to Squantum Air Station just outside Boston. He commuted to Hyannis Port for weekends. Jack, after a few aimless weeks at Stanford Business School the previous fall, had failed both the physical examination for both the Army Officer Candidate School and the Navy because of his back. That summer he devoted himself to a physical program designed to make him acceptable to some branch of the service.

A friend who spent time with the family that summer recalled the magical quality of the Kennedys at home. "It was a scene of endless competition, people drawing each other out and pushing each other to greater lengths," he told Collier and Horowitz. "It was as simple as this: the Kennedys had a feeling of being heightened and it rubbed off on the people who came in contact with them. They were a unit. I remember thinking to myself that there couldn't be another group quite like this one."

Unable to travel that summer, Rose moved to distance herself even further from her children. She built a little shack on the beach, that was off-limits to everyone else.

Jack enlisted in a naval officer's training course and on September 25 he received his commission. Ensign Kennedy was assigned to the Office of Naval Intelligence in Washington. His great friend Lem Billings was disqualified from the service because of his poor eyesight. Joe arranged for Billings to be assigned to the American Field Service, the civilian-manned ambulance corps, in Washington. Jack and Lem were once again inseparable.

Kick was also in Washington. Arthur Krock had found her a job at the *Washington Times-Herald*. Soon she introduced Jack to one of her fellow reporters: beautiful, Danish-born Inga Arvad. As a journalist, Inga had covered the 1936 Olympics where she met Adolf Hitler who invited her to share his box. The fact that she had interviewed both Hitler and Hermann Goering brought her to the attention of the FBI. Her old friend William Cahan insists that she despised Hitler, but she once described him in print as "very kind, very charming . . . not evil as he is depicted . . . an idealist."

Although twenty-eight-year-old Inga was married to Hungarian film director Paul Fejos, she and young Jack soon became lovers. This was not the smartest move for an ambitious young man in naval intelligence. Certainly, J. Edgar Hoover was concerned enough to bug Inga's apartment. By January 1942 his surveillance confirmed that Jack and Inga were having a passionate affair. In such moments he called her "Inga-Binga" and she called him "Honeysuckle." Hoover was informed that the couple had "engaged in sexual intercourse on a number of occasions" and, more seriously, young Jack had shared with Inga "in general terms his tentative official assignment plans" and other sensitive information.

It was Jack's first serious relationship with a woman and they talked of marriage. By the time the young Navy ensign brought Inga for a visit to Palm Beach, Joe's concern had reached flash point.

During one weekend visit, according to Inga, Joe alternately harangued Jack about the relationship and tried to seduce her himself.

When the FBI shared this information with Jack's superior, Capt. Howard Kingman, Kingman wanted him discharged from the Navy immediately. The director of the Office of Naval Intelligence, Capt. Samuel Hunter, intervened on Jack's behalf and had him reassigned to the Sixth Naval District Headquarters in Charleston, South Carolina, where he was supposed to make a fresh start.

That fall the Ambassador, a title he continued to treasure, also moved to deal with the Rosemary problem. Without telling anyone, not even her mother, he arranged for his oldest daughter to have a prefrontal lobotomy at St. Elizabeth's Hospital in Washington, D.C. The experimental operation was believed to work wonders with people who had emotional problems. The sister of playwright Tennessee Williams and film star Frances Farmer were among those forced to submit to the surgery. In Rosemary's case it was a disaster and left her permanently disabled, paralyzed on one side, incontinent and unable to speak coherently. She was never allowed to return home. Instead, she was spirited away to St. Coletta's School in Wisconsin.

For years the family would lie about Rosemary's condition. It is unknown whether any of the children knew the truth. Eunice, who had always been the one closest to Rosemary, apparently visited her regularly, while Teddy, only eleven years old when Rosemary went away, seemed to believe for years that she was dead. And to her father, she was. The family only began to hint that Rosemary was mentally retarded after the 1960 election. Rose Kennedy claimed that she never knew the truth about the operation until 1961.

It was a powerful lesson to the younger Kennedys: If they failed to measure up, if Joe decided that they were losers, they, too, could be sent away.

Happy family pictures from this period mask a group that had become participants in a conspiracy. The family's version of Rosemary's fate would evolve over the years.

Today the official version is that Rosemary was born retarded and that only Rose's herculean efforts made it possible for her to appear normal. But Barbara Gibson, Rose's former secretary, disputes this. She managed to salvage Rosemary's old diaries when they were being tossed out of the Hyannis Port house, and believes that they could not possibly have been written by someone with the "mentality of a four-year-old."

Gibson points out that, given the standards of the time and especially the standards of a strict Irish Catholic family, "there is no way a 'retarded' young woman and her younger teenaged sister would have been allowed to travel to Switzerland unaccompanied by a responsible adult." But Rosemary was nineteen and Eunice only sixteen when they made such a trip.

Rosemary's fate and how it was handled was the ultimate Kennedy deception.

On Sunday morning, December 7, 1941, the Japanese attacked Pearl Harbor. That night, from Palm Beach, the Ambassador sent a telegram to Roosevelt: "In this great crisis all Americans are with you. Name the battle post. I'm yours to command." But no appointment ever came. Nothing but a form letter of acknowledgment from FDR's secretary.

Isolated in Palm Beach, Joe fulminated against "Jews and radicals and certain elements in the New Deal" for putting him "in the leper colony."

Jack and Inga continued to see each other in Charleston, and the FBI continued to record their trysts at the Fort Sumter Hotel. According to Anthony Summers, the surveillance was dropped for a while when Inga began to suspect she was being bugged.

In the spring of 1942, when Inga went to Reno to shed her husband, Jack confided to Lem Billings that he might be getting married. But to his chagrin, Inga chose to marry someone else, cowboy-movie star Tim McCoy. He wrote to Lem, now stationed in Cairo, that she had married "some guy she had known for years who loved her but whom she didn't love."

Years later, when Jack attended a Harvard commencement, "an FBI agent who had known him and had been one of those who listened to a wiretap conversation between Jack and Inga was in a group watching the parade of dignitaries. As Jack passed, the agent whispered to him, 'Whatever happened to Inga?' To which Jack muttered, staring straight ahead, 'You son of a bitch.' "

Joe, Jr., took one big step to catch up with Jack in May when his father presented him with his wings and commission. In July, Jack went to Northwestern University to attend Midshipmen's School. After training at Portsmouth, Melville and Newport, the Ambassador arranged for Jack to be sent to the South Pacific. While Joe, Jr., fretted in training in San Juan, Puerto Rico, and Norfolk, Virginia, his younger brother was already a lieutenant in the South Pacific. Joe, Jr., was proud of Jack but shaken. Joe, Jr., had been the star of the family, the designated heir, the one all the other children looked up to. Now, for the first time, his sickly younger brother had passed him by, and he feared that he might never catch up. For him the war had become a competition with his brother.

That fall, a bitter Joe decided to challenge FDR's personal candidate for the senator from Massachusetts, Joseph Casey. With the aid of his cousin Joe Kane, a powerful Boston politician, he came up with a Casey challenger: his eighty-year-old father-in-law. Running on an anti-New Deal platform, dismissing Casey as FDR's "rubber stamp," Honey Fitz lost by 28,000 votes. The Ambassador did succeed in tearing the Democratic machine apart, insuring the election of the Republican candidate, Henry Cabot Lodge, Jr., in the general election.

Bypassed by the war effort, the Ambassador had to content himself with writing his memoir of his diplomatic years in collaboration with James Landis, dean of Harvard Law School. These papers, never published, are in a sealed file in the John F. Kennedy Library in Boston. The Freedom of Information Act, which applies to the FBI files of J. Edgar Hoover, does not apply to Kennedy's record of his years in public service.

At the end of 1942, Eunice was at Stanford, and Pat had finished high school and was considering taking an apartment in New York.

Late in March of 1943, Kick resigned from the *Times-Herald*. She was finally able to return to England in June to work for the Red Cross. Billy Cavendish was stationed in Scotland with the Coldstream Guards but managed to get to London for their first reunion in four years. They knew immediately that in spite of their national and religious differences, and in spite of the years that had passed, they were deeply in love.

This news set off serious alarms on both sides of the Atlantic. The Cavendish family was a pillar of the Church of England.

Kick's parents, especially Rose, were equally dismayed. They did what they could, even consulting secretly with the powerful Archbishop Francis Spellman, New York's future cardinal.

On June 17, as Kick was boarding the *Queen Mary* bound for England with 160 other nurses and thousands of troops, her brother, Lt. jg John F. Kennedy was entering the front lines of the war against Japan. He had taken command of *PT-109* on the island of Tulagi near Guadalcanal.

On August 2, at 2:30 A.M., Jack's *PT-109* was cut in half by a Japanese destroyer. The following day, the Ambassador was notified at Hyannis Port that his second son was missing in the South Pacific.

For one week Joe kept the news to himself, until informed that Jack had been rescued.

The public image of the Kennedy men, as built and maintained by Joe and Rose, was already so strong that the story was considered worthy of the front page of the *New York Times*.

With a story like this and time on his hands, there was no stopping Joe. He went to work exploiting Jack's authentic heroism for all it was worth. He called in every contact he had, from Secretary of the Navy James Forrestal, for a Navy and Marine Corps medal, to John Hersey for a long *New Yorker* article that officially certified Jack's heroism. The article was then condensed for a larger market via the *Reader's Digest*, making Jack a national celebrity.

Through Joe's efforts, the *PT-109* incident would become as famous as the Normandy invasion.

The experience changed Jack. He had spent most of his life in the shadow of his older brother, but during the days when he and his crew were stranded behind enemy lines and realizing that no one was coming to look for them, he came into his own as a leader of men. One of the men, Ensign Paul Fay, Jr., would remain a friend for life.

On September 6, when the family and friends gathered at Hyannis to celebrate the Ambassador's birthday, the absent Jack's heroism was the main topic. A guest raised a toast not only to the Ambassador, but to "our own hero, Lt. John F. Kennedy of the United States Navy." A friend recalled Joe, Jr.'s, reddened face and frozen smile as he raised his glass to his father and absent brother. But later that night, in the bedroom they shared, the friend could hear Joe crying.

The younger brother he used to bully was now a national hero, and Joe, Jr., was desperate to regain primacy. And desperate times called for desperate measures.

On January 7, 1944, Jack Kennedy returned to the United States. Because of restrictions on wartime travel, neither Joe nor Rose was in San Francisco to greet him. Instead of heading home to Palm Beach, Jack flew to Los Angeles for a visit with Inga. Then it was on to Boston for Honey Fitz's eighty-first birthday, then Palm Beach on January 16.

In England, Kick Kennedy was torn. She loved her Protestant nobleman but she could not bring herself to convert to Anglicism. For him to convert to Catholicism was out of the question. In spite of their religion problem, they became engaged that April and cabled Kick's parents with the news. Rose was horrified and cabled back:

"Heartbroken. Feel you have been wrongly influenced—sending Arch Spellman's friend to talk to you. Anything done for our Lord will be rewarded hundredfold."

Joe, Jr., stepped in. He supported his sister's decision to break with their parents and marry the man she loved. Kick and Billy were married in a civil ceremony on May 6, at Chelsea Register Office. Kick wore a pink crepe suit, a mink jacket and a diamond brooch. Joe, Jr., was the only Kennedy present. Rice being rationed, guests threw rose petals instead. After several days Joe, Sr., stirred himself to send a conciliatory cable to his favorite daughter, but Rose took to her bed and he soon had her hospitalized to keep her away from reporters.

"It's a horrible thing," said Eunice, "but it will be nice visiting her after the war, so we might as well face it."

On D-Day, June 6, 1944, Allied forces launched their massive invasion of Europe along the Normandy coast. Among those manning planes overhead was Joe, Jr. In July he was promoted to lieutenant and transferred to Bombing Squadron 110.

German "buzz bombs" were still hitting London, when volunteers were sought to destroy the launching sites. Joe had already completed two dangerous tours of duty without incident. His gear was packed for him to return home when he heard about Operation Aphrodite and volunteered.

Nancy Gager Clinch believes that Joe had to regain his status in the family at any price, and this was what "drove Joe, Jr., to accept, despite misgivings and actual warnings of failure, the mission that killed him."

On August 12 Joe and his copilot were in the air only twenty minutes when their plane exploded, probably due to an electronic malfunction. No trace of their bodies was ever found.

A pair of priests called on Joe and Rose at Hyannis Port with the terrible news. Most of the children, including Jack, were there with them that Sunday afternoon. Joe proceeded to inform them that their oldest brother had died a hero. He urged them to be brave because that's what Joe, Jr., would have wanted. He urged them to go ahead with their plans to race that day and most of them obediently did so. But Jack could not. Instead, for a long time he walked on the beach in front of their house.

"There were no tears for Joe and me, not then," Rose recalled. "We sat awhile, holding each other close, and wept inwardly, silently."

According to her recollection, Joe then replied: " 'We've got to carry on. We must take care of the living. There is a lot of work to be done.' "

That, at least, was the way Rose saw it. Friends and associates of Joe recall him retreating to his room, locking the door and listening to classical music endlessly and alone. Everyone who knew him agreed that he was never the same again. When Joe, Jr.'s, name did come up, even years later, Joe, Sr., would change the subject, or leave the room.

His heir apparent was dead, but not Joe Kennedy's dream. He turned to his second son.

For all that Joe opposed the U.S. entrance into the war, and although he would spend it banished from the circles of power in luxurious exile at his mansions in Palm Beach and Cape Cod, he could hardly remain untouched by the conflagration. With the death of his oldest and favorite son, he ultimately paid a higher price than most citizens.

———————

Kick, learning of her favorite brother's death, immediately flew home to Hyannis. Weeks later, on September 16, she was notified that her new husband had been brought down by a sniper at Normandy. She returned to England to console her husband's parents and would not return to the States again until the war was over.

Even before peace was declared, the Kennedy family was making postwar plans. When Jack was discharged from the Navy in March 1945, Joe found him a job as a special correspondent for Hearst's International News Service. He covered the founding of the United Nations in San Francisco and Churchill's fall from power in England.

Every one of Jack's columns, carried in every Hearst paper, including Boston's *Herald-American*, included a photo of him in his Navy uniform and this biography: "Lt. John F. Kennedy, recently retired PT-boat hero of the South Pacific and son of Ambassador Joseph P. Kennedy, is covering the San Francisco conference from a serviceman's point of view. Before the war he wrote the bestseller *Why England Slept.*" It might be called the beginning of his presidential campaign.

After closing up the Bronxville house early in 1941, Joe moved the family's legal residence from New York to Palm Beach because Florida, unlike New York, had no income tax. On the advice of Cardinal Spellman, he retained real estate agent John Reynolds to sell his Bronxville estate. Reynolds handled the Diocese of New York's extensive and lucrative real estate holdings. Once again alert to opportunity, Joe teamed with Reynolds to scoop up under valued midtown Manhattan properties and reap yet another fortune in the postwar boom.

Joe paid $600,000 for one property at Fifty-first Street and Lexington Avenue in Manhattan and sold it a few years later for nearly $4 million.

The centerpiece of Joe's real estate empire would be Chicago's Merchandise Mart. Built by Marshall Field for $30 million, it was the world's largest privately owned commercial building: twenty-four stories. But by 1945 Joe was able to pick it up from the financially troubled Field for less than $13 million, putting less than half a million down and borrowing the rest. For Joe it was another insider deal, for he knew from his government cronies that the

Mart's low-rent government leases were about to expire and he believed that they could be replaced with more lucrative ones. Joe ultimately took in each year, in rents alone, more than he paid for the building.

Now that Joe was gone and Kick was making a new life for herself in England, it was time for the next batch of Kennedys to seek their place, as directed by their father.

Never a good student, Bobby had to repeat third grade. He attended a series of lower schools in Hyannis Port, Bronxville, Riverdale, and two different prep schools while the family was living in England. Back in the United States, he had moved from Portsmouth Priory, St. Paul's and Milton Academy before entering Harvard in 1944 as a "legacy." At eighteen Bobby followed his brothers into the Navy and signed up for officer candidate classes at Harvard.

Joe, Jr.'s, shocking death the following year spurred Bobby to resign from officer training, withdraw from Harvard and serve as an enlisted man, a seaman's apprentice, aboard the U.S.S. *Joseph P. Kennedy, Jr.*, the destroyer named for his brother. His shipboard naval career lasted from February to May of 1945, during which time he was assigned to routine details on a short Caribbean cruise that included a trip to the U.S. Navy's base in Cuba. With his discharge papers he was awarded two routine medals and a promotion to seaman second-class. He returned to Harvard in the fall of 1946 for his last two years. "To tell you the truth, I didn't go to class much," Bobby later acknowledged. "I used to talk and argue a lot, mostly about sports and politics." He graduated with a football letter, a prize that had eluded his older, bigger brothers.

PART TWO

THE POSTWAR BOOM

CHAPTER SIX
THE FIRST KENNEDY CAMPAIGN

I never would have imagined before the war that I would become active in politics.

—John F. Kennedy 1960

Early in 1946, after examining the field and warming Jack up with a series of local speaking engagements, Joe informed the family at a Palm Beach gathering that Jack would run for Congress. In April, Jack announced that he was a candidate for the eleventh district in working-class East Boston. The district incorporated the old East Boston wards of P.J. Kennedy and the North End of Honey Fitz. It was natural Kennedy-country and now Honey Fitz's old nemesis James Curley was giving up his seat to run for mayor.

JOE: "WE'RE GOING TO SELL JACK LIKE SOAP FLAKES."

"We're all in this together," Joe told the family. Stealing a glance at her frail, sickly brother, Eunice asked, "Daddy, do you really think Jack can be a congressman?" Joe smiled. "You must remember—it's not what you are that counts, but what people think you are."

Once again Joe turned to his cousin Joe Kane to manage the

campaign. But behind the scenes the Ambassador still called the shots. He devised the strategy, handled the money, picked the key workers, and spent hundreds of hours phoning influential friends, politicians and editors. The first Kennedy campaign included the most elaborate professional advertising effort ever seen in a Massachusetts congressional election. "We're going to sell Jack like soap flakes," said Joe.

Nothing was taken for granted and Jack drove himself hard. On the eve of the June 18 primary, Jack marched in the traditional Bunker Hill Day Parade as commander of the *Joseph P. Kennedy, Jr.* VFW Post 5880, but by the time he had completed the five-mile walk, he was exhausted. Just past the reviewing stand he collapsed and was taken to the nearby home of Boston politician Robert Lee, who later said, "He turned yellow and blue. He appeared to me as a man who had probably had a heart attack."

On primary day the sickly, inexperienced twenty-nine-year-old Jack Kennedy was swept to victory, a victory that landed him on the front page of the *New York Times* and got him a big story in *Time.* The November election would be a mere formality in the heavily Democratic district.

After the election, Joe continued his relentless promotion of his son.

When the new Congress convened in January, Jack rented a three-story brick house in Georgetown (1528 31 Street), where the household included a cook, Margaret Ambrose, who had been with the Kennedys for years; an aide, Billy Sutton, who functioned as a kind of all-purpose assistant in the way Eddie Moore had functioned for Joe; and a valet. Bills were paid by the Park Agency, and Joe and Rose were frequent visitors.

Joe lectured Jack about his spending, especially when he discovered that the freshman congressman was spending $50,000 a year on "incidentals." In 1946 that was enough to keep ten average families going for a year.

Eunice soon joined her brother. Like Jack, she had conquered a series of debilitating illnesses, and with the loss of their brother Joe, he drew closer to her. The consensus among the family was that Eunice had the brains, fire and virtues to make a great elected official. The only one who disagreed was the Ambassador, who felt she lacked the most essential requirement: testicles. He once praised Eunice: "If that girl had been born with balls she would have been a hell of a politician."

At twenty-six Eunice had found herself a job as executive secretary for the Justice Department's Juvenile Delinquency Committee. While working in Washington she met Robert Sargent Shriver, scion of an old Maryland family that had lost its money in the Depression. Jack knew Shriver slightly from Canterbury, the Catholic prep school he had attended briefly, and Kick had met him in Paris. Shriver had attended Yale on a scholarship and was working as an assistant to the editor at *Newsweek* when Eunice was introduced to him by a friend who said he was "a fellow who would like to work for your father." Eunice arranged a meeting and Joe hired Shriver to oversee his real estate holdings.

As a congressman Jack romanced the beautiful green-eyed movie star Gene Tierney, model Florence Pritchett and British tennis star Kay Stammers. The intense romance with Gene Tierney, who was separated from designer Oleg Cassini, lasted a year, but at lunch one day he informed her, seemingly out of the blue, "You know, Gene, I can never marry you." Stunned, Tierney did not respond at first. But when lunch was over, she said simply, "Bye, bye, Jack!" His attempts to see her again failed.

JACK WARNS: "THE AMBASSADOR HAS A TENDENCY TO PROWL."

Womanizing was the hallmark of the Kennedy men. Since ending his affair with Gloria Swanson, the Ambassador had kept up a string of affairs that were no secret to his sons.

Jack liked to tell friends about the time one of his sisters' friends woke in the middle of the night at Hyannis and saw the Ambassador standing next to her bed, beginning to take his robe off as he whispered, "This is going to be something you'll always remember." Jack had watched the scene through a keyhole and took to warning female guests: "Be sure to lock the bedroom door. The Ambassador has a tendency to prowl late at night." Visitors to

Palm Beach often noted that Joe had a series of beautiful house-
mates. When Rose visited, the young women moved out, only to
return after she left.

Rose moved through this atmosphere in total denial, but if this
martyrdom was supposed to inspire her surviving sons, it backfired.

One Washington socialite recalled an encounter with the
Kennedy men on the prowl: "I was at some posh restaurant in
Washington and the waiter brought me a note inviting me to join
friends at another table. It was Joe and his sons, Jack and Bobby.
Jack was a congressman then. When I joined them the gist of the
conversation from the boys was the fact that their father was
going to be in Washington for a few days and needed female companionship. They wondered whom I could suggest, and they
were absolutely serious."

To Jack it was the thrill of the chase that was addictive. The
women hardly mattered. Some women speculated that he was actually disappointed, because he would only have to start hunting
again.

In Jack's world women were for conquest and entertainment.
His serious emotional relationships were with men. "Jack really
wasn't comfortable unless Torby MacDonald or some other male
friend was around to make macho jokes with," one woman recalled for Collier and Horowitz. "He was nice—considerate in his
own way, witty and fun. But he gave off light instead of heat. Sex
was something to *have done*, not to *be doing*. He wasn't in it for the
cuddling."

Supreme Court justice William O. Douglas thought Jack was
bored in Washington and turned to women for amusement. "He
had nothing of consuming interest, he never seemed to get into
the mainstream of any tremendous political thought, or political
action, or any idea of promoting this, or reforming that, nothing.
He was sort of drifting," Douglas said, "and when he started
drifting he became more and more of a playboy."

M.D. WARNS: "JACK KENNEDY DOESN'T HAVE A YEAR TO LIVE."

Kick had been kept in the background and encouraged to stay in England during Jack's congressional campaign. Her marriage to a Protestant Englishman, even a dead war hero, was considered a disadvantage in East Boston. She embraced her life as an Englishwoman and her title, marchioness of Hartington. Living in her own house on Smith Square, she led a glittering social life.

In September of 1947 Kick and friends, including Pamela Digby Churchill, now divorced from the son of Britain's wartime prime minister, were staying at Lismore Castle in County Wexford. The castle had been built by King John in the early thirteenth century, and was the property of Kick's in-laws, the Devonshires.

Pamela had met Jack several times before on visits to the Kennedys but did not get to know him until that visit. "Though he was three years older, he always seemed so very young to all of us," Pamela recalled for her biographer, Christopher Ogden. "In England we dated very much older men and Jack seemed, well, boyish. Skinny and scrawny, actually. Kathleen's kid brother. Not eligible, so to speak."

Jack was not well. His back bothered him and he was unable to join the others riding and playing golf. He and Pamela spent a lot of time together.

One morning he asked if she would accompany him on an expedition to find the "original Kennedys," said to be living about fifty miles from Lismore. They drove over the rutted country roads in Kick's huge American station wagon, finally arriving in New Ross. They were directed to a small cottage with a thatch roof, with pigs, ducks and chickens running in and out of the front door. Eventually they were invited inside for tea while Jack tried to figure out which of the New Ross Kennedys was his ancestor. He never did make a direct connection, but concluded they were probably third cousins. Before leaving, he drove a group of children all around the village in the station wagon, then returned to Lismore.

As they pulled away from the village, Pamela looked at Jack and sighed. "Just like Tobacco Road," she said.

Jack was angry. "I felt like kicking her out of the car," he recalled during a 1963 return to Ireland as President. "For me, the visit to that cottage was filled with magic sentiment."

While in Ireland Jack's health deteriorated, until he was forced to send a coded message to Washington asking for medicine, a precaution so that the ambitious young congressman's condition would not leak to his political opponents.

Returning to London with Kick and Pamela, he was so sick that Pamela had her own doctor, Sir Daniel Davies, see him on September 21. Davies immediately had him hospitalized in the London Clinic. "That young American friend of yours hasn't got a year to live," he told her. His diagnosis was Addison's disease, an illness characterized by a failure of the body's adrenal glands and resulting general weakness, poor appetite, loss of weight, nausea, vomiting and circulatory collapse. Because Addison's disease destroyed the body's resistance to infection, it was considered fatal.

The Ambassador hired a registered nurse to sail home with Jack on the *Queen Mary*. When the ship arrived in New York, a priest boarded and gave him extreme unction, or last rites, before Jack was placed on a stretcher and flown to Boston, where the London diagnosis of Addison's disease was confirmed.

Jack would later describe the illness to columnist Joseph Alsop as "a sort of slow-motion leukemia" and confide that he doubted he would live past forty-five.

The family characterized Jack's illness as a mere recurrence of the malaria he suffered in the South Pacific, a story not questioned until the height of the 1960 presidential primary when some Lyndon Johnson insiders would charge that Jack was suffering from Addison's disease. The family covered up Jack's disability as it had Rosemary's.

The fact that Jack did not die and managed to remain as active as he did is due to the discovery of the "miracle drug" cortisone that gave new hope to Addison's disease sufferers. The discovery set off a great stampede for the drug, a supply of which the Kennedys quickly stored away in safe-deposit boxes around the country so that Jack would never run out.

Doctors at the time were only vaguely aware of the side effects of the miracle drug that included "a markedly increased sense of well-being approaching a state of euphoria accompanied by a real increase in energy, concentrating power, muscular strength and endurance." In the years to come, John F. Kennedy would become a textbook example of the side effects of cortisone. The perpetual tan (really skin discoloration), the thick hair even in middle age, the enhanced confidence and, of course, the boundless libido. But the fact that Jack was on a heavy regimen of cortisone would be kept just as secret as the fact that he suffered from a fatal disease.

A new crisis hit in February 1948, when the family gathered in Palm Beach and Kick joined them for a two-month stay. Just before returning to England, Kick finally found the courage to tell her parents that she was in love with a new man, Peter Milton, Earl of Fitzwilliam, nicknamed "Blood," a war hero and one of Britain's richest peers, a man who traced his ancestry back to William the Conqueror. The earl was not only a Protestant, but a married one at that. Kick assured her parents that they planned to marry as soon as he divorced his wife, a Guinness heiress.

Rose was distraught. A Protestant was bad enough, but a divorced Protestant was out of the question. Rose warned Kick that if she went ahead with this marriage she would be disowned by the family and dead to her. Joe, more realistic, acknowledged that he could not keep her from marrying again. He did manage to keep the romance out of the American press.

When Cholly Knickerbocker, the popular *Journal-American* society columnist, ran an item that Kick was considering a change of religion, Joe tried to have him fired.

Convinced that her place was with Peter, confident that she would still win over her father, Kick sailed back to England that April. Milton went forward with his divorce and they made plans to announce their engagement in May. Joe agreed to meet Kick and her fiancé in Paris on May 15.

On May 13 the Earl of Fitzwilliam chartered a small plane to take him and Kick to Cannes for a holiday and a visit to the horses he kept nearby. Against all advice, Kick and Fitzwilliam chartered a small light plane. A few hours after takeoff, tossed about by high winds, their plane was blown into the Crevennes Mountains in the Ardeche near the small fishing village of Privas. Kick and Fitzwilliam, and the two pilots, were killed instantly.

The Ambassador got the news at the George V hotel in Paris. He hurried south to Privas, hoping there was some mistake, and insisted on waiting in the rain until a peasant's cart, bearing the bodies, came down from the mountain. When it reached Joe he identified his favorite daughter.

The man who had everything had lost the two children most like him, the two he loved the most.

Kick was buried at Chatsworth, the Devonshire estate, under a stone that reads: "Joy she gave, and joy she has found."

Jack was notified of Kick's death in Washington. He was in the Georgetown house, lounging on a couch, listening to a record of the musical comedy *Finian's Rainbow*, with his aide Billy Sutton. He insisted on confirmation. A second call came a few minutes later, informing him that Kick's body had been identified. He made a remark about the sweetness of the soprano singing "How Are Things in Glocca Morra?," turned his head and began to cry.

Of all his brothers and sisters, Jack was the one most profoundly affected by Kick's death. He turned to Lem Billings.

"He was in terrible pain," Billings recalled for historian Goodwin. "He told me he couldn't get through the days without thinking of Kick at the most inappropriate times." They were all gone: Joe, Kick and Rosemary.

According to Billings, "The only thing that made sense, he decided, was to live for the moment, treating each day as if it were his last, demanding of life constant intensity, adventure and pleasure."

Many friends were shocked at Rose's attitude. She seemed to regard the airplane crash as a judgment from God.

There can be no doubt that Kick's death had a profound impact on her younger sisters, Eunice, Patricia and Jean. Their oldest sister Rosemary had been a low-achiever and worse, rebellious and given to wandering Washington late at night. When it began to seem that she was becoming sexually active, she was forced to submit to a dangerous operation that completely disabled her and was sent away for good.

No doubt Rose reminded them that their favorite sister, the lively Kick, had married outside the Church, defying her parents and their clerical advisors. And the marriage had lasted less than two years before God took her young husband.

In spite of God's punishment, Kick had, in Rose's eyes, defied the Church again when she made plans to marry a *divorced* Protestant and even went off for a dirty weekend with him before marriage. For that, Rose could conclude, God had taken her life. The lesson seemed to be: Disregard your Catholic training once for a man and God will take him; disregard it twice and God will take you. No wonder the girls grew up into docile women, saintly and long-suffering. Even Eunice, the most active, pledged herself to a life of good work among the retarded, as if to atone for the family's treatment of Rosemary.

No such lessons were ever held out to the Kennedy men.

Since graduating from Harvard in March 1948, Bobby had followed Jack's example and put in a stint as a journalist overseas. He was sent to the Middle East by the *Boston Post*. An Israeli tank captain offered him a ride from Tel Aviv to Jerusalem in his tank; the convoy he would otherwise have taken was wiped out.

Poor grades kept Bobby from following his brothers into Harvard Law School, but family friend James Landis, former dean there, arranged instead for him to be admitted to the University of Virginia Law School. Bobby was already courting Ethel Skakel, an energetic madcap, one of seven children of the founder of Great Lakes Carbon Corporation, and a Manhattanville College friend of his sister Jean.

At law school Bobby was undistinguished, except for his work revitalizing the Law School Forum. He brought many important speakers to Charlottesville, among them family friends like Supreme Court justice William O. Douglas and Senator Joseph McCarthy. No one caused the sensation that Ralph Bunche, the black diplomat, did when he appeared in the segregated college town, but Bobby refused to cave in to protesters who objected to his mixed-seating plans.

On June 17, 1950, Bobby married Ethel Skakel in St. Mary's Church in Greenwich, Connecticut. The wedding was followed by a lavish reception at the Skakel estate. Their first child, Kathleen Hartington, was born in 1951, the same year Bobby earned his law degree. The following year, on September 24, their first son, named Joseph Patrick for Bobby's dead brother, was born.

In late 1951 Bobby became a Justice Department attorney in Brooklyn, New York. As a federal lawyer, he worked for the

Criminal Division uncovering evidence against grafters and tax evaders. This was his first glimpse into the underworld he would later explore as chief counsel for the Senate's McClellan Committee on labor racketeering. Investigative work appealed to him, fulfilling his almost religious drive to hunt down evil.

"With Bobby, it's always the white hats and the black hats, the good guys versus the bad guys," his bride, Ethel, explained.

Jack had faced only token opposition when he ran for a second term in congress in 1950 and almost immediately after the election he began to lay ground for a challenge to Henry Cabot Lodge, Jr., Massachusetts's incumbent Republican senator. To build up his foreign relations credentials, he planned an October 1951 trip to Israel and Japan, accompanied by his sister Patricia. The Ambassador insisted that he also bring Bobby along. In India they dined with Prime Minister Nehru. They visited Saigon, but the trip ended in Japan where Jack became ill with an infection that caused his fever to shoot up to 106 and once again made the family fear for his life. He seemed to take strength from Bobby's presence and was on his feet by the time they reached home.

Never forgetting that all politics is local, Jack kept up a busy schedule of speaking tours of Massachusetts. He accumulated a large index-card file of just about everyone he met in the thirty-nine cities and 312 towns he visited. That became the core mailing list for his next campaign.

When Jack's senate campaign began, his longtime advisor Kenneth O'Donnell insisted that Bobby was the only one to run it. Bobby resisted. He and his growing brood were living in New York and he was making a name for himself with the Justice Department. Besides, Bobby pleaded that he knew nothing about electoral politics.

O'Donnell persisted, predicting a humiliating defeat if matters were allowed to drift. Finally Bobby relented and agreed to leave for Boston.

As a campaigner, Bobby's greatest value may have been his willingness to be the driven, ruthless pragmatist, so Jack could stay above that kind of thing and be perceived as pure. Soon Jack came to see his younger brother as "the only one I can count on when it comes down to it."

In the campaign itself, personality emerged as the key issue, with the dignified aristocrat Lodge no match for the media-wise Jack. Looking ahead, the Ambassador was seen wearing a deep blue tie with the silver inscription "Kennedy for President," a gift from friends.

The Kennedy campaign released 900,000 copies of an eight-page tabloid on Jack with the photos of Joe, Jr., and Jack on the cover under the headline: JOHN FULFILLS DREAM OF BROTHER JOE WHO MET DEATH IN THE SKY OVER THE ENGLISH CHANNEL. Inside were drawings of Jack Kennedy rescuing shipmates in the South Pacific and a reprint of John Hersey's article on the saga of the *PT-109*. The Kennedys spared no expense to get the publication into circulation. The tabloid was sent out to every registered voter in the state of Massachusetts.

The Ambassador exerted his power in subtle but important ways. According to J. Edgar Hoover's biographer Anthony Summers, Joe had been a Special Service contact of the FBI since 1943. Knowing of Hoover's jealousy of the CIA, he kept the FBI chief informed of what he learned as a member of Dwight Eisenhower's board on Foreign Intelligence.

Because of Joe, from 1951 on the FBI would maintain a Resident Agency, staffed by four agents, at Hyannis Port. Its only reason for existence seemingly to keep the Kennedy family happy. But if the Ambassador was on good terms with the bureau chief, his son Jack was not. He had never forgiven Hoover for breaking up his youthful idyll with Inga Arvad.

JACK: "PEOPLE WILL SAY I'M QUEER IF I DON'T GET MARRIED."

The endorsement of the *Boston Post* was critical for Kennedy and Lodge. Lodge estimated it was worth forty thousand votes. Although the *Post*'s owner, John Fox, a passionate anti-Communist Republican, had privately promised to support Lodge, he was desperately short of cash.

A loan of $500,000 inspired Fox to endorse Jack's candidacy. Fox and Joe denied any connection.

With Jack's election on November 4, 1953, it was clear that

Kennedy, Inc., had forged a political machine that was unstoppable.

The next step was to find a bride for Jack. This was an important part of Jack's image. He told aide Ruth McMillan: "People will say I'm queer if I don't get married."

CHAPTER SEVEN

JACK AIMS FOR VICE PRESIDENT AND TAKES A BRIDE

How long do you have to live in this country before you become an American? We've been here for two generations. Isn't that enough?

—Joseph P. Kennedy, 1953

From here on, you must think of Jack less as a friend and more as a potential candidate for the presidency of the United States.

—Joseph P. Kennedy's advice to Lem Billings, 1957

Jacqueline Lee Bouvier was the daughter of a socially ambitious mother and an incorrigible rake with impeccable social credentials. Jackie's maternal grandfather James Thomas Lee was a brilliant second-generation Irishman who put himself through City College and Columbia Law School and made a fortune in New York City real estate and banking. By the time his daughter Janet met John Vernon Bouvier III, most of the Bouvier money was long gone and "Black Jack" would squander the rest. Black Jack Bouvier was sixteen years older than his bride when they wed in East Hampton in 1928 and he was unfaithful to her on their honeymoon cruise. But he had the social connections Janet yearned for. Their daughter Jacqueline Lee was born the following July 28, 1929, just months before the stock market crash that would change their world forever.

After several separations and the birth of a second daughter,

Caroline Lee (known simply as Lee), on March 3, 1933, Janet and Black Jack divorced in 1940. Two years later Janet married Hugh Dudley Auchincloss, a wealthy stockbroker (Auchincloss, Parker and Redpath), with impeccable social lineage. "Hughdie," as he was known, came with a Park Avenue apartment and two waterfront estates, forty-six-acre Merrywood on the Potomac in McLean, Virginia, and ninety-seven-acre Hammersmith Farm in Newport, Rhode Island.

Although nowhere near the libertine Black Jack Bouvier was, Hughdie had one indulgence. He was an obsessive collector of pornography in all forms, with one of the largest collections in the world.

Auchincloss had been married and divorced twice before. By his first wife, Maria Chrapovitsky, the daughter of a Russian naval officer, he had a son, Hugh Dudley III, known as Yusha. By his second, Nina Gore Vidal, daughter of Senator Thomas P. Gore of Oklahoma, he had two more children: Nina Gore ("Nini") and Thomas Gore. He had also acquired a stepson, Gore Vidal. Auchincloss and Janet had two more: Janet Jennings (1945) and Jamie (1947).

Black Jack sank into alcoholic self-indulgence and although there were many women in his life, he never married again. In 1944 he spent eight weeks in the alcohol rehabilitation program at luxurious Silver Hill, where his brother Bud had been treated sixteen years earlier. Bud died of alcoholism at the age of thirty-six. Silver Hill was equally unsuccessful in treating Black Jack, who would return there in 1946 and 1947.

JACKIE: "THE KENNEDYS ARE REALLY TERRIBLY *BOURGEOIS.*"

Jackie was educated at the exclusive Miss Porter's. In her graduation entry in the yearbook, she said her ambition was "not to be a housewife." In 1947 she was named "Queen Deb of the Year" by Hearst columnist Cholly Knickerbocker. She made the dean's list at Vassar College. She beat out 1,280 entrants to win the *Vogue* Prix de Paris writing contest with an essay in which she named Sergey Diaghilev, Baudelaire and Oscar Wilde as the persons she wished she might have known. Her stepfather persuaded her to decline the prize, a one-year trainee position with the magazine that included a six-month stint in the Paris office. He seemed to fear that she might stay in France permanently. She spent the school year 1949–50 at the Sorbonne in Paris, and went on to earn a degree in French literature from George Washington University.

After graduation she took a $42.50-a-week job as the Inquiring Camera Girl of the *Washington Times-Herald*. She met the rising young Massachusetts senator at a Georgetown dinner party and asked to interview him, asking the question, "Can you give any reason why a contented bachelor would want to get married?"

Although Jackie and Jack had been dating since June 1951, both saw others and by the summer of 1952 Jack was too immersed in his first senate campaign to get involved. Only after the election, when he escorted Jackie to Dwight Eisenhower's inaugural ball and invited her to the opening session of the Eighty-third Congress, did things get serious.

Jack, who had once told a newspaper interviewer that he wanted a wife who was "something nice. Intelligent, but not too brainy," was smitten.

One of the first insiders to realize that the relationship between the senator and the debutante was serious was Jack's secretary, Evelyn Lincoln. Her job had always included juggling the many women he was seeing and to call them for him. Jackie stood out because she wasn't on Lincoln's telephone list. "When he didn't ask me to call Jackie, I knew that she had to be someone special," Lincoln recalled. "One day, he came in and said: 'I'm going to have an engagement party on June 25th.'

"I said 'Who?' And he said: 'Jacqueline Bouvier.' "

Yet around that time Jackie confided to her cousin John Davis that Jack was so vain "he goes to a hairdresser almost every day to have his hair done, so it'll always look bushy and fluffy." She also claimed that if no one recognized him at a party or a reception, or a photographer failed to take his picture, "he sulks afterwards for *hours.*" As for the rest of the family, "the Kennedys are really terribly *bourgeois.*"

As for Jack, Jackie's cousin John H. Davis writes: "If he had not come from such a social-climbing family and did not have such powerful political ambitions, he would probably never have got married at all."

On the whole, the cousin found Jackie's attitude toward her beau, "blasé and condescending," so he was surprised to learn the following spring that they had become engaged.

"JACK KENNEDY WAS TERRIBLY FOND OF HIS MALE FRIENDS."

Almost immediately problems emerged. The young couple was rarely alone together. Jackie discovered that her fiancé preferred the company of men. "Jack Kennedy was terribly fond of his male friends and his family," recalled Davis. "He had this damnable tendency to always have people around."

On May 23, following a seven-year courtship, Eunice Kennedy married Sargent Shriver at St. Patrick's Cathedral in New York. At the reception Eunice toasted her new husband: "I searched all my life for someone like my father and Sarge came closest."

Jack, possibly moved by the occasion, soon proposed to Jackie by telegram. She was in London photographing the coronation of Queen Elizabeth II. "He knew in his gut that Jackie, a free spirit, could not be tamed to behave like other Kennedy wives and women," said his longtime friend George Smathers. When Jackie accepted he gave her an emerald-and-diamond ring. They did not announce the engagement immediately because Jack and his father did not want to overshadow a big story in the upcoming *Saturday Evening Post* on "The Senate's Gay Young Bachelor."

On June 25 the engagement was officially announced at a party given by Janet and Hugh D. Auchincloss at Hammersmith Farm. Jack was well aware that Janet did not consider him good enough for her daughter.

Yet weeks before the wedding, Jack took off for a European idyll with another male friend, his old Harvard roommate Torbert Macdonald. The two bachelors charted a yacht and sailed off the coast of France, and visited Stockholm and London. Much to Jackie's shock, her future husband was gone for weeks without a word.

At their rehearsal dinner, where he gave her a diamond bracelet, she would claim that throughout their entire courtship the nearest he ever came to a love letter was a single postcard from

Bermuda. She held it up for the guests to see. It read: "Wish you were here."

JACK BOUVIER'S DISGRACE

On her wedding day Jackie wore a floor-length veil of rosepoint lace that had been worn by her grandmother, her mother and Lee. The ceremony was held at St. Mary's Roman Catholic Church in Newport on September 12, 1953. It was a clear and windy day. Unfortunately, Black Jack, fresh from drying out in a French clinic, fell off the wagon in a big way and had to be confined to his hotel room during the service. Jackie's stepfather Hughdie stepped in and walked her down the aisle. Lee (who had married in spring 1953) was matron of honor and her new husband, Michael Canfield, was an usher. The 750 guests included everyone from notorious senator Joseph McCarthy to screen star Marion Davies. Jackie's wedding gift to her new husband was a St. Christopher medal.

The newlyweds spent their wedding night in New York at the Waldorf-Astoria and left the next day for a honeymoon in Acapulco. One of her first moves was to write her father a long letter, forgiving him for the wedding no-show.

On April 24, 1954, Patricia Kennedy married movie star Peter Lawford in a ten-minute ceremony at St. Thomas More church in New York. The wedding was followed by a reception for three hundred at the Plaza Hotel.

Joe had no objections to his fourth daughter marrying a bisexual British-born actor. He did not even insist on a prenuptial agreement. Rose was distressed because Lawford was Anglican, but relented when he agreed that the children would be raised as Catholics.

In many ways Lawford was a Kennedy man. He began sexual relations at age ten, frequented prostitutes and had loathed his eccentric, self-centered mother from childhood.

Almost immediately Lawford proved his usefulness as a member of Kennedy, Inc., by introducing Jack to Marilyn Monroe. It was at a party at the home of agent Charles Feldman. Marilyn was with Joe DiMaggio, her husband of six months, and the marriage was already showing signs of strain.

During spring and early summer Jack suffered from increasing trouble with his back. He was forced to use crutches and was in excruciating pain. When Congress adjourned that August, he headed straight for the Cape to confer with a team of specialists. He had been managing to live with his Addison's disease for years on a program of cortisone implanted every three months, supplemented by oral doses daily. They recommended a complicated and extremely risky operation. Any surgery for someone with Addison's disease was dangerous. After his experience with Rosemary's disastrous brain surgery, Joe tried to discourage his son from having the risky operation, but Jack could not live with the pain.

Jack was admitted to the New York Hospital for Special Surgery on October 10. As usual, the Kennedy family floated a false cover story, through the *New York Times*, that he would undergo a spinal operation "to clear up a wartime injury." He was not operated on until October 21, and after several rocky days he was given the last rites of the Church. By late December, still weak, he was removed to his father's house in Palm Beach. The following February he returned for a second operation in New York and then back to Palm Beach for a long convalescence.

The devoted Lem Billings took a leave of absence from his marketing business to spend a month with Jack there.

Throughout this ordeal Jack put his time to good use by working on a book. Theodore Sorensen and several university professors including Jules Davis of Georgetown, Arthur Schlesinger, Jr., James MacGregor Burns and Allan Nevins, collaborated to help him produce *Profiles in Courage*, the book he dedicated to Jackie.

Profiles in Courage related the stories of eight political leaders, from John Quincy Adams of Massachusetts to Thomas Hart Benton of Missouri, whose political courage led them to defy their constituents and their colleagues in order to serve the national good.

In March 1957, after much vigorous lobbying by Arthur Krock, *Profiles in Courage* won a Pulitzer Prize.

JACKIE LEAVES JACK: "I'M NEVER GOING BACK."

The first few years were difficult. There were Jack's two spinal operations and Jackie's 1955 miscarriage. When his health permitted, Jack was totally focused on his next step: the quest for the presidency. This required a great deal of self-absorption. For one thing, Jack was obsessed with how he photographed. His father had not spent years in the movie business for nothing. In the mid-1950s, Jack visited fashion photographer Howell Conant at his studio on Manhattan's West Thirty-fifth Street. Conant had built his reputation photographing some of the most beautiful women of his time, among them Grace Kelly, Janet Leigh and Doris Day. He also had important advertising accounts, from Ponds cold cream to Eastman-Kodak. He was the perfect combination for Jack: someone who knew how to capture sex appeal and how to sell a product.

Jack spent an entire day with Conant, posing, then studying the contact sheets to decide on his best angle. Together they settled on a pensive look into space that conveniently hid the fact that his eyes were a bit too close together.

In August 1956, shortly after Jack lost a hard-fought struggle for the vice-presidential nomination at the Democratic convention in Chicago, Jackie gave birth to a stillborn daughter. But by that time Jack was off sailing with Teddy and friend George Smathers on the Mediterranean.

Marriage had not dampened Jack's lust for other women, and he even had relationships with some of Jackie's friends. One of them acknowledges that she was one of "a cast of thousands."

In July 1955 Jackie walked out and went to visit her sister, who was living in London with her husband, publishing heir Michael Canfield. Lee was equally unhappy in a different way and the two sisters went off to Paris. Peter Ward, brother of the Earl of Dudly, recalls sailing with the sisters in the south of France that summer. "Jackie left Jack Kennedy at that time," claims Ward. "They were split. Jack was having trouble with his back, and Jackie had rather a bad conscience about that, but that was all. She said 'I'm never going back' in my presence several times. She wasn't the least upset and seemed to be having a very good time."

As for Jackie, she soon discovered she was not cut out to be a political wife. "Jackie didn't like people in the political world, and she never wanted to go campaigning with Jack, ever," recalled Evelyn Lincoln. "So he lived a life of his own. He was gone quite a bit, and she traveled a lot. She would go to Europe, and Hyannis Port . . . or Palm Beach. . . . But in their way, they loved each other."

Jackie, who had already experienced one miscarriage during the first year of their marriage, could no longer bear to be in the big house she and Jack had purchased in Virginia. Four months after the stillbirth, they sold the house to Bobby and Ethel and moved back to Georgetown. Bobby and Ethel were glad to move in with their growing family. Ethel had given birth to their third child, Robert F. Kennedy, Jr., on January 17, 1954, and a fourth, David Anthony, on June 15, 1955.

According to a friend of the couple, Jack and Jackie separated three years after their marriage.

Joe, concerned about his son's political future, met with Black Jack Bouvier and together the two forged a reconciliation between their children. "The agreement was that Jackie would go back to Jack, but he wouldn't fling his affairs in her face," says the friend.

On May 19, 1956, Jean Kennedy, twenty-seven, married Stephen Edward Smith at St. Patrick's in New York. Smith was a graduate of Georgetown University and an executive in his family tugboat-based transportation company. Grandson of a three-term congressman, he was once described as "John F. Kennedy crossed with Frank Sinatra." Impressed, Joe put his son-in-law in charge of the Park Agency.

That summer, at the Democratic convention in Chicago, Jack was asked to make the nominating speech for presidential candidate Adlai Stevenson. He did so well, he was encouraged to campaign for the vice-presidential nomination. For the first time, Jack defied his father's advice. The Ambassador was convinced that he would be committing political suicide. Stevenson was sure to lose in the general election against the popular incumbent, Dwight D. Eisenhower, and the Ambassador believed that the party would blame Jack. But although Jack did not win the nomination, the exposure established his image as a youthful, determined fighter, and Bobby's experience on the convention floor, desperately scouring for votes, would be invaluable four years later.

Black Jack died in August 1957 at the age of sixty-six. Jack Kennedy was ailing himself, but knowing how much it meant to Jackie, he was determined that his father-in-law would get a prominent obituary in the *New York Times*. He went in person to the office of the managing editor of the *Times*, accompanied by Jackie's uncle, and carrying the obituary Jackie had written herself and a photograph obtained from one of Black Jack's last girlfriends. The obituary ran, but not the photo.

The funeral for Black Jack was held on August 6 in St. Patrick's Cathedral in New York. He was laid to rest at St. Philomena's Cemetery in East Hampton.

By that time Lee Bouvier Canfield was seeing Stanislas Radziwill, a Polish prince known as "Stas." Cut off from his country and fortune, first by the Nazi invasion of Poland and then the Russian occupation, Stas had settled in London, recouped a modest fortune in real estate, acquired British citizenship, and maintained the honorific title of prince.

By February 1958 Lee and the prince had decided to leave their mutual spouses. They married quietly on March 19, 1959, in a civil ceremony at Merrywood. Their son, Antony (later Anthony), was born in Switzerland on August 4, 1959.

Even before the marriage, Lee and Stas sought to have her marriage to Michael Canfield annulled by the Catholic Church. This was done for Stas, who sought to please his devout father. In 1961 the Supreme Tribunal of the Holy Office in Rome refused the annulment, with no possibility of appeal. But by then Lee's brother-in-law was President of the United States and ultimately, and very quietly, an annulment was obtained and she married Radziwill again, this time in a Catholic ceremony in 1963. Ironically, by that time the marriage to Radziwill had also begun to fade. They would grow apart and finally divorce in September 1974.

Jack and Jackie's first child was born on November 27, 1957. Caroline Bouvier Kennedy was delivered by caesarian section. She was christened not in the senator's home state, Massachusetts, nor in Washington, D.C., but in St. Patrick's Cathedral in New

York on December 13, possibly to position Jack for maximum media exposure.

That same year, Jack won a seat on the Senate Foreign Relations Committee and was the subject of a *Time* cover story. (Henry Luce was, after all, a close friend of Joe's.)

After working on Jack's 1952 senate campaign, Bobby had to decide on the next step for his own career. In 1953 he worked briefly for the Hoover Commission headed by former president Herbert Hoover. Then Bobby learned that the Senate's Permanent Subcommittee on Investigations, under Senator Joseph McCarthy, wanted an assistant counsel. The idea of uncovering conspiracies and corruption appealed to him. Encouraged by the Ambassador, he joined McCarthy's staff. He was there on and off until 1959. Several of his departures were precipitated because of clashes with fellow staff member and rival Roy Cohn.

It was Bobby's pursuit of Teamster leader Jimmy Hoffa that would establish him as a national figure in his own right. For most of 1956, except for his efforts to help Jack gain the vice-presidential nomination, Bobby was absorbed in preparations for the Hoffa investigation. In mid-September, the Government Operations Subcommittee (soon known nationally as the Rackets Committee) began its long investigation.

In January 1957, the Senate expanded the special McClellan Committee; Senator John F. Kennedy, who was on the parent Government Operations Committee, joined the eight-member subcommittee as one of four Democrats.

For the next three years, the labor hearings would dominate Bobby's life. There is no doubt that Bobby Kennedy's war on Jimmy Hoffa was a personal vendetta. Psychohistorian Nancy Gager Clinch believes that Hoffa held an undeniable fascination for Bobby, partly because the two men closely resembled each other in many ways. Neither was a big man physically. Both were driven, as demanding of others as they were of themselves. Each inspired intense love or hate in his associates. Privately, they lived lives of intense self-discipline. Neither smoked. Bobby seldom drank, Hoffa never did. Separately, journalists had compared each man to a coiled steel spring.

Jack's 1958 campaign for a second senate term was vigorously managed by Bobby. Brother Ted and brother-in-law Stephen

Smith participated for the first time. Jack racked up the necessary big victory.

JOE: "JACK IS THE GREATEST ATTRACTION IN THE COUNTRY TODAY."

Major features on Jack and Jackie and the rest of the family soon appeared in *Life, Redbook,* the *Ladies' Home Journal, Look,* the *Washington Post* and the *Reader's Digest.* Kennedy was also prominent in the bookstores. In 1958 there was an "authorized" biography by James MacGregor Burns and articles ghosted for Jack in the *New York Times Magazine, The Reporter,* and *Foreign Affairs.*

Joe could rightfully boast that "Jack is the greatest attraction in the country today."

In the spring of 1958 Jackie and Jack were invited to a cocktail party for Sir Winston Churchill on the *Christina,* Aristotle Onassis's yacht, docked at Skorpios. Ari was not impressed with Jack, who was already being touted as a presidential candidate, but the fifty-eight-year-old tycoon was quite taken with the twenty-nine-year-old Jackie. "There's something provocative about that lady," he later told a friend. "She's got a carnal soul." Their paths would not cross again until 1963.

Jackie's "carnal soul" was apparently wasted on her Kennedy man. That summer when she took baby Caroline to Hyannis Port, Jack conducted at least one affair.

Not every fascinating story about the young senator made it into the popular media. Some stories got no farther than the secret files of J. Edgar Hoover. There was, for instance, the story of the Georgetown couple that became obsessed with Jack's philandering. One night in 1958, Leonard and Florence Kater were disturbed by the sound of pebbles being thrown at an upstairs window. The window belonged to twenty-year-old Pamela Turnure, a receptionist in Jack's Senate office, who rented a room from them. The man Turnure let in that night was Senator John F. Kennedy and he became a regular nocturnal visitor.

Deeply offended and deeply Catholic, the Katers rigged up a tape recorder to pick up the sounds of the couple's lovemaking and even photographed Jack sneaking out in the middle of the night. According to journalist Anthony Summers, they spied on the couple for months, even after Turnure had moved out of their house.

THE ROSEMARY PROBLEM SURFACES AGAIN

Dealing with media at this level was a tricky game. It required creating an impression of openness and candor while maintaining the secrecy around such matters as Jack's poor health. Above all, there was the Rosemary problem. She remained the madwoman in the attic.

As late as 1958 the family was maintaining the fiction that Rosemary had become a quasi nun, content to renounce the glamorous world of her siblings to teach less fortunate children. In the *Saturday Evening Post* story on Jack, Rosemary was described as "a schoolteacher in Wisconsin." In Joseph Dineen's *The Kennedy Family* he describes Rosemary as having a "vocation," the traditional Catholic term for a call to the religious life, and writes: "It was inevitable, perhaps, that she should study at Marymount convent in Tarrytown, New York, and devote her life to the sick and afflicted and particularly to backward and handicapped children. She is the least publicized of all the Kennedys. She prefers it that way and her wishes are respected." Poor Rosemary.

That summer, Robert's merciless grilling of Jimmy Hoffa before a national television audience earned him a reputation as an implacable prosecutor. Bobby, too, converted his experience to a book, *The Enemy Within*, written with John Seigenthaler.

In the spring of 1959, with the presidential election campaign approaching, the Katers were still obsessed with Jack's reckless behavior. They mailed details of the "adulterer's" conduct to the newspapers, including audiotapes and a photograph of Jack emerging from Pamela Turnure's apartment at one A.M. on July 11, 1958. Naturally, the papers had no interest in such a story about a Kennedy. Only the *Washington Star* ran a small item on the couple. According to Anthony summers, one company, Stearn Publications, sent the Katers' letter to J. Edgar Hoover. He quietly obtained a copy of the sex tapes and offered them to Lyndon Johnson.

The Katers now took their campaign to the streets and began showing up at Jack's political rallies with hand-fashioned signs denouncing him as an adulterer. They followed him to Independence, Missouri, when he called on former president Harry S. Truman. They telephoned the Ambassador and Cardinal Cushing, but neither patriarch nor priest was any more interested than the media. Mrs. Kater took to picketing the White House with a sign saying "Do you want an Adulterer in the White House?" None of this ever made it into the popular press.

The Katers were apparently unaware that their tapes and photographs were just a small part of the rapidly expanding file that J. Edgar Hoover was keeping on Jack Kennedy. Already accumulating in there was the March 1960 report that Jack "had been compromised with a woman in Las Vegas" and visited by an airline hostess in Miami. There was the framed photograph on the senator's desk that showed him and several other men entertaining several nude women aboard a yacht, and the "affidavits from two mulatto prostitutes in New York."

On September 11, 1959, days after Ethel gave birth to their fifth child, Mary Kerry, and one day after the Senate Rackets Committee concluded its three-year inquiry, Bobby resigned as chief counsel, stating that the committee's purpose had been "fruitfully realized" with passage of a labor reform bill and exposure of union corruption and racketeering. Bobby took time out to write his own bestseller, *The Enemy Within,* then he was free to focus on Jack's next step—the presidency of the United States.

Jack and Bobby had turned the potentially dangerous investigation into a personal triumph that brought them the attention of the important press. They appeared on television's *Meet the Press* and *Face the Nation,* and on the covers of national magazines.

CHAPTER EIGHT
Jack's Presidential Campaign

Jack and Bob will run the show, while Ted's in charge of hiding Joe.

—Republican jingle, circa 1960

I think it's so unfair of people to be against Jack because he's a Catholic. He's such a poor Catholic. Now, if it were Bobby, I could understand it.

—Jacqueline Kennedy, 1960

Jack Kennedy's campaign was based on a New Frontier and his favorite campaign slogan became "It's time to get this country moving again." And move he did, but few realized that he was fueled by potent chemicals.

Sometime on the eve of the 1960s, John F. Kennedy discovered speed. Since his childhood he had managed to function in spite of his terrible health. Cortisone had been a godsend, but he was about to get hooked on something even more powerful. He was introduced to the legendary Max Jacobson, a Manhattan doctor who had fled Germany in 1936, set up practice in New York, and became the physician to the stars. Jacobson's fame as "Dr. Feelgood" was based on his "miracle tissue regenerator," shots that were actually a secret combination of vitamins, painkillers, human placenta and amphetamines. His patients included Truman Capote, designer Emilio Pucci and Tennessee Williams.

John and Jacqueline Kennedy began taking his shots during JFK's presidential campaign in 1960, and he would become indispensable to Jack's future.

EUNICE: "WE DON'T TALK ABOUT CABINET JOBS AT HOME—ALL WE TALK ABOUT IS WINNING."

On January 2, 1960, in the caucus room of the Senate, Jack declared he was a candidate for the presidency.

The quest for the nomination would be a struggle. Likely contenders for the Democratic nomination included Adlai Stevenson, Averell Harriman, Hubert Humphrey and Senate majority leader, Lyndon B. Johnson.

Bobby, thirty-four, was managing Jack's campaign. And for the first time, Teddy took on a responsible role in a Kennedy campaign. Fifteen years younger than Jack, he was, in every sense, part of another generation. He had always been the chubby little brother, barely noticed and never taken seriously.

In Chicago, Eunice denied rumors that her husband had his eye on the post of Secretary of Health, Education and Welfare. "We don't even talk about cabinet jobs at home," she said. "All we talk about is winning." Then she picked up her year-old son, Timothy, held him aloft and cooed to him in a chanting fashion, "Win, win, win."

MONEY TALKS

One of the first, and most important, contributions Joe Kennedy made to his son's campaign was to form the Ken-Air Corp., purchase for it a $385,000 Corvair propeller airplane, and then lease it to the candidate at $1.75 a mile. The plane, which Jack Kennedy named the *Caroline*, became a tremendous advantage. While Hubert Humphrey either wasted time waiting around airports for commercial flights or lumbered about in his campaign bus, Jack Kennedy tore here and there in the *Caroline*, covering more territory in less time and at less expense.

Jack Meets Judy

On February 7, on a campaign stop in Las Vegas, Jack was introduced to Judith Campbell by Frank Sinatra. After Sinatra's show at the Sands, the party went to the Copa Room for drinks. Judy was seated next to Ted, who was campaign coordinator for the Rocky Mountain states. After a few drinks, she would later recall, Ted "leaned over to ask if I would show him the town." Judy agreed, flattered that Ted seemed to want to know everything about her, and unaware that the young and handsome Ted was already married. "He was the baby brother," she said, "walking in his older brother's shadow."

Later that night Ted escorted Judy to her room and although he attempted to join her inside, she stopped him at the door. When he pressed the issue, she warned, "I know you want me to lose my patience."

"Oh God, no," young Ted laughed, "that's the last thing I want you to lose." He finally said his good-night, adding, "You can't blame a guy for trying."

But Ted wasn't through with Judy. He would keep after her to fly back with him to Denver, where he was working on the campaign. He phoned her several times from the airport as he was leaving, unaware that Judy's affair with his big brother had already begun.

Jack and the beautiful young woman, recently divorced from leading man William Campbell, clicked immediately. Soon there were daily phone calls and a rendezvous at the Plaza Hotel in New York City on March 7. According to Judy, the sex that first time was disappointing but Jack continued to call her regularly from his campaign stops in Wisconsin, West Virginia, Indiana and Washington.

Judy continued to see others, and in April, at the Hotel Fontainebleu in Miami Beach, Sinatra introduced her to Sam Giancana, one of the most powerful men in organized crime. Giancana also had a long relationship with the popular singer Phyllis McGuire. But once he learned of Judy's close friendship to John F. Kennedy, she represented more to him than a young and pretty face.

Small, dapper, weasel-faced Sam Giancana was the head of the Chicago Mafia, credited with two hundred killings. He controlled betting, prostitution, loan sharking and owned interests in three Las Vegas hotels, the Riviera, the Stardust, and the Desert Inn.

Jack and Bobby identified the West Virginia primary as key to winning the nomination. The state's nomination was ninety-five percent Protestant and a win there would convince convention delegates that Jack's Catholicism would not be an issue in the presidential election.

Jack's opponent in the primary was Hubert Humphrey, the senator from Minnesota, beloved by West Virginia coal miners for his longtime union support and folksy, old-fashioned campaign style. But Humphrey's small-town ways were no match for the Kennedy bandwagon's deep pockets and high technology. There's no doubt that Jack's big TV budget helped, as did his courageous appearance on television to declare: "... when any man stands on the steps of the Capitol and takes the oath of office of President, he is swearing to support the separation of church and state; he puts one hand on the Bible and raises the other hand to God as he takes the oath. And if he breaks his oath, he is not only committing a crime against the Constitution, for which Congress can impeach him—and should impeach him—but he is committing a sin against God. A sin against God, because he has sworn on the Bible."

The Kennedy men were not content to rely on statesmanship alone. At Jack's request, Judy Campbell arranged a meeting for him with Sam Giancana at the Fontainebleu. Giancana agreed to use his influence with West Virginia officials to ensure victory there.

Giancana sent his lieutenant, Paul "Skinny" D'Amato, into West Virginia to get out the vote. D'Amato met with the sheriffs who controlled the state's political machine. He forgave debts many of them had run up at his 500 Club in Atlantic City and handed cash payments to others.

FBI wiretaps reveal that Frank Sinatra also disbursed large mob donations to pay off election officials.

On election night, fearing that he would lose the state, Jack stayed in Washington, and he and Jackie went to the movies with Ben and Toni Bradlee. Bradlee was the Washington bureau chief of *Newsweek*. When they returned home they learned that Jack had won and immediately flew off to Charlottesville in his private plane. Hubert Humphrey conceded and withdrew from the presidential race.

Defeating Hubert Humphrey was the single most important victory of Jack's campaign.

Giancana apparently believed that in helping Kennedy's campaign, he was gaining a friend in the White House and protection from future prosecution by the government. He was in for a rude awakening.

HARRY TRUMAN: "I'M NOT AGAINST THE POPE, I'M AGAINST THE POP."

After the first convention session, Jack returned to his suite at the Beverly Hilton and spent some private time with Judy Campbell. He tried to talk her into a three-way with a pretty black woman, but she declined.

On July 11 the Democratic National Convention at Los Angeles nominated John F. Kennedy for president.

Party leaders were still leery of Jack. Truman opposed him, telling reporters, "I'm not against the Pope, I'm against the Pop." Eleanor Roosevelt regarded him as one of "the new managerial elite that has neither principles nor character."

Joe and Rose stayed secretly at the Santa Monica mansion of Marion Davies, and kept in touch with Jack's headquarters at the Biltmore Hotel sixteen miles away via a battery of poolside telephones. But by the time Jack gave his acceptance speech before the convention, Joe was already on his way back to New York.

Always conscious of Kennedy, Inc.'s, image in the media, Joe, Sr., made it a point to call his old friend Henry Luce from the airport and arrange to watch his son's acceptance speech in the latter's apartment. The founder of *Time* and *Life* was arguably the most powerful publisher in America, and Joe had cultivated their relationship since his Roosevelt days. Luce had always been alternately appalled and fascinated by Joe's cynicism. The two men discussed their sons, and Joe suggested what Henry should do for his own son: "Why don't you just buy him a safe congressional seat?" Luce was shocked. "What do you mean by that? You can't do *that!*" "Come on, Harry," said Joe, "you and I both know how to do it. Of course it can be done."

ANGIE DICKINSON: "THE MOST REMARKABLE SIXTY SECONDS OF MY LIFE."

Jack is said to have celebrated his nomination by skinny-dipping in the Lawfords' swimming pool with star Angie Dickinson and his equally nude brother Bobby. Although she once called being with Jack "the most remarkable sixty seconds of my life," the star has usually been mum on the subject. Her silence only fed the rumors that surround their relationship.

Another relationship was heating up that was far more potentially explosive. Days after Jack won the Democratic nomination, Marilyn Monroe invited her friend Jeanne Carmen, a beautiful blond golfer and actress who had appeared opposite leading men from Ricardo Montalban to Jerry Lewis, to what she promised would be "the wildest party" at the Lawfords' Santa Monica beach house. Jack had specifically asked Peter Lawford to have Marilyn there.

On the drive down Carmen asked how Jack was in bed. "Well, let's put it this way"—Marilyn shrugged—"I've had better. He's a little too quick to suit me. But he seems to be a fast learner."

At the beach house Carmen was introduced to the candidate. "I could tell right off the bat he was the type of guy who was playing a numbers game," she recalled, but acknowledged his charm. "Jack was such a gentleman, I was really impressed with him— and attracted to him, I have to admit."

Carmen was taken by surprise later that day when Marilyn dropped by her room with news that Jack was suggesting she join them in a threesome.

"We can think of it as helping out the country," Marilyn suggested.

It was all Carmen could do to keep from laughing. She dismissed the idea as crazy.

Not one to take no for an answer, Jack showed up, too.

"Just think of it as standing on the edge of a New Frontier," Jack told her. "The frontier of the 1960s. A frontier of unknown opportunities and perils. Jeanne, I'm asking you and Marilyn both to be new pioneers on that New Frontier."

The night of September 26, Jack and Richard Nixon appeared in Chicago in the first of their so-called Great Debates. Nixon labored under a serious handicap: He had a light, naturally transparent skin. On an ordinary camera it photographed well. But television cameras had almost an X-ray effect, creating, for one thing, the unshaven appearance that came to haunt him. Nixon came off looking haggard and seedy; Jack was fresh and clean-cut.

THE $500,000 PALIMONY PAYMENT

Jack's sexual antics frequently threatened to torpedo the campaign, but related problems were quietly handled behind the scenes with a check or a threat. One of the few affairs that worried him was the record of his wartime romance with Inga Arvad. He knew by now that J. Edgar Hoover had tapes of his trysts with Inga in Washington and Charleston.

One former girlfriend sued Jack for breach of promise, claiming she had been engaged to him in 1951. She was quietly paid off with a $500,000 payment by Robert in early 1961. Little note was made at the time, although J. Edgar Hoover, always fascinated with the sexual escapades of the Kennedy family, quietly noted the payment in Jack's growing FBI file.

The Ambassador continued to pull his son's strings. He had his own man in Jack's Boston office to report who came and went, and a maid in the Georgetown house reported back to him regularly.

Late in the campaign Bobby discovered a Nixon infiltrator in his own home. His five-year-old son David told visiting newsmen that he was supporting Nixon. "Now, David," Ethel chided him in front of a reporter. "You know you don't mean that!" "Yes, I do," the boy said. He insisted until his mother made it clear that she had had enough. "All right, then—Kennedy," David said in surrender.

KEEPING SECRETS

The Rosemary charade continued. A *Look* magazine article that fall about "The Kennedy Women" characterized Rosemary as "a victim of spinal meningitis, now in a Wisconsin nursing home."

But there were so many secrets to be kept by now. Shortly before election day, Walter H. Judd, a Republican congressman and former medical missionary, demanded that candidate Kennedy confirm or deny that he had Addison's disease and was the patient described only as "a man thirty-seven years of age" whose case history appeared in the November 1955 edition of the *American Medical Association Archives of Surgery*. Jack, of course, continued to deny that he had the illness or was the patient in the article. (In 1967 the patient in question was finally and definitely identified as John F. Kennedy.)

MICKEY COHEN: "THE PRESIDENCY WAS STOLEN IN CHICAGO."

On election night, November 8, the entire Kennedy family gathered at Hyannis Port to await the election returns. Jack received 34,226,731 votes to 34,108,157 for Nixon. His Electoral College majority was 303 to 219. The popular vote margin, 118,574, was the equivalent of a win by one vote in every precinct in America.

Of the eleven states assigned to Teddy, mostly in the Republican West, Jack lost eight.

Early in the evening Jack called Chicago mayor Richard J. Daley, who told him that "with a bit of luck and the help of a few close friends, you're going to carry Illinois," a state crucial to victory. Praise be! In the eleventh hour, the votes that came in from Cook County's mob-dominated West Side put Jack over the top.

"Actually, and this goes without saying, the presidency was really stolen in Chicago, without a question, by the Democratic machine," recalled mobster Mickey Cohen. "I know that certain people in the Chicago organization knew that they had to get John Kennedy in . . . But nobody in my line of work had an idea that he was going to name Bobby Kennedy attorney general. That was the last thing anyone thought. In fact, he had just openly promised in his campaign that he wouldn't name Bobby as attorney general."

JACK: "I NEVER HAD ADDISON'S DISEASE . . . MY HEALTH IS EXCELLENT."

The day after the election, a jubilant Jack Kennedy met with four hundred reporters at the National Guard Armory near Hyannis Port and announced that his first telephone calls as President-elect had been to J. Edgar Hoover and Allen Dulles, asking them both to stay on. Then he told his first lie as President.

Reporters asked about the persistent rumors that he had Addison's disease. Jack, who had been diagnosed with the illness in 1947 and on a doctor-prescribed regimen of cortisone ever since, replied: "I never had Addison's disease. In regard to my health, it was fully explained in a press statement in the middle of July, and my health is excellent."

In the weeks before his inauguration Jack began interviewing candidates for more than seventy key posts in the new administration. At one point he complained to his father, "Jesus Christ, this one wants that, that one wants this. Goddamn it, you can't satisfy any of these people. I don't know what I'm going to do about it all."

Old Joe, sitting in the front seat of the limousine, turned around and said: "Jack, if you don't want the job, you don't have to take it. They're still counting votes up in Cook County."

As if the year had not been successful enough, Jackie gave birth to their second child and first son on November 25. They would name him John F. Kennedy, Jr.

PART THREE

LIVING ON THE NEW FRONTIER

The inauguration of President Kennedy proclaims a new era for Washington, the nation and the world. But his ascension to power is more than just a change-over of administration and a party victory; it is the proclamation of a new American dynasty—the Kennedys.

—Cholly Knickerbocker,
New York Journal-American

CHAPTER NINE
DAYS OF HEAVEN: LIFE IN THE KENNEDY WHITE HOUSE

I don't see anything wrong with getting Bobby a little legal experience as attorney general before he goes out to practice law.

—John F. Kennedy,
at a luncheon one week after
Bobby was confirmed as Attorney General

Sex to Jack meant no more than a cup of coffee.

—Nancy Dickerson

I think the major role of the President's wife is to take care of the
President and his children.

—Jacqueline Kennedy, 1960

It's possible that the Kennedy dynasty, still powered by the Ambassador, made its most reckless move at this time. Heady with
their narrow victory, they turned their back on the organized
crime figures who had made it possible. The national game was
now being played by Kennedy rules.

Mickey Cohen, Sam Giancana and other mobsters believed that
by helping to elect Jack Kennedy they were putting a friend in the
White House. They should have listened to Eunice Kennedy who
knew that her father planned to place her younger brother Bobby
in the Justice Department.

"Bobby we'll make Attorney General so he can throw all the

people Dad doesn't like in jail. That means we'll have to build more jails," Eunice Kennedy had once boasted. And nowhere else was Joe's control over his son more evident than with this appointment.

George Smathers, one of Jack's closest friends, recalls lounging beside the pool at Palm Beach with Jack shortly after the 1960 election. The President-elect confessed that his father had been pressing him to name Bobby Attorney General. Jack was aware that if he did choose his brother, he would invite charges of nepotism. Moreover, Bobby had never practiced law; he had only served on Senate investigating committees.

Smathers suggested an alternative: name Bobby Assistant Secretary of Defense. The job, he pointed out, carried minor responsibilities, and, within a year or two, he could be promoted to Secretary of Defense. Bobby would not be in the cabinet—at first—thus muting the critics, but would nonetheless be close to his brother, as an advisor.

Jack liked the idea and encouraged Smathers to pitch it to the Ambassador when he arrived a half hour later.

Joe listened but did not reply. Instead, he turned to Jack. Shaking his finger under the nose of the next president of the United States, Joe barked: "I want Bobby to be attorney general. He is your blood brother. Nobody has sacrificed more of his time and energy in your behalf than your brother Bobby. And I don't want to hear any further thing about it."

It was at the Palm Beach mansion, now dubbed "the winter White House" that President-elect Kennedy was briefed on November 27 by CIA director Allen W. Dulles and Richard M. Bissell, deputy director for plans, about a secret operation that had been authorized by President Eisenhower in March. The plan was to have a brigade of CIA-trained Cuban exiles invade Cuba and to assassinate Cuban president Fidel Castro. A thousand Cuban exiles were already being trained by the CIA in Guatemala.

The plan appealed to all the worst in Jack: a love of secrecy, a love of danger. And since the plan, as presented to him, seemed foolproof, it would be the first great success of his administration and launch it with glory.

One reason that Bobby resisted accepting the Attorney General post at first was that he was thinking seriously about going back to Massachusetts and running for governor there. But by mid-December, with most of his other cabinet appointed, and all of them strangers, Jack saw the wisdom of having Bobby on the inside with him. On December 15 he had breakfast with his brother in Georgetown to discuss it.

If at first Jack was not anxious to have Bobby in the cabinet, Bobby, likewise, was not all that eager to be there. "I need someone I know to talk to in this government," he told Bobby. "If you announce me as Attorney General, they'll kick your balls off," Bobby warned. Jack replied, "You hold your balls and I'll make the announcement." Bobby agreed to take the post of attorney general.

As Attorney General, Bobby came into immediate conflict with J. Edgar Hoover. The longtime head of the Federal Bureau of Investigation was nominally his subordinate, but in fact the most powerful man in the country.

In his first interview as Attorney General, Robert told journalist Peter Mass that he would make organized crime his "number one concern." In his first speech after joining the cabinet, he declared: "Organized crime has become big business."

Hoover, on the other hand, had maintained for years that there was no such thing as organized crime. He was, and always had been, far more concerned with the Communist menace.

Hoover had built his power over three decades, through seniority, political expertise and the most sophisticated information-gathering machine in history. He had been gathering information on Jack since the President's Inga Arvad days, and he was aware of all his important relationships up to and including Judy Campbell and the $500,000 palimony payment.

Ethel, sometimes described as the most Kennedy of the Kennedy wives, soon proved herself every bit the master of media that the Kennedy men were. Washington correspondent Douglas Kiker, who had worked for the *New York Herald-Tribune* and NBC, acknowledged that "it's never been a secret that relationships between reporters and their sources often become incestuous, but the situation at Hickory Hill between Ethel, Bobby, and the press was extreme. As a result many of those people in their reporting wound up promoting the Kennedys and building false images and myths about them that became part of Kennedy history and legend.

"A lot of big-time journalists played by Ethel's rules and compromised themselves to be part of that circle," says Kiker.

In the 1990s Sophy Burnham would become famous as the author of *A Book of Angels*, but in those years she was just another magazine journalist who also visited Hickory Hill and recalls the adulation. The Kennedys, she said, "knew perfectly how to charm the press. There they were—Ben Bradlee, all those guys—being charmed by John Kennedy and Bobby. The adulation was shameful."

The night before his inauguration, Jack Kennedy celebrated at a round of parties. Jackie was stunning in a white gown and he insisted that their driver turn on the lights inside their limo so that the crowds lining the Mall could see her. Even after an exhausted Jackie went home, Jack was accompanied on his rounds by his old navy buddy Paul "Red" Fay. The former ensign's chief assignment that night, and the day and night that followed, was to escort Angie Dickinson, with whom Jack slipped away to private rooms a couple of times during the ceremonies.

John F. Kennedy was sworn in as the thirty-fifth president of the United States on January 20, 1961. His day began with mass at Holy Trinity Church near Georgetown University. Later that morning, as he stood to take the oath of office on a freezing winter day, he was the picture of youthful vigor. Looking at photographs taken at the time, one sees the permanent suntan, the thick hair, the smile that radiates an enhanced sense of confidence and, of course, the sex appeal. But as mentioned time and again, all those qualities were also the symptoms of heavy cortisone use. Like so much about the Kennedy family's public image, appearances were deceiving.

Among the honored guests in a section just below the podium, among Ted Sorensen, Mayor Richard Daley, union leaders George Meany and Walter Reuther, and Angie Dickinson and Red Fay, was Dr. Max Jacobson.

"Let the words go forth from this time and place, to friend and foe alike, that the torch has been passed to a new generation of Americans," began the President. "Let every nation know, whether it wishes us well or ill, that we shall pay any price, bear any burden, meet any hardship, support any friend, oppose any foe to assure the survival and success of liberty. . . ."

During the inauguration festivities Jackie's cousin, historian John Davis, congratulated Joe on his son's success. "I asked him point-blank if he personally had some great vision for America that his son could help realize, and he laughed at me as if I were naive. Joe Kennedy's vision of America, I eventually realized, was simply to have his son President, to have the Kennedys at the summit of political life. What vision he had was for a family, not a people."

At another ball at the Statler-Hilton, Jack left Jackie in the presidential box with the Johnsons and slipped upstairs to a party given by Frank Sinatra for stars who had performed at the inaugural gala the night before, including Dickinson, Kim Novak, Gene Kelly, Tony Curtis and Janet Leigh.

Judy Campbell, although invited, had opted not to attend. She explained in her memoir: "Too many people already knew about our relationship without my flaunting it before his wife on this most important day of their life."

JACKIE COLLAPSES—JACK PARTIES ON

An exhausted Jackie retreated to the White House at midnight, but Jack continued on for two more balls, finally ending his rounds with a visit to a party at the Georgetown home of columnist Joseph Alsop. There he is said to have had a secret tryst with Angie Dickinson. "I will never confirm or deny the rumors about me and him," Dickinson maintains to this day. "That's something I would only discuss with my confessor. The exact nature of my relationship with him is something I'll take to my grave. Everyone was in love with him."

Finally heading home shortly before dawn, Jack spent his first night in the White House alone in the Lincoln bedroom. Or was it in a ménage à trois with two of six Hollywood starlets Peter Law-ford had brought in for the occasion at Joe Alsop's?

On January 25, John F. Kennedy became the first president to hold a live televised press conference. This first exchange between the quick-witted young president and the press was witnessed by sixty million people.

The media romance with the Kennedys reached full flower dur-ing Jack Kennedy's reign in the White House, but it was not achieved without a price. The price was journalistic integrity. Typical of respectable journalists who fell into the Kennedy thrall was Joe McCarthy, who wrote *The Remarkable Kennedys* in 1962, followed by many other such books with the cooperation of the family.

Years later, visited by fellow journalist Lester David, McCarthy would recall interviewing Old Joe for *The Remarkable Kennedys*. The Ambassador let his guard down, and spoke at length about his plans for all three of his sons.

McCarthy recalled, "I was taking notes, but then I stopped be-cause it was getting clear to me that Joe wasn't even aware of what he was saying and certainly never intended me to put his remarks in a book. I never wrote what he said because I didn't think it was fair to take advantage of the old man that way. He was a tough SOB, that's for sure, and I knew he broke people in business and never missed a second's sleep. But still, I had this journalistic in-tegrity hang-up. Besides, I knew that if I wrote it, the old man would deny he ever said it.

"I don't recall his exact words, but they went like this: 'Each of those three kids is going to be president of the United States. There would have been four if Joe had lived. Hell, Joe, that's three presidents named Kennedy going down in the history books, one after the other.'

"He gave a little laugh when he said that three Kennedys beat two Adamses."

Joe had been dead for years when McCarthy shared that story, but still he asked his friend not to print it while he was alive. "The Kennedys wouldn't like it at all and I'm still writing about them," he explained.

The President soon advised editors that he preferred to be referred to as JFK in their headlines rather than Jack. It was an obvious reference to the still popular FDR.

Once he moved into the White House, Jack made sure that there was a bedroom set aside for Lem Billings, who came down every weekend.

Like his sister Rosemary, Jack had a restless temperament and had no intention of being confined to the White House. He made the rounds of events at the Alfalfa Club and the National Press Club and parties until dawn at the homes of his Georgetown friends. One night he slipped out to see the movie *Spartacus* at a downtown theater; and other times, much like Rosemary, he strolled along public streets around the White House, usually after dusk. Needless to say, such recklessness concerned the Secret Service.

JFK was even more reckless at home, maintaining simultaneous affairs with two White House secretaries the Secret Service dubbed Fiddle and Faddle. The duo, one blonde, one brunette, were said to engage in threesomes with Jack and nude swims with him in the White House pool. "Aren't you afraid Jackie will come back earlier than you expect and catch you with these broads?" he was asked in the Oval Office. Jack merely smiled. "Jackie can't get within two hundred yards of this place without my knowing about it."

As the elected leader of the most powerful nation in the free world, he was now free to fully indulge his priapic tendencies in ways his father never dreamed of. According to British journalist Glenys Roberts: "He seduced his own secretaries and baby-sitters, who became pregnant by him and had to go to Puerto Rico for abortions. He ordered up prostitutes like most Americans sent out for sandwiches."

And Jackie knew what was going on. On one occasion she was escorting an Italian journalist named Benno Gaziani around the White House when she pointed to two young secretaries and said, "Those are my husband's lovers." She knew about the affairs with Marilyn Monroe and Jayne Mansfield, as well as the parade of nameless flings. "She would find hairpins and bobby pins in his bedroom and, of all things, a radio under his bed."

In the spring, a few weeks before the CIA's elaborate Cuban invasion was to begin, Jack finally brought Bobby in on the scheme.

For the first time in United States' history, the government backed and launched the invasion of a sovereign state with which we were not at war and which was not threatening our national security.

The Bay of Pigs invasion was a disaster. The President had to appear on television and tell the nation that he took full responsibility for the failure of the operation. Afterward Jack assigned Bobby, CIA director Allen Dulles and others to investigate why U.S. intelligence experts had so badly underestimated Cuba's power to crush the invasion.

Eleven days after the fiasco, on April 28, Judy Campbell was present when Jack met with Sam Giancana in her suite at the Ambassador East Hotel in Chicago. Determined not to be humiliated again, he directed Operation Mongoose, an undercover effort to oust Castro by any means necessary: sabotage, guerrilla warfare, even assassination. By now, all methods of eliminating Fidel, his brother Raul and strategist Che Guevara, including poison pills and exploding cigars, had failed or been aborted. In June, Los Angeles-Las Vegas capo Johnny Roselli organized an assassination team to ambush the Cuban dictator, an effort that also failed.

In all, Judy Campbell arranged ten meetings between the President and the mob boss. She acted as their courier, carrying plain sealed manila envelopes among JFK, Giancana and Roselli. She was young and naive. "Sam was one of the nicest, kindest people I knew," she said later. "I didn't know he was a murderer. I wouldn't have believed it." In fact, she didn't have a clue what she was involved in until fifteen years later, when she was called before the Senate Intelligence Committee. "It finally dawned on me that I was probably helping Jack orchestrate the attempted assassination of Fidel Castro with the help of the Mafia."

In June, Jackie and JFK made their first state visit to Paris and Vienna.

By this time Dr. Jacobson and his magic shots had become so indispensable that they chartered an Air France jet to fly him to Paris. Dr. Feelgood was so much a part of the inner circle that he was included in the family pictures in *John F. Kennedy: A Family*

Album by Mark Shaw. According to journalist Michael Gross, after Shaw died in 1969 of acute and chronic amphetamine poisoning while under Jacobson's care, the government raided the doctor's office. Six years later his license to practice medicine was revoked after he had been found guilty of fraud and forty-eight counts of unprofessional conduct.

Accompanied by Dr. Jacobson, the President flew to Vienna for a summit meeting with Khrushchev. Although fortified by a Jacobson injection, he had a hard time coping with Khrushchev's crude barbs. He was out of his league. According to journalist James Reston, who interviewed him, immediately after at the U.S. Embassy, Jack slumped down on a couch, pulled his hat over his eyes and dwelt on Khrushchev's humiliating treatment.

"He thinks because of the Bay of Pigs that I'm inexperienced. Probably thinks I'm stupid. Maybe, most important, he thinks I have no guts." No Kennedy man could live with that kind of perception. The solution was action.

"We have to confront them," Kennedy said of the Soviets. "The only place we can do that is Vietnam. We have to send more people there."

JOHN'S OTHER WIFE

In August rumors about Jack Kennedy's first marriage began to surface. *The Blauvelt Family Genealogy*, privately published in 1957, included a paragraph listing a Blauvelt descendant, Durie Malcolm, who, it said, had been married to John F. Kennedy.

In a memoir of his years as an intimate of the president, *Conversations with Kennedy*, former *Washington Post* editor Ben Bradlee claimed that when he first learned of the rumors he tried to get a copy of *Genealogy* out of the Library of Congress, only to be told pointedly that the book was out, and that the waiting list included ten members of Congress.

A compilation of descendants of Gerrit Hendricksen (Blauvelt) who came to America in 1638, the book represented thirty years of research by genealogist Louis Leon Blauvelt.

The relevant entry read:

"Durie (Kerr) Malcolm. We have no birth date. She was born Kerr, but took the name of her stepfather. She first married Firman

Desloge IV. They were divorced. Durie then married F. John Bers-
bach. They were divorced, and she married, third, John F.
Kennedy, son of Joseph P. Kennedy, onetime Ambassador to England. There were no children of the second or third marriages."

According to Bradlee, "It wasn't until August 20 that I got what
I believe is the complete story from the President himself, and
from other sources."

Bradlee's "other sources" seem to have consisted solely of
White House press secretary Pierre Salinger. It turned out that the
author of the genealogy, Louis Blauvelt, was dead, but his son-in-
law, William K. Smith, of East Orange, New Jersey, the new
keeper of the Blauvelt records, had allowed Salinger to examine
all the records from which Blauvelt had written the book. "Again,
at Salinger's request, Smith executed an affidavit stating there was
no evidence in those records of any such marriage," Bradlee reported. "Smith told Salinger that he had found a yellowed, 1947
clipping from a Miami newspaper, reporting that John F.
Kennedy had been seen in a Miami nightclub with Durie Malcolm. Kennedy later confirmed to me that he had dated her once,
but that she had been a girlfriend of his brother, Joe."

In 1961 Durie Malcolm was married to Thomas Shevlin and living in Palm Beach. Salinger told Bradlee that Mrs. Shevlin had
also executed an affidavit, swearing she had never been married
to John F. Kennedy. Bradlee does not indicate that he ever saw
such an affidavit. He did try to call Mrs. Shevlin every day for at
least a week, and in each case the operator reported that her telephone had been disconnected at "the customer's request."

According to Bradlee, "The records show that this woman was
unmarried—and thus technically in a position to marry
Kennedy—twice. Once between the summer of 1938 and January
1939, when Kennedy was a junior at Harvard. And once between
January and July of 1947, the first six months of Kennedy's first
term in Congress."

All this was enough to convince Bradlee that the story had no
basis in fact. Later, when he did mention it to Jack himself, the
President told Bradlee that he had met Durie one day while they
played golf at the Seminole Club in Palm Beach. "She was a girlfriend of my brother Joe," Jack went on, "and I took her out a couple of times, I guess. That's all."

Here is where the President's behavior gets interesting. "You haven't got it, Benjy," he told Bradlee. "You're all looking to tag me with some girl, and none of you can do it, because it just isn't there."

"Jackie just listened with a smile on her face," Bradlee recalled. "And that is the closest I ever came to hearing him discuss his reputation as what my father used to call 'a fearful girler.' "

What makes this report so astounding is that at the same time Bradlee was having this conversation with the President, JFK was also in the middle of a long and serious romance with Bradlee's sister-in-law Mary Pinchot Meyer. Although he refers to Mary Meyer's appearance at no less than five social occasions in his memoir, Bradlee never once seems aware of her special relationship with the President. If Bradlee could miss what was happening right under his nose, it's hard to have confidence in his version of the Durie Malcolm story, especially since Bradlee's only sources seem to have been the adulterous President and his devoted press secretary.

In reports about this rumored marriage, speculation usually centers on the idea that Joe, Sr., with his money and church connections, could have bought a Catholic annulment. But no such annulment was ever necessary. This was an elopement between a twice-divorced heiress and a rich young Harvard man. It was most likely conducted in haste by a justice of the peace. Such a minor official could easily be encouraged to lose the paperwork for the reward of a judgeship. It's most likely that scenario happened. Sam Giancana claimed to have obliterated all records of the marriage, clearing the way for Jack to run for the presidency.

In 1992, FBI files obtained by the *Globe* revealed that the marriage had occurred in 1939 when Jack was twenty-two. Since the dissolution of her marriage to Jack Kennedy, the still-beautiful Durie married twice more and today lives in Palm Beach as Mrs. Frank Appleton.

"The fact that JFK was married before he even met Jackie has been a well-kept secret in Palm Beach for almost forty years," said one longtime resident of the resort town. "My father is eighty-two and still talks about it. He knows JFK's first wife—they used to be neighbors."

The FBI file indicates that Jack first tried to get a divorce in Reno but the proceeding was invalidated. "An attempt was made to get a divorce in New Jersey, but apparently this did not work out. He is alleged to have gotten a sealed divorce in early 1953," says the secret government file.

Veteran investigative reporter Leo Damore has no doubt that the family's power in 1960 allowed them to erase any trace of the marriage and divorce.

"The story I got was that the affair was a weekend fling that led to an elopement," says Damore. "They went to New Jersey because you could get married without a waiting period. They wed in Fort Lee, right across the Hudson River from New York City."

Joe, of course, was furious and immediately moved to hide the records of the marriage and subsequent divorce.

Today, as always, Durie Malcolm Appleton declines to discuss the matter. "She just doesn't want to talk about that," said her current husband. "You must appreciate the way we feel about this."

When the story of "John's other wife" first surfaced, Kennedy loyalists like Bradlee dismissed it and embraced the White House version. But in the years since, as more details emerged about disinformation and suppression surrounding Rosemary's disability, Jack's illnesses, Jack and Bobby's adulteries, Teddy's accident at Chappaquiddick, Joe II's Jeep accident on Cape Cod and the Good Friday rape, among other incidents, it becomes easier to conclude that the family's version could be another Kennedy deception.

JACK & JUDY & MARY & MARILYN

Even while Jack was assuring journalists that they would never catch him with a woman, he was maintaining simultaneous affairs with Judy Campbell, Mary Meyer and Marilyn Monroe. After the inauguration, Jack's relationship with Judy Campbell was conducted mainly by phone. Judy later told a senate committee that the most intense period of the relationship was between April 29, 1961, and March 22, 1962. She spent her free time with mobster Sam Giancana.

Two weeks after the Bay of Pigs, on May 5, Jack invited Judy to Washington while Jackie and the children regularly decamped for weekends at Glen Ora, an estate in the Virginia horse country. Judy stayed at the venerable Mayflower Hotel. She kept a rendezvous with the President at the White House that afternoon.

In her memoir Judy recalled being met at the Mayflower by a White House car and met at the White House by Dave Powers, who escorted her to the President, who was taking his customary prelunch nude swim. Afterward they shared a private lunch.

Although she declined to reveal it in her memoir, Judy later acknowledged that she told the President about her relationship with Giancana. Naturally, he was jealous.

On August 8 Jack asked a surprising question. "Has Teddy phoned you?"

"No, why?"

"Boy, if Teddy only knew," he gloated, "he'd eat his heart out!"

On August 24, after frozen daiquiris in the family quarters, the President presented Judy with a diamond-and-ruby brooch. There were more meetings—at the Plaza in New York, at her apartment in Los Angeles, in Palm Beach and the White House.

Jackie took a worldly view of such activities. Her own father had conducted an open affair on his honeymoon cruise that lasted for the entire voyage. It's said that she once discovered a woman's undergarments under a pillow in the President's bedroom. She held them out to him, saying, "Would you please shop around and see who this belongs to? It's not my size."

Like Rose, Jackie decided to turn a blind eye to her husband's infidelities. Unlike Rose, she was very much a hands-on mother. Once in the White House, she discovered her biggest problem was maintaining privacy for her children. To protect Caroline, she established a school inside the White House, with the help of Susan Wilson, a former Vassar College classmate. "I think the school was indicative of Jackie's desire to create an environment where her children could have access to other kids," said Wilson. Comprised of twenty-one students, the school occupied two rooms above the Oval Office; its students were the offspring of the President's New Frontiersmen or personal friends of the Kennedys.

Most mornings when Jackie was in town, she could be found there, watching the children. "Jackie had a knack with kids, *all* kids," said one friend. Susan Wilson recalls: "Her public persona is cool, cerebral. But you saw another side of her with children, especially *her* children. When she was with them, she showed an intense, loving concern. When you can make a child feel so precious to you, I think that's what gives confidence and self-esteem."

The cool, elegant international fashion plate could be seen hitching Caroline's pony, Macaroni, to a sleigh and giving the children rides around the White House grounds. Like his father, Jack sincerely loved children. "The President always had the children come down to the Oval Office before they left for the day," recalls broadcaster Sherrye Henry, whose daughter went to the White House school. "He'd keep candy in his pockets, and if it was a pretty day he'd lead them outside like the Pied Piper. Then he'd roll on the ground, and the children would tumble on top of him, digging in his pockets for the candy."

One reason Jack's passion for Judith Campbell began to cool in early 1962, was that he had begun a serious affair with the aforementioned Mary Pinchot Meyer, ex-wife of Cord Meyer, a high-ranking CIA official. They even smoked pot together in the White House.

Blond and beautiful Mary Meyer was part of Washington society. In fact, when Pamela Turnure was forced to leave her room at the Katers' because she was seeing the married Senator Kennedy, she moved in with her friend Mary Meyer. Mary regularly attended many White House events with her sister Tony and brother-in-law Ben Bradlee. According to her friend James Truitt, the President first propositioned Mary in December 1961, but she was involved in a serious relationship with the painter Kenneth Noland at the time and declined.

In January 1962 the relationship with JFK went from friendship to an affair. "She said she had to tell someone what was happening," Truitt recalled. "So she confided in me and my former wife Ann."

She told Truitt that JFK felt "no affection of a lasting kind" for Jackie. By July, Mary introduced him to marijuana. They shared two joints. "This isn't like cocaine," he concluded. "I'll get you some of that." Mary also told the Truitts that she was keeping a diary about the affair.

Despite his countless relationships with women, Jack Kennedy remained a man most comfortable in the company of men, especially his longtime friend Lem Billings. Restless and bored in the horse country around Glen Ora, he would often bring Billings along as company. The two men would golf together. On Sundays he would go to mass with Billings, and usually borrow $10 from Billings for the collection plate. He would rarely pay it back.

With his dream realized and his son in the White House, Joe Kennedy was content to take a backroom position. At seventy-three the Ambassador had finally learned the wisdom of the course his father, P.J., had chosen and he relished the power without the limelight. Movies still fascinated him and he personally supervised the production of *PT-109*, based on Jack's wartime experience. When Bobby signed a studio contract for a film based on his book, *The Enemy Within*, Joe phoned to revise the agreement. A startled executive replied that his son, the Attorney General, had been satisfied. Joe snapped back, "What the hell does he know about it?" and improved the deal.

It had long been his habit to spend winters in Palm Beach and it was there on December 19, 1961, that Joe collapsed on the golf course and asked his niece Ann Gargan to drive him home. Rose told the servants that he would be fine and went out for a golf game of her own. Hours later a worried Ann Gargan called an ambulance and he was rushed to St. Mary's Hospital. In spite of his robust appearance, Joe had long suffered from stress-related illnesses including ulcers and neuritis. He had had warnings of a stroke but refused to take the prescribed anticoagulents. Now, near death, he was given the last rites.

Joe did not die. He had suffered a massive stroke, he had an inoperable blood clot on an artery of the brain, and he was paralyzed on his right side and unable to speak. Initially, he participated in a program of physical therapy and rehabilitation, but he would never recover or return to his leadership of the family. For the next eight years he would be confined to a wheelchair and unable to speak intelligibly. Ironically, his condition was not very different from Rosemary's.

Frank Saunders, onetime Kennedy family chauffeur, recalled that whenever Rose entered her husband's room, he became visibly upset. "Before, he had been the Supreme Being in the Kennedy house," Saunders said. "But after the stroke it was like a little smile came over her face, as if to say, 'Gotcha now.' "

But before he was incapacitated, Joe had made one final demand.

THE AMBASSADOR TO THE PRESIDENT: "NOW IT'S TED'S TURN!"

Since Jack's election, Teddy and Joan settled in at 3 Charles Square in Boston with their infant daughter, Kara Anne, born February 27, 1960. Joan kept house with the help of two maids. She gave birth to their first son, Edward M. Kennedy, Jr., there on September 26, 1961. Teddy went to work as an assistant district attorney in Suffolk County (Boston) for a salary of one dollar a year.

Ted and Joan talked of leaving Boston and making a fresh start in the West. They settled instead for a modest rebellion, acquiring a summer house outside the family compound. In the spring of 1961 they bought a house on Squaw Island, about a mile from Hyannis Port. The four-bedroom, gray shingle house was linked to the Ambassador by a special telephone line.

Joe told the President: "You boys have what you want now and everyone else helped you work to get it. Now it's Ted's turn." Joe still wanted to collect on all he had invested in getting Jack the seat in the Senate. "Look, I paid for it," he explained. "It belongs in the family."

But Teddy would not be eligible to fill Jack's vacant seat until February 22, 1962, when he would turn thirty. The Massachusetts governor was persuaded to name a family friend to fill out Jack's term.

After Joe suffered his December 19 stroke, Teddy seemed to feel he had to fulfill his father's dream. But another ambitious man with family connections also aspired to the senate seat. Edward L. McCormack, thirty-eight, nephew of Speaker of the House John McCormack. McCormack had been editor in chief of *Law Review* at Boston University School of Law, graduated first in his class there, served three terms in the Boston City Council, and had been an outstanding Massachusetts attorney general since 1956.

There was little in Teddy's previous life that had prepared him for this primary campaign, but on March 14, he announced that he was a candidate. Almost immediately the *Boston Globe* unearthed a dark episode in his past: He had been expelled from Harvard for cheating.

Robert L. Healy, political editor of the *Globe,* found the story, but in order to get it into the paper he had to get some confirmation. He asked the White House to open up the Harvard record and was immediately summoned to the Oval Office. "I had three meetings there with the president, Ted Sorensen, McGeorge Bundy, Kenny O'Donnell and Arthur Schlesinger, Jr.," he recalled. "Jack was pretty shrewd. He would have liked the story included in some kind of profile of Ted, which would have buried it, but I said 'no soap.' "

The President and his aides kept pressing Healy to play down the story but he stood his ground. "So finally, Jack gave me access to the whole thing," Healy said.

On March 30 the *Globe* ran the story. Ted immediately issued a statement accepting full blame. "I made a mistake," he said. And went on:

". . . What I did was wrong. I have regretted it ever since. The unhappiness I caused my family and friends, even though eleven years ago, has been a bitter experience for me, but it has also been a valuable lesson. That is the story." This was the first of what would become the three historic apologies of Ted's career.

The cheating story died. During the hard-fought primary Teddy's sisters Patricia and Eunice, wife, Joan, and sister-in-law Ethel worked every county in the state.

Even the admiring journalist Joe McCarthy had no illusions about young Ted. "He isn't very heavy mentally," he acknowledged. "He's a bright and capable guy but nothing like his brothers. In many ways he's a fathead, a little bit conceited, a little bit cocky, the kind of guy who'd never finish a sentence when you asked him a question. He simply didn't think things through as Jack and Bobby did."

Teddy's slogan: "He can do more for Massachusetts." He took sixty percent of the votes (559,303 to McCormack's 247,403). In the subsequent general election he soundly trumped George Cabot Lodge, the Republican candidate whose father had been defeated by Jack back in 1952.

JOE ON TEDDY: "HE ISN'T A BRIGHT STUDENT, HE'S A GOOD SALESMAN."

Even Joe seemed to acknowledge his youngest son's lack of mental gifts, once remarking, "If he isn't a bright student, he's a good salesman."

Nothing demonstrates the differences between the male and the female Kennedys better than the fates of Rosemary and Ted. For Ted only managed to graduate from Milton Academy in 1950 with a C average. Despite terrible grades, Teddy (like brother Robert) was admitted to Harvard as a "legacy" because his older brothers and father had graduated.

Yet even at Harvard, young Ted floundered. Unable to pass a freshman Spanish test, he paid a friend who was recognized when he handed in his exam book. Both lads were expelled, but advised that they could apply for readmission in a year if they demonstrated responsible citizenship.

Young Ted spent a month in Hyannis, pondering his future, then enlisted in the Army, unaware that he had signed up for a four-year stint, not two. His father stepped in and arranged for Ted's enlistment period to be shortened. He never rose above the rank of private and was discharged in 1952 and returned to Harvard, as did his test-taking friend, and they graduated together.

JACK AND MARILYN ON TAPE

Sometime in the late 1950s, the future President was introduced to Marilyn Monroe in Hollywood by his brother-in-law Peter Lawford. After the nomination the two began a series of seaside flirtations at Pat and Peter Lawford's Santa Monica mansion. The world's most famous film star and the soon-to-be president of the United States. The relationship eventually moved on to a series of assignations at the Beverly Hilton Hotel and meetings aboard *Air Force One*.

"Of all Jack's women, I think Marilyn complemented him most," observed Peter Lawford. "They both had a sense of humor that clicked."

While Jackie and the children remained back East, the President attended a glittering 1961 Christmas party at the Lawfords' Santa Monica home. Everything was lavishly decorated for the holiday season: there were poinsettias and holly everywhere, and a tall beautifully trimmed tree in the living room. But the President and the superstar had seen Christmas trees before, and they soon slipped away to a bedroom suite. After a bubble bath, during which Monroe poured champagne over the President's shoulders, they shared a languid hour in bed.

Their tryst would have been spoiled had they known that it was all being taped. Fred Otash, the renowned private detective whose client list included gangsters, union bosses and stars from Rock Hudson to Frank Sinatra, had been retained by Teamster boss Jimmy Hoffa to tape the romantic exchanges between Marilyn and Jack.

Marilyn was a good friend of the Lawfords, and was fascinated with the Kennedy family. After four miscarriages and seven abortions, she still yearned for a child. The large, boisterous Kennedy family must have represented this; not only the family she had yearned for as a child growing up in a series of foster homes, but the children she was unable to bear. Pat Lawford confided to friends that "Marilyn seemed haunted by her childlessness, asking endless questions about my children and about all of the Kennedy children." Peter sometimes found her in the playground of their Santa Monica house "silently admiring my children's toys and books."

As 1962 opened, an ebullient President gave his six-year-old nephew David Kennedy a photograph of the boy posing in front of the White House, which he had inscribed "a future President inspects his property." Apparently, his uncle had forgiven David the skepticism he voiced earlier in the campaign.

At the same time Bobby and Ethel were off on a month-long world tour that took them from Tokyo to Berlin, Hong Kong to Italy. Pat and Peter Lawford threw a going-away party for them in California. It was there, on February 1, that Ethel was introduced to Marilyn Monroe for the first time. Pat had invited all the important "young Hollywood," including Kim Novak, Janet Leigh, Natalie Wood, all of whom were outdazzled by Marilyn. She claimed she was dying to meet Bobby. (Some friends, though, claim to have seen her with him long before the party.) Pat obligingly seated her brother between Marilyn and Kim Novak.

Bobby and Marilyn sat together at dinner, passing notes on cocktail napkins, and later dancing the twist together, while Ethel stoically watched it all from across the room.

According to Marilyn's confidant Rupert Allan, she and Bobby talked of how few really big stars remained. Marilyn was immensely flattered when Bobby told her that she and Elizabeth Taylor were the only stars left.

Marilyn prepared for the party by reading intensively and finding out everything she could about the Attorney General and his work. She was especially fascinated by the Kennedy family, both the relationship between Bobby and his brothers, and his relationship with his many children.

Bobby, who had up until now been the most chaste of the Kennedy men, had met his femme fatale in Monroe. Marilyn had such a good time, in fact, that she got high on champagne and had to ask Bobby to take her home. He insisted that his press aide, Ed Guthman, accompany them. The three of them, Bobby driving, Marilyn beside him and Guthman in the backseat, drove directly to her new home in Brentwood, where they turned her over to her housekeeper.

The next day, Ethel and Bobby left for Honolulu, the first stop on their itinerary, and Marilyn reported for her costume fittings on *Something's Got to Give.*

BOBBY LEARNS ABOUT JUDY

On February 27, returning to work at the Justice Department, Robert Kennedy received a memo from FBI Director Hoover informing him that a woman associated with mobster Johnny Roselli had called the White House on an average of two times a week. It's possible that at this point the Attorney General didn't even know who Judy Campbell was.

The Kennedy-Campbell idyll ended March 1962, after a four-month FBI investigation of phone records showing Campbell's calls to Kennedy's secretary at the White House. That month, FBI Director J. Edgar Hoover and Kennedy had lunch. Two hours later Kennedy placed his last call to Campbell.

Next to go was the man who had introduced them: Frank Sinatra.

For years Sinatra had enjoyed a special relationship with the Kennedy family, but once Jack was in the White House, he may have pushed it too far.

According to the flamboyant mobster Mickey Cohen, the singer went to Jack "in connection with someone's problems in Chicago. So John says to him, 'Go talk to Bobby about it.'

"But Bobby was really insulting to Frank and very unreceptive. So Frank went back to John Kennedy and relayed to him what took place.

"So Jack told Frank, 'Tell you what you do. Why don't you go see Dad, go talk to Father about that,' " because, according to Cohen, Joe was "the only one who could talk to Bobby.

"So the way I get the story is that Frank went to Joe Kennedy and that Bobby still took a stand which was very, very unreceptive all the way around. But later on, something was done for the person, you know, he beat the beef. I think the help finally came from the President himself. See, he was indebted to Frank in every possible way that you could think of."

And what had Frank done for Jack? According to Cohen, "Besides being a complete friend, Frank got him all the broads he could ever have used. And these girls were not unknowns. They were all starlets that I kept company with. They weren't prostitutes, wouldn't go to bed with any Tom, Dick or Harry. I guess they preferred to go to bed with John Kennedy instead of Mickey Cohen, you know—or Frank Sinatra instead of Mickey Cohen. The girls were very discreet. It was very much in confidence when some of them discussed with me what was going on at Marion Davies' house. . . ."

EXIT FRANK

On February 28, just weeks before the President was to make a weekend visit to Sinatra's Palm Springs hideaway, Jack's political advisors declared that the singer was "an undesirable person."

At a state dinner, Bobby snapped, "This man is involved with criminal elements, you can't afford to be seen with him." The President turned red and changed the subject.

FBI Director J. Edgar Hoover always the consummate bureau-
crat, had rapidly grasped that if he were to outlast President
Kennedy as he had outlasted four of Kennedy's predecessors, he
would have to play ball and acknowledge organized crime. And it
gave him a wonderful opportunity to tweak the Kennedy brothers. By now he had prepared three reports on Sinatra charging
that he had "personal ties to ten leading figures of organized
crime." The President read the memos, filed them and refused to
sever his friendship with Sinatra. He wasn't ready to swear off the
heavy doses of glamour and gossip the entertainer brought to his
life.

An irate Bobby called Peter Lawford away from the set of his
television series. "Tell Sinatra that the President can't stay at his
compound in March," said Bobby. "And find another house for
the Palm Springs visit."

Aware of Sinatra's work, his power and how much the President's visit meant to him, Lawford tried to change Bobby's mind,
but Bobby was adamant. "It's too dangerous."

Lawford appealed to the President. "Don't do it, Mr. President.
You owe Sinatra."

"I can't stay at Sinatra's," Jack insisted. "Not while Bobby is investigating Giancana. Frank is too close to this man."

It fell to Lawford to break the news to Sinatra, who had built
special cottages for the President and the Secret Service and a helicopter pad at a cost of $1.2 million.

Instead of honoring Sinatra with a visit, the President stayed
with Bing Crosby.

"The Kennedys damn near broke Sinatra's heart," recalled
longtime Hollywood columnist Dorothy Manners. "They cruelly
dropped him overnight. Perhaps he knew they would do the
same thing to Marilyn and wanted to warn her."

But Marilyn was in no mood to listen. And ironically enough,
the move from Sinatra's Palm Springs home to Bing Crosby's provided an even more comfortable setting for the President to conduct his affair with the movie star.

Hollywood, like Washington, is a small town and insiders from
Beverly Hills to Topanga Canyon were sharing sightings of the
President and Marilyn. Early in 1962 they were said to have spent
a night at the Beverly Hilton, dining on room-service lobster ther-

midor. There was an after-midnight assignation in a penthouse at the Beverly Hills Hotel and a tryst on Santa Monica Beach.

That March, after *Air Force One* dropped the presidential entourage in the desert, it diverted to Los Angeles to pick up Peter Lawford and a disguised Marilyn and bring them to Palm Springs.

The President was in the heavily guarded Bing Crosby mansion, but he slipped away several times for assignations with Marilyn. Reporters saw them arm in arm in the desert sunsets. During one exclusive party in the secluded guest house, Marilyn seemed to act as unofficial hostess, much as Gloria Swanson had sat at Joe's side during his Hollywood stay. It was obvious to everyone that she was there for the night.

As the affair continued, Marilyn began to confide dreams of marriage to friends. Ridiculous as it might seem that anyone could believe that a Catholic president would divorce his popular wife to marry a three-times divorced movie star, the fact is that Marilyn's whole life had defied reality. "After all, what were the odds of this little girl from nowhere marrying the world's greatest athlete, Joe DiMaggio? But she did," said *Something's Got to Give* associate producer Gene Allen. "And what were the chances of her marrying the world's greatest playwright, Arthur Miller? But she did it. Given those successes, maybe she could have become First Lady—if it had all worked out perfectly."

The relationship with Jack had progressed to such an extent that in mid-April 1962, Marilyn flew to New York for a private fundraiser, a ten-thousand-dollar-a-plate affair, for Jack's biggest supporters.

Marilyn's entrance, in skintight sequins and glittering aquamarine earrings, brought the party to a stop. "Dinner was forgotten, and nobody paid attention to the musical quartet; every eye was on Marilyn," guest Rupert Allan told journalists Peter Harry Brown and Patte B. Barham. "When Marilyn finally moved close to the President and they exchanged a few words, I suddenly realized that she had fallen in love with him. It frightened me, because I knew Marilyn never did anything by halves."

After the fund-raiser ended around 4 A.M., the presidential limousine returned Marilyn to her Fifty-seventh Street apartment, where she soon changed to casual clothes and taxied over to Jack's rooftop hideaway at the Carlyle Hotel.

Her April 15 appearance at Jack's fund-raiser seemed to give

Marilyn new confidence and she became even more public about their relationship. Up until then, she had always been careful to telephone Jack from the privacy of her bedroom. Suddenly she began openly calling the Oval Office from her bungalow on the Fox lot, where she was making *Something's Got to Give*. These calls to the White House went through the Fox switchboard.

If the President was "too busy" to take her call, she would chat with his longtime secretary, Evelyn Lincoln. "He said he was too busy to talk about it right now. Said he was involved in crucial business" she said, winking at Fox choreographer Stephen Papich, who witnessed such a call. "But, Stephen, as you know, he's never too busy for 'you know what.'"

Even jaded Hollywood-types were surprised, however, when Marilyn's planned appearance at the President's upcoming birthday gala at Madison Square Garden was trumpeted in the local trade papers. "This was deliberately bringing the rumors into the public," said screenwriter Nunnally Johnson. "Many of us felt that her appearance at Madison Square Garden would be like Marilyn making love to the President publicly after doing it privately all these months."

"She told me she had a private number to Jack in the Oval Office," said actress Terry Moore, a friend. "She was proud and that was a very, very exciting thing for her."

One friend who tried to warn her was Frank Sinatra.

"Marilyn told me that Sinatra called her with a warning, advising her against further intimacy with the Kennedys," Robert Slatzer said. "He particularly advised her to back off from John Kennedy. It was obvious that he would drop her. With another election year coming up, what choice did he have?"

The FBI increased its surveillance of Sam Giancana. Bobby Kennedy ordered FBI agents to pursue Judy Campbell everywhere. "I was followed, hounded, harassed, accosted, spied upon, intimidated, burglarized, embarrassed, humiliated, denigrated, and . . . finally driven to the brink of death," she wrote in her memoir.

This only solidified her loyalty to Giancana. "Okay, Sam, I'm with you," she told him. "If you have to fight them, I'll fight them too."

THE PRESIDENT SECRETLY TAPED JACKIE

By the summer of 1962 Jack had upgraded and expanded the audiotaping system originally installed in the Oval Office by FDR. In a room beneath the Oval Office, a tape machine—installed at the President's direct request by Secret Service agent Robert I. Bouck—secretly recorded his meetings.

According to journalist William Safire, the President was so pleased with the notion of being the only one in a meeting aware of being recorded that he extended the taping to telephone conversations. He touched a button that signaled his secretary, Evelyn Lincoln, to record on a Dictabelt the calls he selected.

The first telephone caller the President taped was his own wife. According to Safire, "This tape was later removed from the [JFK Library] files, along with four numbered audiotapes of official meetings that Kennedy family members and their lawyers presumably felt showed embarrassing or illegal actions."

"I want you to be careful about your profanity," Jack warned his friend Dave Powers, in the Oval Office one day, "because I don't want to hear your bad words coming back at me." Powers soon learned about the taping system. Safire called it "the first systematic invasion of privacy by a United States president."

None of those taped, from Jacqueline Kennedy to former presidents Truman and Eisenhower, nor friends Senator George Smathers and Ted Sorensen, were aware that their conversations were being recorded. "Hundreds of people who spoke to the President with the reasonable expectation of privacy were betrayed," said Safire. "And a nation that was dismayed and infuriated at the revelation of the Nixon taping system in 1973 can see today where that sleazy business began in earnest: in 1962 at the personal direction of John Fitzgerald Kennedy."

The act of secretly taping those closest to him shows a dark side of Jack Kennedy. "Kennedy's precedent-setting actions were rooted in mistrust of loyal colleagues and the absence of an ethical compass," concludes Safire. "He probably rationalized this systematic wrong as being 'for history.' But it backfired; his secret taping impugns his character far more than any peccadillo."

Early in 1962, accompanied by her sister, Lee, Jackie made a semiofficial visit to India and Pakistan, with a stopover for an audience with Pope John XXIII in Rome.

MARILYN MONROE: "HAPPY BIRTHDAY, MR. PRESIDENT."

On Thursday, May 17, 1962, a helicopter borrowed from Howard Hughes landed on the cement courtyard adjacent to Twentieth Century Fox Soundstage 14, and out stepped Peter Lawford. He rushed into the building and soon emerged with Marilyn Monroe in slacks, high heels, mink coat and sunglasses. Bringing up the rear were her publicist Pat Newcomb and her acting coach and confidante Paula Strasberg. The foursome were soon carried aloft to Los Angeles Airport and from there to New York.

Defying orders from Fox's top management, Marilyn left the troubled set of *Something's Got to Give* to appear at the President's birthday party two days away.

According to Brown and Barham, for two weeks Fox's New York office had used every means at its disposal to prevent her from appearing at the star-studded gala. It had become a bitter contractual dispute—with the Fox board of directors on one side and Marilyn's lawyers and the Kennedy brothers on the other. Finally Marilyn was notified in writing that if she left the set for the party, she would be fired.

Marilyn, who had spent $12,000 on a Jean Louis gown of silk and beads and a matching ermine stole, panicked and telephoned the White House. The President promised to work it out, and apparently turned the matter over to Bobby.

The Attorney General first contacted Peter Levathes in Hollywood, then Milton Gould, the most powerful man at Fox. The discussion degenerated to the point of Bobby screaming, "You'll be sorry for this, you fucking bastard. You're dealing with the First Family of America."

Fox's position was unbending, but somehow the Kennedy brothers allowed Marilyn to believe that they were working it out. And so she went forward.

Marilyn was introduced to the Garden crowd by Peter Lawford.

Just as Lawford said, "Mr. President, never in the history of the world has one woman meant so much—" Sick with a respiratory infection and sinusitis, stoked with amphetamines, she had never looked more beautiful.

The crowd gasped, then roared as Marilyn moved through the circles of light, swathed in the ermine wrap, until she reached Lawford and let it slip into his hands, revealing her gown. The crowd went wild.

In the presidential box Jack looked over his shoulder at writer Gene Schoor, "Jesus Christ, look at that dress," he said.

Schoor noticed that the President was staring. "What an ass, Gene," Kennedy said. "*What* an ass." Seated next to him, Bobby betrayed no trace of emotion.

When Marilyn finished singing "Happy Birthday, Mr. President," Jack walked on stage and told the audience, "I can now retire from politics after having 'Happy Birthday' sung to me in such a sweet, wholesome way."

After the gala Marilyn arrived at an exclusive party at the apartment of Democratic party leader Arthur Krim on the arm of her former father-in-law Isidore Miller. She moved through a crowd of two hundred of the most powerful men in America, most of whom were awed to be in her presence.

Finally, the President could not wait any longer. He pulled her away from the other guests and into a corner, where they were soon joined by Bobby. The three huddled together in an intimate conversation for fifteen minutes.

Dorothy Kilgallen, the *Journal-American* columnist, would advise her readers that Marilyn and Bobby danced five times during the evening, while an angry Ethel Kennedy looked on.

Shortly after one A.M., Secret Service agents escorted the President, the movie star and a handful of others through the crowded apartment and into a private elevator, which descended to the basement of Krim's apartment house. From there they moved through a series of tunnels that connected the Carlyle Hotel with nearby apartment houses. The crush of reporters in the hotel lobby never saw the private band of revelers who crowded into the penthouse, where some of them remained until dawn.

"I learned from an FBI agent that they remained in the suite for several hours," said columnist Earl Wilson later. "It was the last prolonged encounter between them."

Marilyn flew back to Los Angeles early Sunday afternoon, May 20.

Five days later Marilyn tried calling the President on his private line, and discovered that it had been disconnected. When she tried to reach him through the White House switchboard, operators refused to put through her calls. "She was angry when the phone connection was cut," Robert Slatzer recalled. "It was a terrible shock." Terry Moore told ABC News producer Sylvia Chase, "[She] was devastated when he cut it off."

At the same time Marilyn discovered that Fox had not approved her appearance at the presidential birthday, as Bobby and Peter Lawford had led her to believe. And the studio was abuzz with rumors that she was about to be fired in the middle of *Something's Got to Give.*

Depressed and adrift, Marilyn retreated to her secluded Brentwood bungalow in a haze of champagne and barbiturates.

On June 1, she turned thirty-six. She managed to pull herself together and continue filming, but soon fell ill again. On June 4 she was notified at home that she was fired. The studio announced that she would be replaced by Lee Remick, but when Marilyn's costar Dean Martin declared days later he would not continue without her, they were forced to shut down production.

On June 11 Marilyn sent two wires to Robert Kennedy, one to his home in Arlington, Virginia, and the other to his office in the Justice Department. The cable to Arlington officially declined an invitation to a formal dinner for Peter and Pat Lawford. It read: "Dear Attorney General and Mrs. Robert Kennedy: I would have been delighted to have accepted your invitation honoring Pat and Peter Lawford. Unfortunately, I am involved in a freedom ride protesting the loss of the minority rights belonging to the few remaining earthbound stars. After all, all we demanded was our right to twinkle."

According to Brown and Barham, no trace of the second cable survives, but it was undoubtedly a plea for Bobby's help in her battle with Fox.

And Bobby apparently did try to help, contacting first Judge Samuel Rosenman, chairman of the board of Twentieth Century-

Fox. Rosenman, a former Franklin Roosevelt speechwriter, was an old and close friend of the Kennedy men and agreed to reconsider Marilyn's case. Bobby informed him that the President would be grateful for any help he could provide.

In the third week of June, Bobby Kennedy arrived at Marilyn's house in a white convertible. His visit was both personal and political, his first private meeting with the star.

Soon the two of them were walking hand in hand around Marilyn's pool while Bobby tossed a small white ball for her small white poodle, "Maf."

Marilyn later told both Eunice Murray, her nurse-housekeeper, and Robert Slatzer what Bobby had told her during their ninety-minute visit. "I'm a lawyer and a politician. And I live in my work. You're an actress, and you live in your work as well. Besides your work is important to the whole world. Stick with it." Shortly after that, he was gone.

He was also there, of course, to get Marilyn to stop dunning the White House with phone calls. To appease her, he ended up giving her his own private number at the Justice Department. Marilyn was soon calling him three and four times a week.

Marilyn was convinced that Bobby was going to rescue her.

That summer, Marilyn would place at least eight telephone calls to the Attorney General's office, seeking advice and support. On June 25 Marilyn called his office to confirm his presence at the Lawfords' two nights later and to invite him and the Lawfords to visit her home for a drink before dinner; she spoke only with his secretary, Angie Novello, for one minute. On Monday, July 2, she placed two calls, again to Novello and for the same length of time. The remainder of the calls were placed during the last two weeks of July, only one of them lasting more than a minute: On July 30 Marilyn called Bobby to say she was sorry to have missed his Los Angeles speech the previous weekend; she had gone to Lake Tahoe.

But those were not isolated phone calls. According to journalists Brown and Barham, between June 20 and July 15, Marilyn mounted a full-tilt media campaign to rescue her career. She gave ten interviews ranging from sessions with her friend and columnist Sidney Skolsky to extravagantly produced photo shoots with Bert Stern of *Vogue* and with Douglas Kirkland. During the interviews reporters were surprised that no topics were off limits, and that Marilyn was eager to talk about Fox and their mistreatment of her over the years.

Marilyn's media campaign, supported by Bobby and Fox executives Darryl Zanuck and Spyros Skouras, was successful. She was reinstated at *Something's Got to Give*, and at better terms.

At this point in the history of the Kennedy family, and especially the Kennedy administration, it was entirely reasonable for Bobby to regard himself as the invincible family fixer. He had successfully delivered a half-million-dollar palimony payment to save Jack's presidential campaign, suppressed all evidence of his brother's affair with Judy Campbell, and now he had weaned Marilyn away from Jack.

He regarded himself as a paragon of morality, repelled by the behavior of his father and brothers. The story is told that at one party, Teddy threw his arms around Jack and Bobby and said, "We three." Bobby backed away in obvious distaste, saying, "No, you *two*." Bobby was the one who warned brother-in-law Peter Lawford to watch his step, or he would damage the family image, and Bobby was the one delegated by Rose to talk to brother-in-law Stephen Smith about rumors that he was cheating on Jean.

But with Marilyn, what started out as merely another errand to smooth over a minor Kennedy peccadillo became, for Bobby, a passionate affair. According to Brown and Barham, Bobby and Marilyn began a long-distance relationship so intense and passionate that Hazel Washington described it as "making love over the phone. And I do mean making love."

This might have been a short-lived affair, between two people based on opposite coasts, committed to very different worlds. But that summer, Bobby Kennedy was often on the Fox lot, arriving by helicopter and guarded by Secret Service agents. He was consulting on the film version of *The Enemy Within*, which veteran producer Jerry Wald was preparing. The film was to profile Bobby's attempts to curb organized crime within the labor movement, and his war with Jimmy Hoffa.

The Attorney General and the movie star sometimes spent the night in the presidential suite at the Beverly Hilton, where staff remember that elaborate meals were brought in from La Scala.

They were seen at at least four parties where many guests recognized that the two were infatuated with each other. In fact, with the help of her longtime psychiatrist, Dr. Ralph Greenson, Marilyn was able to feel sexually fulfilled for the first time. Her friend Jeanne Carmen, who had known her since the mid-1950s, agreed that Bobby Kennedy was the man who awakened the sex goddess.

"It certainly wasn't JFK," Carmen said. "He could have read the paper while he was having sex with her. With the President, she told me, it was 'a minute on and a minute off.' " But Marilyn confided that Bobby was "marvelous in bed—sweet and loving as no man had ever been. She often said, 'He's my little love.' "

Years later a BBC investigative team probing Marilyn's death uncovered a handwritten note from Jean Smith that seemed to validate the affair. Written from the Kennedy mansion in Palm Beach, it told Marilyn "Understand that you and Bobby are the new item" and invited Marilyn to come East for a visit.

When the note came up for auction in 1994, Jean Smith faxed the *Washington Post*, claiming that any conclusion that the note verified an affair was "utter nonsense."

NUDE BOBBY TO MARILYN: "I HAVEN'T HAD THIS MUCH FUN IN A LONG TIME."

According to Jeanne Carmen, she and Marilyn introduced Bobby to the lighter side of life when, during one of his increasingly frequent visits to Los Angeles, they invited him to a secluded nude beach near Malibu.

To protect his identity, Marilyn and Jeanne fitted him with a false beard, cap and sunglasses, and minutes later they were driving to the beach.

"By the way he was trembling, Marilyn and I both thought he was going to pass out," Carmen recalled. "When we were done, he looked up like he was in a daze and said over and over again: 'I can't believe I'm doing this! I just can't believe it.' "

As the afternoon idyll drew to a close, Bobby assured Carmen and Marilyn, "I haven't had this much fun in a long time."

The relationship with Marilyn continued. On June 26 she and

Bobby had dinner together at the Lawfords' beach house and spent the night. Weeks later she discovered she was pregnant, and the father was most likely one of the brothers. On July 20 she had an abortion. And then, as suddenly as it began, her affair with Bobby was over.

Like his brother, he simply stopped taking her calls. She telephoned his private line and received a taped message informing her that she had reached a nonworking number. She even tried to reach him through the main switchboard of the Justice Department. She was told that the Attorney General was unavailable. He ignored her notes and curtailed his trips to the West Coast.

Friends tried to explain to her that the affair had been doomed from the start, but she was distraught.

And she began to talk.

She told columnists Sidney Skolsky, Earl Wilson and James Bacon about her affair with Bobby, and the gossip was rampant in Washington, D.C. The Washington press corps was abuzz with it, as well.

When Marilyn persisted, Peter Lawford was delegated to get her to back off. It did no good.

Finally, she called Bobby at Hickory Hill.

This was going too far. Kennedy mistresses were supposed to know their place and it was not to break into the privacy of the home without an invitation.

Dorothy Kilgallen ran a blind item about their relationship: "Marilyn Monroe is cooking in the sex appeal department. She has appeared vastly alluring to a handsome gentleman. A handsome gentleman with a bigger name than Joe DiMaggio in his heyday—so don't write her off."

The same day, Marilyn learned that Bobby and Ethel and several of their children had flown to San Francisco, where the Attorney General was scheduled to address the American Bar Association. Marilyn made many calls to the St. Francis Hotel where they were staying, but never managed to get through to Bobby.

In addition, Marilyn had started to receive mysterious harassing calls. A woman's voice was calling all night long, always with the same message: "Leave Bobby alone, you tramp. Leave Bobby alone." Marilyn did not believe it was Ethel's voice, but it was a vaguely familiar voice that she had heard before.

It is now conceded that on August 4 Bobby flew to Los Angeles and had an ugly showdown with Marilyn. According to Anthony Summers, the quarrel sent Marilyn into hysterics and her psychiatrist had to be called.

Marilyn had been expected to have dinner with the Lawfords that night, but after her spat with Bobby, she could not face him. Instead, she stayed home, making a series of calls to Dr. Greenson and friends. Her last call, to Peter Lawford, was made around ten P.M. "Say goodbye to Pat," she said. "Say goodbye to Jack, and say goodbye to yourself because you're a nice guy." Suddenly there was silence. Lawford tried to call her back, but the phone was off the hook. By the time she was found a few hours later, she was in a coma. She died in the early hours of August 5.

A distraught Lawford called Fred Otash and begged the private detective to case her bungalow and clear out any evidence linking Marilyn to the President and the Attorney General.

To complicate matters, a crumpled piece of paper, found in Marilyn's bedclothes, bore a White House telephone number. A classic cover-up followed. The scrap of paper and other evidence disappeared. Records of Marilyn's last phone calls disappeared from the offices of General Telephone, possibly confiscated by the FBI.

After the news of Marilyn's death was made public, her half sister, Berniece Miracle, asked Joe DiMaggio to make the arrangements. The baseball hero had never stopped loving her and he blamed Hollywood and the Kennedys for her fate. Only thirty people were allowed to attend the services at Westwood Memorial Park chapel. The Lawfords, Sinatra, and Sammy Davis, Jr., were all barred.

Lee Strasberg gave a brief eulogy and someone sang "Over the Rainbow." Then the coffin was opened so her friends could get a last look at Marilyn. She was wearing a green Pucci dress, lying on a bed of champagne velvet, a bouquet of roses from DiMaggio in her hands. He sobbed, "I love you," and kissed her one last time.

Was Bobby's affair with Marilyn Monroe a one-shot slip? Many who socialized with him and Ethel in those days were not convinced. Like the Ambassador and the President, the Attorney General seemed to prefer the quick hit.

"I have a friend who was in the library with him," Jeanne Martin, ex-wife of Dean, claimed, "and before she knew it the door was locked and he threw her on the couch. It was so blatant." Bobby even propositioned a former convent school classmate of his sister Jean. "Why don't you come home with me?" he asked. "I have my car outside. Ethel's away."

Ethel didn't have to be out of town. One shocked Washington reporter at a festive luau watched as Bobby groped a dancer under her grass skirt.

But Kennedy rules were for the Kennedy men only. When Bobby saw Ethel dancing at a party with a family friend, he created an ugly scene. "Bobby came over and grabbed Ethel and said, 'Listen, why are you acting like a whore? I don't want to be married to a whore. Get out of here. You're not dancing with anybody.' I was just so surprised at the way he behaved. It was shocking. Ethel looked dumbfounded."

CHAPTER TEN
DARK CLOUDS GATHER

The year 1963 began auspiciously. The whole Kennedy family welcomed the new year with a party in Palm Beach. Among the guests were Kick's old friend Pamela Churchill, now the wife of prominent Broadway producer Leland Hayward.

One week later thirty-year-old Teddy took office as the junior senator from Massachusetts. This marked the first time in American history that three brothers simultaneously held high government office.

PUBLISHER REVEALS JFK'S AFFAIR—IS REMOVED FROM CONVENTION IN STRAITJACKET

The mysterious death of Marilyn Monroe was followed by another tragic casualty of the Kennedy administration.

Jack had learned from his father the importance of cultivating the press and by developing a passionate friendship with Philip Graham, publisher of the *Washington Post*, he could not have made a more powerful ally. Henry Luce, William Randolph Hearst and the columnist Arthur Krock belonged to the Ambassador, but Phil Graham belonged to Jack. The alliance began when Jack joined the Senate's prestigious Committee on Foreign Relations. And was cemented when the two men shared women while they were neighbors in Georgetown.

An alcoholic and a manic-depressive, Graham was also a brilliant publisher and had revitalized the *Post*. According to Deborah Davis, author of a biography of Katharine Graham, Phil's close relationships with JFK and another master politician, Lyndon B. Johnson, then chairman of the Senate Armed Services Committee and eventually the Senate's majority leader, "corrupted his publishership and contributed to his destruction."

In his drive to be a political power, Graham was eager to claim credit for helping to elect JFK by teaming him with Johnson on the 1960 Democratic ticket. He liked to imply that only he could have managed it. Jack had learned from his father how to play the press and allowed Graham to think he could have a role in creating national policy. Graham and his wife, Katharine, were included on the short list for JFK's "Hickory Hill seminars," informal weekend meetings at Bobby's home. (The Lyndon Johnsons were not.)

Graham, who had previously been hospitalized for his manic-depressive illness, soon lost perspective on the Kennedys. He was convinced he had put JFK in the White House, and now he, Phil Graham, was one of the powers behind the President.

But except for feeding him off-the-record information to encourage Graham's pro-Kennedy editorials and features, Jack had lost interest in Graham as he had earlier lost interest in Marilyn Monroe. His usefulness was limited. "Something as simple as giving a job in the Attorney General's office to one of Phil's old law-school friends, a well-known and excellent lawyer, which was the most standard kind of political payola, turned out to be beyond Kennedy's debt to him," says Deborah Davis.

Graham's friend was briefly and reluctantly hired, then fired by the Attorney General.

Like Jimmy Roosevelt and others before him, Phil Graham had learned that Kennedy relationships flowed one way. There was no payback for Kennedy pocket people. As Jack asserted his new power from the Oval Office, Graham found himself shut out, unable to exercise even minimal clout.

Graham's condition, exacerbated by Jack's rejection, deteriorated, until in early 1963, in the middle of an ugly divorce, he flew to Phoenix, Arizona, on a Gulfstream jet leased by the *Post* and set up residence there with his mistress.

Coincidentally, there was a journalists' convention going on in Phoenix. Phil Graham had not been invited, but when he learned about it he showed up in the banquet room during a speech, grabbed the microphone, and drunkenly announced to the crowd, many of whom knew and admired him, that he was going to tell them exactly who in Washington was sleeping with whom, beginning with President Kennedy. "His favorite," screamed Phil, "was now Mary Meyer...."

As Phil ranted, Davis reports, one of the newsmen called Kennedy, who immediately called Katharine, wanting to know if, as a friend, there was anything he could do to bring Phil under control. The call came as Katharine was meeting with the *Post* executives in her home, planning to bring Phil back forcibly and commit him to a psychiatric hospital. She declined the President's offer; Kennedy had done enough. Phil's assistant James Truitt took the phone and asked the President to send Phil's psychiatrist, Leslie Farber, to Phoenix on a military jet. Phil was brought back to the motel, where he was injected with a heavy sedative, and he was then taken to the airport in an ambulance.

A sedated Graham, in a straitjacket, was taken back to Washington and committed to Chestnut Lodge, one of the most expensive psychiatric hospitals in the country. Phil Graham never again returned to the *Post* and on August 3, 1963, while on a weekend visit to the family farm, he took a shotgun and blew his brains out. He died two days short of the first anniversary of the "suicide" of Marilyn Monroe.

JFK AT BERLIN WALL: "I AM A JELLY DONUT."

In May, Jack celebrated his forty-sixth birthday quietly in Washington, a sharp contrast to the previous year's gala. This time he opted for a dinner cruise around the Potomac aboard the presidential yacht, *Sequoia*.

On June 26 Jack made his second presidential tour of Europe, but this time Jackie, pregnant with their third child, did not accompany him. Jack did not possess his wife's gift for languages. When he visited the Berlin Wall and gave a rousing speech defending the rights of West Berliners against the Soviets, declaring "*Ich bin ein Berliner*," it was unfortunately interpreted as "I am a jelly donut," *berliner* being a local pastry. The correct phrase, Dr.

Jacobson told him when they returned to the United States, should have been "*Ich bin Berliner.*"

From Germany, JFK moved on to four days in Ireland and concluded his trip in Italy, where he met with the new Pope, Paul VI, and attended a session of NATO.

Jackie's sister Lee took time out from a cruise aboard Aristotle Onassis's yacht to substitute beside Jack in Germany and Ireland. She returned to the *Christina* but left again when word arrived that Jackie's baby Patrick had died.

Jackie had been staying in Hyannis Port and spent the morning of August 7 horseback riding with Caroline. On returning to the compound, she felt labor pains and summoned her obstetrician, John Walsh, who was vacationing nearby. He called for a helicopter and she was taken to the military hospital at Otis Air Force Base near Falmouth where a floor had been prepared for just such an emergency. Jack, who had remained in the White House, was notified immediately and flew to Otis to be by her side.

At 12:52 P.M. the hospital announced that Mrs. Kennedy had given birth by caesarian section to a boy weighing four pounds and 10 1/2 ounces. He was 5 1/2 weeks premature and in such danger that he was baptized in the hospital and named Patrick Bouvier for his paternal grandfather and Black Jack.

By the time Jack arrived, he was informed that Jackie was doing fine, but that little Patrick had hyaline membrane disease, a serious respiratory problem common in premature babies. The doctors recommended that the infant be taken to Children's Hospital Medical Center in Boston where he could get the best treatment. Jack conferred with Jackie and had the baby brought to her. That night he accompanied the infant in an ambulance to Boston, where he visited the hospital four times during the next day to check on Patrick's condition. He spent the next night on a cot near the baby. The following day Patrick slipped into a coma and died.

"I was with him in the hospital when he was holding Patrick's hand," said Evelyn Lincoln, Jack's longtime secretary, "and the nurse said, 'He's gone!' Tears came into his eyes. I had never seen tears in his eyes before." No one in the Kennedy inner circle had ever seen Jack react so emotionally. "He just cried and cried and cried," said Dave Powers.

Jack returned to Otis where he broke the news to Jackie. They spent an hour alone in her hospital room. It was during that time that she told him: "The one thing I could not bear would be to lose you."

While Jackie recovered, the rest of the family attended the funeral mass in Boston celebrated by Cardinal Cushing. Instead of a solemn requiem mass with its black vestments, Cushing wore white vestments for the Mass of the Angels. The President carried the small casket in his arms and placed inside it the St. Christopher medal that had been Jackie's wedding present to him. He was the last to leave the church after the mass, clutching the casket and seeming disoriented. Cushing had to restrain him. "Come on, Jack, let's go," he said. "God is good." The baby was buried in the family's new plot at Holyrood Cemetery in Brookline. Jack touched the tiny coffin as it was lowered into the grave. "Goodbye," he whispered. "It's awfully lonely down there."

For most observers it was the first time they had seen the cool, distanced President lose his composure. He seemed on the brink of collapse.

Jackie remained in bed at Otis hospital for a week, then spent the remainder of the summer in Hyannis Port. As she left the hospital, she thanked the nurses. "You've been so wonderful to me that I'm coming back here next year to have another baby. So you better be ready for me."

The loss of his infant son was probably the greatest emotional blow Jack had experienced since the wartime death of his older brother. It altered forever the delicate relationship between Jack and Jackie and drew them closer than they had been. Observers at his inauguration had commented on the lack of affection between the two of them. Now, as they left Otis hospital, the President took his wife's hand for the first time in his public career, and led her to the car.

On September 12, Jack and Jackie marked their tenth anniversary. He presented her with a catalog from J. J. Klejman, a New York antiques dealer, and told her to pick out what she wanted. She selected a coiled serpent bracelet. Her anniversary gifts to him were a gold St. Christopher medal to replace the one he had placed in little Patrick's coffin, and a red-and-gold leather scrapbook of photographs of the White House rose garden taken during its restoration. On each page were before and after pictures of the garden taken every day during its renovation, plus a copy of the President's schedule for that day and a quotation on gardening written by Jackie in longhand.

JACK TO JACKIE: "I'D LIKE TO SEE A LITTLE MORE ABOUT CAROLINE, A LITTLE LESS ABOUT ONASSIS."

Those closest to Jackie, including the President and her sister, Lee, were aware that she was still in a depression. Lee invited Jackie to join her and Onassis on a cruise aboard the *Christina*. Ari was instantly smitten.

Jack was not thrilled at his wife's new friend. It was common knowledge that in 1954 Onassis had been indicted by the federal government on criminal charges of falsifying the ownership of a number of Liberty ships. The United States claimed that Onassis had used American cohorts as "fronts" to buy up, at low prices, the surplus Liberty ships which, by law, could only be purchased by Americans. Onassis had been arrested and released on $10,000 bail. He eventually paid a $7-million fine but avoided jail.

To improve the image of what might look like a frivolous cruise, Jack pressured his undersecretary of commerce, Franklin D. Roosevelt, Jr., to go along with his wife as a de facto chaperone.

The *Christina* was stocked with eight varieties of caviar, the finest vintage wines. A crew of sixty included two hairdressers, three chefs, a Swedish masseuse and a small orchestra for dancing in the evenings. Ari and his guests sailed from Piraeus at the beginning of October for wherever Jackie wanted to go. "Mrs. Kennedy is in charge here," Ari told a crowd of reporters witnessing the departure.

Photographs of Jackie and Ari together disturbed Jack, but there was nothing he could do. Photographs of Jackie sunbathing on the deck of the *Christina* were bad politics, and the photographs of her water-skiing in a bikini were even worse. "Does this sort of behavior seem fitting for a woman in mourning?" asked an editorial in the *Boston Globe*. If they were meant to make Jack nervous and jealous, they succeeded. From the ship she wrote letters to the President that began: "My dearest, dearest Jack." He called her several times late at night. Once he cabled her: "What I'd like to see in the headlines is a little more about Caroline and a little less about Onassis."

On the last night of the cruise, Ari presented the women with gifts. Lee received three diamond bracelets, and Jackie got a diamond-and-ruby necklace, which could be converted to two bracelets. "Ari has showered Jackie with so many presents I can't stand it," Lee wrote to the President. "All I got is three dinky little bracelets that Caroline wouldn't even wear to her own birthday party."

When the cruise ended, Jackie was still not ready to return home. Instead, she and Lee stopped off in Marrakesh to attend the birthday celebration of the king's firstborn son.

If she was trying to bring Jack into line, the ploy worked. He was waiting at the airport with Caroline and John, Jr., when she returned.

Jackie returned to Jack and the White House, but a few months later, at a Washington dinner party, she vehemently defended Onassis, calling him "an alive and vital person who has come up from nowhere."

The White House staff and the press noted a new cooperation and openness about Jackie in the months after the cruise. Having exerted her independence and charmed a dangerous and enormously wealthy tycoon, she had once again aroused Jack's fascination. He not only wanted her, he realized that he needed her, and he asked her to accompany him on a campaign trip to Texas that November. She agreed.

JFK: "WE'RE HEADING INTO NUT COUNTRY TODAY."

The President's trip to Dallas was purely political. The Democratic party in Texas was split by a feud between the conservative governor, John Connally, and a liberal senator, Ralph Yarborough. Even with Texas's own Lyndon Johnson on the ticket, Jack had barely carried Texas in 1960 with a mere 46,233 votes. It was critical that the Democratic party be united before his next presidential campaign. The fact that he intended to run again, although he had not yet announced, was taken for granted.

Throughout his career Jack and the Ambassador had put great

store in polls. Now the Belden Poll showed his approval rate in Texas was at fifty percent, down from seventy-six percent in 1962. Not everyone thought the Texas trip was a good idea. When Adlai Stevenson was there for United Nations Day in October, he had been booed and spat on. Dallas was considered a stronghold of the ultraconservative John Birch Society. Reactionary Dixiecrats were still fuming at the President's decision to desegregate the University of Mississippi. But Jack was determined to make the trip and delighted that Jackie had agreed to go. It would be her first political trip since the 1960 election campaign.

Early in November the White House announced that the President and the First Lady would be making a two-day swing through the Southwest, stopping in San Antonio, Houston, Fort Worth and Dallas. They intended to spend the weekend at the LBJ Ranch outside Austin.

They flew to Texas on November 21. The President dedicated the Aerospace Medical Center in San Antonio, then attended a testimonial dinner for Rep. Albert Thomas. From there they went on to spend the night in Fort Worth.

The next morning, November 22, Jack was surprised and pleased by the size of the crowd that was already gathering in the rain outside his Fort Worth hotel.

The *Dallas Morning News* was not nearly so enthusiastic. For months *News* editorials had been calling Jack "fifty times a fool" for signing the nuclear test ban treaty. That Friday the *News* front-page headline: PRESIDENT'S VISIT SEEN WIDENING STATE DEMO-CRATIC SPLIT. On page 14 was a full-page advertisement, paid for by H.L. Hunt and other conservative businessmen, asking the President twelve questions, most notably: "Why has the Foreign Policy of the United States degenerated to the point that the CIA is arranging coups and having staunch Anti-Communist Allies of the U.S. bloodily exterminated?" Jack read it with interest, then muttered, "We're heading into nut country today."

Before they left Washington, there had been some discussion about whether to use the bubbletop on the President's limousine. Jackie wanted it, to protect her hairstyle. The Secret Service, of course, wanted the bubbletop for security reasons. But Jack insisted on an open car and he insisted that the scheduled route of his Dallas motorcade be released to the press. "If you want people to turn out," he said, "they have to know where to find you."

After breakfast at the Texas Hotel, Jack and Jackie flew to Love Field in Dallas. There they entered the open top, bubble-free blue Lincoln Continental.

The admiring crowds that greeted Jack at Love Field and awaited him in downtown Dallas had no reason to imagine that his youthful, vital appearance was a sham. The night before he had slept on a special wooden board for his bad back. Now, under his shirt, he was wearing a back brace, and in his left shoe, a quarter-inch remedial lift.

Like his brother Joe before him, he seemed to take an almost fatalistic view of danger. He was less concerned with his personal safety than with politics and appearances. Concerned about the rift in the local Democratic party, he insisted that his aide Kenneth O'Donnell get Lyndon Johnson and Senator Ralph Yarborough into the same car, even if he had to shove them in. Governor and Mrs. Connally rode in the front seat of the Lincoln, with Jack and Jackie in the back.

JACKIE: "HIS BLOOD AND BRAINS WERE IN MY LAP!"

The presidential motorcade traveled down a ten-mile route through downtown Dallas on its way to the Trade Mart, where the President planned to speak at a luncheon.

As the presidential limousine turned onto Elm Street, near the nondescript Texas Book Depository, Nellie Connally remarked to Jack: "Mr. President, you can't say Dallas doesn't love you."

"No, you can't," he said. "No, you can't."

In the next few seconds, as the motorcade slowed down to negotiate the turns in Dealey Plaza, shots rang out. Witnesses remembered that it sounded like a car backfiring. Jackie screamed, "Jack, what have they done to you?"

At approximately 12:30 P.M. two bullets struck the President. "My God, I'm hit," he said, holding his throat.

America's President lay dying in his wife's arms.

Days after the President's death, in the rainy seclusion of her Hyannis Port house, Jackie sat down with journalist Theodore

White and poured out her immediate impressions of what had happened. White promised her that his notes would not be released until a year after her death.

Recalling the fatal motorcade, Jackie said that the shots "sounded like a backfire."

"Then Jack turned back, so neatly—his last expression was so neat. He had his hand out—I could see a piece of his skull coming off.

"It was flesh-colored, not white," she continued. "He was holding out his hand and I could see this perfectly clean piece detaching itself from his head. Then he slumped in my lap. His blood and his brains were in my lap . . . All the ride to the hospital, I kept bending over him, saying, 'Jack, Jack, can you hear me? I love you, Jack.'

"I tried to hold his head down. Maybe I could keep it (his brain) in." She promised herself she would take care of him every day of his life. She would make him happy. But in her heart she knew he was dead.

At the hospital she resisted the efforts of interns to lead her away from her husband's body. "There was a sheet over Jack," she said. "His foot was sticking out of the sheet, whiter than the sheet."

She took his foot and kissed it. Then she pulled back the sheet. "His mouth was so beautiful. His eyes were open. They found his hand under the sheet, and I held his hand all the time the priest was saying extreme unction."

Hours later, aboard *Air Force One,* Jackie was still wearing her blood-spattered pink Chanel suit as Lyndon B. Johnson was sworn in as President.

Teddy got the news in the Senate.

Bobby got a call from J. Edgar Hoover at Hickory Hill. He immediately went to join Jackie and her children. He insisted that Ethel go through with her car pool that afternoon so that she could tell their children herself.

Sargent Shriver would handle the funeral arrangements. Ted and Eunice would fly to Hyannis Port to be with their parents.

"Your father has gone to look after Patrick," her nanny, Maud Shaw, told Caroline.

Peter Lawford got the news in Lake Tahoe, where he was appearing at the Desert Inn. He flew back to Santa Monica to join Pat. Together, they and their seven-year-old daughter Sydney flew back to Washington. (Eight-year-old Christopher refused to join them.)

In Hamburg, West Germany, Ari Onassis learned of the shooting and immediately telephoned Lee Radziwill in London. She asked him to accompany her and her husband to the funeral. The next day Ari received an invitation from the chief of protocol not only to attend the funeral but to be a guest at the White House while in Washington. He accepted.

Rose got the news from her radio. The Ambassador, now an invalid, was the last to be told. The servants told him that his television was out of order. Ted confirmed that, even surreptitiously unplugging his father's television. He could not bring himself to tell his father what had happened.

Eunice took the lead: "Daddy. Daddy, there's been an accident. But Jack's okay. Jack was in an accident, Daddy. Oh Daddy, Jack's dead. He's dead, but he's in heaven. Oh God, Daddy, Jack's okay, isn't he?"

Rose, Eunice and Ted left for the funeral, leaving the Ambassador behind. But the enormous drive still lived in his crippled body and the old man struggled into his clothes and insisted that his niece Ann Gargan take him to the airport. By the time they got there, the *Caroline* had left. He was driven home and put to bed. From there he watched the nationally televised funeral for his son, the President.

The autopsy on the President was so botched that it left a permanent legacy of doubt that would feed conspiracy theorists for years. Doctors at Parkland in Dallas had wanted to conduct the autopsy there, but the Secret Service insisted on removing the body and returning it to Bethesda Naval Hospital. Jackie accompanied the body to Bethesda.

It was apparently Bobby who allowed the autopsy to go forward without a forensic pathologist. It is also believed that he was responsible for the disappearance of vital organs and tissue samples that should have been kept for future study. Even in death, the Kennedy code of deception ruled.

JACKIE: "I WANT JOHN-JOHN TO BE A FINE YOUNG MAN."

In spite of her grief, Jackie knew that she had to go on for the sake of her children. "I'm going to bring up my son," she told Theodore White. "I want him to grow up to be a good boy. I have no better dream for him. I want John-John to be a fine young man."

When Caroline asked her what kind of prayer she should say for her father, Jackie almost broke down. "I told her to say either 'Please, God, take care of Daddy,' or 'Please, God, be nice to Daddy.' "

Before the funeral Jackie wrote a farewell letter to her husband and told Caroline, "You must write a letter to Daddy now, and tell him how much you love him." Caroline printed, "Dear Daddy: We are going to miss you. Daddy I love you very much. Caroline." John was not old enough to write, but he signed Caroline's letter with an X. Their letters were placed inside the President's coffin.

The day of the funeral was John, Jr.'s, third birthday. Although many people suggested his party be postponed, Jackie insisted that it go through as planned. Two days later, on Caroline's birthday, Jackie gave another party. "Of course, all of us adults were in tears," recalls Sherrye Henry, "but not Mrs. Kennedy. She did what I couldn't have done."

The President's body lay in state in the East Room of the White House, flanked by an honor guard representing each branch of the armed forces. One observer saw Bobby enter and throw his arms over the coffin and start talking to his dead brother. "It broke my heart," he recalled. Before the funeral mass Bobby placed his *PT-109* tie clip, a silver rosary and a lock of his own hair into his brother's coffin.

A horse-drawn caisson bore the body of the slain president to the Capitol rotunda on Sunday. On Monday a twenty-one-gun salute was fired while fifty jet planes flew overhead and *Air Force*

One dipped a wing in tribute. A solemn requiem mass was celebrated at St. Matthew's Church.

JFK REHEARSED HIS OWN ASSASSINATION

As shocking as the assassination of John F. Kennedy was, it is even more shocking to discover that he rehearsed the event just a few months earlier. It was during Labor Day weekend in 1963, that the President, a James Bond fan, joined with friends to make an amateur film, not far from Hammersmith Farm in Newport, Rhode Island. The presidential yacht, *Honey Fitz,* docked nearby, and a Navy photographer filmed what happened next. Jack came off the boat, walked down the long pier, then suddenly clutched his chest, and fell over, flat, across the pier. A beautiful woman, Countess Consuelo Crespi, and her young son, emerged from the yacht and stepped over him as they walked toward shore. Next, Jackie came out and she, too, stepped over Jack's "body." Finally his friend Red Fay came along and pretended to stumble over the body. As he did, he fell on top of Jack. Red liquid spurted from Jack's mouth and all over his T-shirt.

This weird scene was observed by veteran reporters Frank Cormier and Merriman Smith. Cormier related it to author Ralph G. Martin, recalling that when he wrote about the Kennedy home movie, "Kennedy was absolutely furious. He liked to keep what he considered his private life separate from his official life." After Cormier wrote a small piece about the home movie, he found himself "in the doghouse." Months later he ran into Pierre Salinger and Ken O'Donnell. Salinger informed him that the White House considered him a Peeping Tom and his story was in terrible taste.

"Well, if it was in terrible taste for me to write about it, it was in terrible taste for the President to do it," Cormier replied.

Ken O'Donnell agreed.

ROSE KENNEDY: "NOW IT'S BOBBY'S TURN."

The effect of the assassination on Joseph Kennedy can only be imagined. For the second time, one of his sons had deliberately and recklessly put his life on the line, and the resulting tragedy had dashed Joe's triumphant conquest of the White House. But the founder of the dynasty, incapacitated by his stroke, could not communicate his reaction, and the family could no longer benefit from his counsel. His 1961 stroke broke his body, but the assassination of his son broke his spirit. After this, he gave up.

Rose's own dynastic ambitions remained undimmed.

After the funeral, guests returned to the White House for a reception, later, to celebrate John's third birthday. John Davis recalls that before leaving, he found Rose standing alone and went over to her to offer his condolences.

"She looked smaller and more inconspicuous than usual," he writes, "as if her son's tragedy had somehow shrunken her. But she was outwardly calm."

"Oh thank you, Mr. Davis, but don't worry. Everything will be all right. You'll see. Now it's Bobby's turn."

John F. Kennedy was buried at Arlington on Monday, November 25. The following Thursday was Thanksgiving Day, and most of the Kennedy family gathered at Hyannis Port for the weekend. Only Bobby and his family couldn't face it. They stayed at Hickory Hill and in December headed for Palm Beach.

In the aftermath a wave of memorializing that verged on canonization would begin. It is widely accepted that Jackie, in her sessions with reporter Theodore White, first compared the Kennedy administration to King Arthur's Camelot when she told how the President had loved to listen to the Lerner and Loewe cast album.

This is not accurate.

According to journalist L. Fletcher Prouty, during the 1962–1963 period, the U.S. Army had a contract study called "Camelot" under way in a think tank group associated with American University in Washington. Neither the President nor his Secretary of Defense, Robert S. McNamara, was popular with army officials and those who were members of the think tank used the word "Camelot" to characterize the administration in a derogatory sense.

The mobster Mickey Cohen was more earthy than most in expressing his admiration for the slain president. "I don't want to take anything away from John Kennedy being President," he said. "Needing broads two, three times a day—doesn't take away from him being President. Because being President of the United States doesn't still make him anything less than a man. I admired Kennedy because, well the son of a bitch was not only a man—he was *all* man, and that's good. If a man's got to get laid three times a day, fine and dandy. He was a guy just like me."

PART FOUR

AFTER CAMELOT

All arrogance will reap a harvest rich in tears. God calls men to a heavy reckoning for overweening pride.

—Herodotus

CHAPTER ELEVEN
BOBBY'S BRIEF MOMENT

We had to be first in sailing and skiing races. We had to beat our opponents in tennis and get more runs than the other team in softball. And if we didn't he'd get mad. Very, very mad! It was made clear that we weren't to take these sports halfheartedly.

—Kathleen Kennedy Townsend,
recalling life with her father,
Robert F. Kennedy

Bobby Kennedy had been hit hard. For ten years he had devoted himself to his older brother's career. Now Jack was gone, and all the power they had struggled together to achieve was in the hands of Lyndon B. Johnson, a man they both distrusted. Bobby took to leaving Hickory Hill in the middle of the night and driving deep into the countryside, returning at dawn, looking haggard and heading for his job as attorney general. Inside his office he would sit at his desk, staring out the window.

"I was the seventh of nine children," Bobby once said, "and when you come from that far down you have to struggle to survive." Lem Billings believed that Bobby felt "the least loved" of the sons and in reaction he became "a devoted observer of all the clan rules," becoming the most serious and religious of the boys.

Friends noticed that he began to unconsciously assume Jack's mannerisms; his cigar smoking, even donning an old tweed coat of Jack's.

Not even the conviction of his longtime adversary Jimmy Hoffa could rouse him. Bobby's obsession with Jimmy Hoffa had continued throughout his term as Attorney General. As Prof. Monroe Friedman later wrote in the *Georgetown Law Journal*, "From the day that James Hoffa told Robert Kennedy that he was nothing but a rich man's kid who never had to earn a nickel in his life, Hoffa was a marked man." When Bobby became Attorney General, he made satisfying this vendetta the public policy of the United States. But by the time Hoffa was convicted of attempted jury bribery in early 1964, Bobby no longer cared. His mental and emotional energy was concentrated on psychological survival.

Jackie moved with her children into the Georgetown mansion of Averell and Marie Harriman. They happily turned their home over to them while Jackie planned her future, and the Harrimans moved into a nearby hotel.

Jackie did everything possible to maintain continuity for her children. She asked Dave Powers to come over every day and play soldier with John, as he used to in the White House. "He'll remember his father through associations with people who knew Jack well," she told him.

But Washington soon became impossible. "The crowds were too much," Letitia Baldridge recalled. "Tour buses went by and said, 'This is the home of Jacqueline Kennedy.' It was just awful, so she got out of Washington."

WARREN COMMISSION

On November 29, 1963, Lyndon Johnson appointed a presidential commission, chaired by Supreme Court justice Earl Warren and including two senators, Richard Russell (D., Georgia) and John Sherman Cooper (R., Kentucky), and two congressmen, Gerald Ford (R., Michigan) and Hale Boggs (D., Louisiana) to investigate the assassination of President Kennedy. Also on the commission were John J. McCloy, former head of the World Bank, and Allen Dulles, former director of the CIA. Among the young investigators supporting them was assistant counsel Arlen Specter, an assistant district attorney from Philadelphia.

Bobby told Warren Commission investigators that "I would like to state definitely that I know of no credible evidence to sup-

By the 1930s Joseph P. Kennedy looked like the man who had everything: a fortune that survived the Great Depression, a powerful political connection with Franklin D. Roosevelt, nine handsome and promising children, and a tolerant spouse who turned a blind eye to his endless affairs. (*AP/Wide World*)

Betty Compson, star of stage and screen, was one of Joe's liveliest conquests. (*The Bettmann Archive*)

Gloria Swanson, the first superstar, was a woman who lived life on her own terms, the opposite of the dutiful Rose. No wonder Joe was smitten, and no wonder their notorious affair could not last. (*The Bettmann Archive*)

Nancy Carroll, a brunette comedienne, replaced Gloria Swanson in Joe's affections. (*The Bettmann Archive*)

Constance Bennett was another screen star who caught Joe's attention. (*UPI/Bettmann*)

Dime-store heiress Barbara Hutton sought help from Ambassador Kennedy in London and ended up being propositioned. (*UPI/Bettmann*)

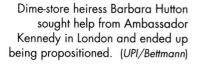

Kennedy men traditionally shared their women, and the legendary Marlene Dietrich boasted that she had made love with three of them: Joe, Joe, Jr., and Jack. (*Star Press*)

The rules were different for Kenne women. Here the long-suffer Rose is flanked by her t oldest daughters: Kick (l.) a Rosemary (r.) in 1938. Each g would rebel in a different way a meet a tragic fate. (*UPI/Bettma*

Naval Lt. Joseph P. Kennedy, Jr., was killed in action in 1944 while on a secret bombing mission. He was the family's prince, their best hope. (*UPI/Bettmann*)

President John F. Kennedy, the most powerful man in the world, brought the Kennedy rules to the White House. (*UPI/Bettmann*)

Inga Arvad, the beautiful Danish journalist and suspected Nazi sympathizer, who was Jack's first serious romance. (*UPI/Bettmann*)

Gene Tierney, one of the great screen beauties of the 1940s, did not reveal her 1949 affair with Jack until she published her autobiography in 1979. (*AP/Wide World*) [Shown here in 1950]

Angie Dickinson in 1962. She has always remained coy on the subject of her relationship with the President, but there is no doubt he respected her talent enormously. (AP/Wide World)

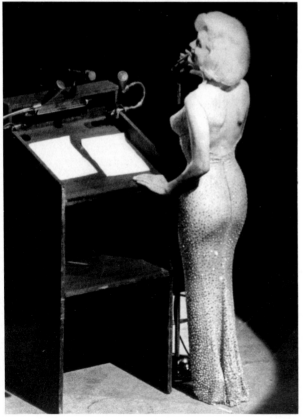

Marilyn Monroe, the May night she sang "Happy Birthday, Mr. President," at Madison Square Garden. Days later, Jack had her private line to him in the Oval Office disconnected, and by August she would be dead. (UPI/Bettmann)

Judith Campbell Exner was one of several mistresses Jack balanced while in the White House. Beautiful and well-connected, she was introduced to Jack by Frank Sinatra and was also a longtime mistress of Chicago mob boss Sam Giancana. (*UPI/Bettmann*)

Strong-willed and enigmatic, Jacqueline Kennedy never publicly discussed her years with the Kennedy men. (*UPI/Bettmann*)

Peter Lawford's 1954 marriage to Patricia Kennedy would revitalize the family's Hollywood connections. Handsome, troubled, and irresistible to women, Lawford could always be relied on to provide female companions for the Kennedy men. (*The Bettmann Archive*)

Lawford even brought out a rarely-seen fun side in his brother-in-law Robert, who was usually the conscience of the Kennedy men. (*The Bettmann Archive*)

Kennedy Men, 1960: Teddy once threw his arms around his two older brothers and said: "We three." Bobby pulled away in mock horror, joking, "No, you two." (Nelson Tiffany/Gamma-Liaison)

In the wake of the assassination of his brother, Bobby Kennedy moved to New York and in 1964 ran successfully for the U.S. Senate. Here he is shown with his wife Ethel, and their son David. There is no hint in this photograph of the tragedies that awaited them all. (UPI/Bettmann)

Mary Jo Kopechne's 1969 death on Chappaquiddick Island put an end to Senator Edward M. Kennedy's presidential hopes. *(UPI/Bettmann)*

Senator Teddy, wearing his controversial neck brace, leaves St. Vincent's Church with his wife, Joan, after the funeral Mass for Mary Jo. *(UPI/Bettmann)*

Spectators look on as police work near Senator Teddy's Oldsmobile which had just been exhumed from Poucha Pond, too late to save Mary Jo Kopechne. (*UPI/Bettmann*)

More than anyone else in the family, the ailing Joseph P. Kennedy recognized that Chappaquiddick was a death blow to his dreams of a Kennedy dynasty. Shown here a few weeks after Chappaquiddick, he would be dead by fall.

While preparing for his 1980 presidential bid, Teddy and Joan tried to at least give their marriage some sense of life. Few were convinced. (Joel Landau/UPI/Bettmann)

Former Olympic skier Suzy Chaffee, shown in 1985, has often been linked to the Senator. (AP/Wide World)

Lacy Neuhaus of Houston in 1981.
(*AP/Wide World*)

New York socialite and city planner
Amanda Burden in 1976.
(*AP/Wide World*)

Helga Wagner, Palm Beach jewelry designer, who was one of the first people Teddy Kennedy called from Chappaquiddick and who has remained a good friend. (*UPI/Bettmann*)

Teddy is said to have finally found happiness with Washington, D.C. attorney Victoria Reggie, a divorced mother of two, whom he married in 1992. (*Reuters/Bettmann*)

port the allegations that the assassination of President Kennedy was caused by a domestic or foreign conspiracy."

Jackie soon realized that she and the children had to escape from the well-meaning public in Washington and from the Kennedys as well. "Jackie understood the importance of creating a family unit apart from the larger Kennedy family," historian Doris Kearns Goodwin told *Ladies' Home Journal*. "She recognized that the children would get strength from the grandparents and cousins, aunts and uncles, but it was growing up with a feeling of belonging to their own small family that would give them stability."

So, in September 1964, the three moved to New York. Jackie took a fifteen-room apartment on Fifth Avenue, overlooking Central Park.

When she learned that Caroline's classmates at the Convent of the Sacred Heart were not inviting her to their parties, she called the other mothers and told them she understood that they probably didn't want it to seem as if they were inviting Caroline simply because she was famous. But "after all, Caroline's only a little girl," she said. After that, Caroline was always included.

John, meanwhile, was enrolled at St. David's, a Catholic boys' school.

"One of my mother's favorite times of the year was spring in New York when [the] ballet came to town," Caroline recalls. "She would let my brother and me stay up late and take us to each year's new production. The world of classical dance—its princes, sorcerers, cruel spells and true love—was very real to my mother and we all lived in that magical world each time we went to the ballet."

Gradually, Jackie grew closer to Bobby, who replaced her sister, Lee, as her confidant. She gave him a copy of Edith Hamilton's *The Greek Way*, which he read from cover to cover, underlining and making notes. He was especially moved by some lines from Herodotus: "All arrogance will reap a harvest rich in tears. God calls men to a heavy reckoning for overweening pride."

Insiders were speculating about the true nature of the intense friendship between RFK and his widowed sister-in-law. Taki Theodoracopulos, who was involved with Lee Radziwill and sharing an apartment with Peter Lawford at the Sherry Netherland, recalls Lawford confiding that Bobby and Jackie were having an affair.

JFK MISTRESS MURDERED AND HER DIARY DESTROYED BY CIA

On October 12, 1964, at forty-four, Mary Meyer became another Kennedy intimate to die mysteriously. She was murdered on the towpath near her Georgetown studio, apparently shot in a botched robbery. A young man was arrested and charged with first-degree murder.

Some time before she died, Mary Meyer confided to her friends James and Anne Truitt that she was having an affair with the President and keeping a diary about it. Truitt was then vice president of the *Washington Post;* his wife Anne was a sculptor and confidante of Mary. Following the 1963 suicide of Phil Graham, Truitt was sent to the Tokyo bureau of *Newsweek,* a *Post* company. Before they left for Japan, Mary discussed the disposition of her diary in the event of her death. She asked the Truitts to entrust it to James Jesus Angleton, chief of counterintelligence for the CIA.

The Truitts were still in Tokyo when they received word of the towpath murder, but the Saturday after Mary Meyer's murder, five other friends, including Angleton and his wife Cicely, gathered at her Georgetown home to search for her diary.

They knew that Mary usually left her diary in the bookcase in her bedroom, where she also kept clippings about the assassination of JFK, but the diary was not there.

Drawing on his training and all the specialized tools at his disposal, Angleton combed her deep, narrow town house. But it was her sister, Tony, who finally found the diary in Mary's studio, locked in a steel box filled with hundreds of letters. She turned it over to Angleton and asked him to burn it. According to a November 12, 1995 letter to the *New York Times Book Review* jointly signed by Cicely Angleton and Anne Truitt, Angleton followed this instruction in part by burning the loose papers. He also followed Mary Meyer's instruction and safeguarded the diary. Years later, he honored a request from Tony Bradlee that he deliver it to her. Subsequently, Tony Bradlee burned the diary in the presence of Anne Truitt.

On July 19, 1965, Raymond Crump went on trial for the murder of Mary Meyer.

The prosecutor, Albert Hantman, told the jury that "this is a classic textbook case of circumstantial evidence."

Ten days after the trial began, the case went to the jury which took less than a day to reach a verdict of not guilty.

The acquittal left Mary Meyer's murder officially unsolved. Washington police never reopened the investigation.

Several years after Mary Meyer's death, some of her inner circle gathered at a seance in Upper Marlboro, Maryland, to attempt to establish contact with her departed spirit.

But the affair continued to be a secret known only to a tight inner circle until it burst forth as a headline in the *National Enquirer* in 1976.

Fourteen years after the murder, the *National Enquirer* published a story headlined JFK 2 YEAR WHITE HOUSE ROMANCE . . . SOCIALITE THEN MURDERED AND DIARY BURNED BY CIA. The main source for the story was James Truitt. The former publishing executive had been motivated, he said, by Ben Bradlee's lack of candor in his own book, *Conversations with Kennedy.* "Here is this great crusading Watergate editor who claimed to tell everything in his Kennedy book," said Truitt, "but really told nothing."

The *Post's* reaction to the story was to smear Truitt in a February 23 story that cited a doctor's certifications contained in court records that Truitt had suffered from a mental illness "such as to impair his judgment and cause him to be irresponsible." It quoted an anonymous Washington attorney to the effect that Truitt had threatened Bradlee and others in recent years with exposure of the "alleged scandals."

Journalists Ron Rosenbaum and Philip Nobile wrote about the mystery in *New Times* and concluded that: "the *Post*, while giving admirable play to an extremely touchy subject, created the hard impression that Truitt was an unreliable source—even though Bradlee knew that Truitt was essentially truthful about Mary Meyer and JFK."

Bobby also began to take up other prerogatives of Kennedy men. Sometime in the early 1960s he and Ethel had befriended the singer Andy Williams and his beautiful French wife, Claudine Longet. The two couples skied, sailed and traveled together. By the time he was elected to the Senate, some astute observers were convinced that Bobby and Claudine, fifteen years his junior, were lovers. Peter Lawford, for one, was convinced that they shared a "brief, rather intense affair." Years later, in an interview, Claudine did acknowledge that they shared a special closeness.

"We could talk in the way a girl and a man can talk, the way women are almost never able to talk, the way I was never able to talk to Ethel . . . not chitchat," she said. "When Bobby died I lost interest in the Kennedys. There was no one for me to talk to. I drifted away. There was just no one there."

[In 1977, two years after her divorce from Williams, Claudine Longet was convicted of criminally negligent homicide in the fatal shooting of her lover, Vladimir "Spider" Sabich.]

Bobby now found himself locked in a power struggle with Lyndon Johnson and Hoover. Once Johnson announced that no member of his cabinet would be eligible to run as his vice president, Bobby took the hint and on August 22, 1964, announced he would run for the Senate in New York. He was elected that November.

"I have absolutely no presidential ambitions," Bobby declared hours after he was sworn in as a United States senator, "and neither does my wife—Ethel Bird." Six days later, on January 10, 1965, Ethel delivered their sixth son and ninth child. Matthew Maxwell Taylor, named for their close friend, the Ambassador to South Vietnam, was christened at St. Patrick's in New York.

For the next two years, Bobby, now recognized as the heir apparent, spoke out on national issues and traveled frequently abroad. From 1965 on, his anti-Vietnam position would become more pronounced. He would increasingly address the problems of blacks, the poor and student radicals.

BOBBY WARNS: "STOP SEEING MY SISTER OR WE'LL FIX YOUR GONDOLA!"

There were rumbles of change among the Kennedy women. The shy and quiet Jean, who had written so charmingly to Marilyn Monroe, had suffered in silence as her own husband, Stephen Smith, fully embraced the Kennedy rules by his wildly indiscreet philandering. But in 1965, according to author Lawrence Leamer, she took a lover of her own: the brilliant, troubled and many-times-married lyricist Allan Jay Lerner. With his creative partner, Frederick Loewe, they created some of the most popular Broadway musical comedies of all time, including *Brigadoon* and *My Fair Lady*. Their 1960's hit, *Camelot*, based on the legends of the knights of the Round Table, became Jackie's choice for a metaphor for her husband's administration.

"Jean was daring in her choice," wrote Leamer. "Lerner was as dangerous to the Kennedy image as any of Jack's involvements." For once in her life, Jean showed a flash of the Kennedy wild streak. She courted exactly the kind of danger her brothers did. "Steve could stride into Bobby's headquarters with his mistress on his arms," said Laurence Leamer, author of *The Kennedy Women*, "but Jean had to be far more furtive in her involvement."

According to Leamer, the lyricist rented a yacht that August while his newest musical, *On a Clear Day You Can See Forever*, previewed in Boston. The boat became a floating love nest for the couple, at least until Lerner got a call from an angry Bobby Kennedy, who advised him, "Stop seeing [Jean]. Or we'll fix your gondola!"

That summer, Jean left her husband and two sons behind while she went to rendezvous with Lerner in Paris. Lerner never showed up. On her return to New York, he sent her a letter ending their affair. Jean reconciled with her husband and they subsequently adopted two daughters, Amanda and Kym. [Jean Smith has denied this story.]

Jean's sister Pat also tried to strike out on her own. A year after Jack's assassination, she separated from Peter Lawford. The issue was his drinking, drugging and womanizing, and the separation had been discussed then postponed so as not to interfere with Jack's reelection campaign. On December 17 they signed a legal separation agreement. A month later, after spending the Christmas holidays in Sun Valley, Idaho, with Jackie and Bobby and Ethel and their children, she appeared before a local judge to petition for divorce on grounds of mental cruelty.

Pat's only son Christopher took the collapse of his parents' marriage very hard. He was nine at the time and the dissolution of the marriage meant the end of his life among the movie stars of southern California. Patricia moved to New York City with Christopher and his three sisters, Sydney, Victoria and Robin. But now he would grow up closer to his male Kennedy cousins, hell-raising with Joe II and Bobby, Jr., and David. Especially David.

Bobby took time out in 1966 to attempt to suppress a memoir about Jack. He got an early look at the manuscript of Red Fay's *The Pleasure of His Company* and became irate, demanding that Fay cut forty percent of the book. Ethel was especially upset about Fay's recollection of the Kennedy family dinner where the Ambassador criticized his children's spending habits. Fay refused, but did prune a few bits.

BOBBY: "AT STAKE IS OUR RIGHT TO MORAL LEADERSHIP!"

Bobby's power base was growing. By 1967 he had the largest staff in the Senate. On March 24 Ethel gave birth to their tenth child, breaking Rose's record. Douglas Harriman was named for former Secretary of the Treasury Douglas Dillon and Ambassador at Large Averell Harriman. The weekend of June 17 Bobby and Ethel celebrated their seventeenth anniversary and Douglas's christening, unaware that this would be their last such celebration together.

By the midsixties Bobby was determined to unseat President Johnson, yet he waffled, despite the urging of close advisors who were convinced that LBJ had been seriously damaged by the Vietnam War.

In January 1968 Bobby announced that under no circumstances would he be a candidate for president. But after Senator Eugene McCarthy of Minnesota took twenty of twenty-four delegates in the New Hampshire primary, he reconsidered. On March 16, four days after McCarthy's victory, Bobby declared himself a candidate. "I do not lightly dismiss the dangers and difficulties of challenging an incumbent President; but these are not ordinary times and this is not an ordinary election. At stake is not simply the leadership of our party or even our country—it is our right to moral leadership."

Two days later he denounced the Vietnam War, in much the same terms that the Ambassador had denounced Great Britain and supported the Nazis: "I am concerned—as I believe most Americans are concerned—that our present course will not bring victory, will not bring peace, will not stop the bloodshed . . . and will not advance the interests of the United States or the cause of peace in the world." He took responsibility for participating in some of the early decisions on the war, but insisted that "past error is no excuse for its own perpetuation."

On March 31 Lyndon Johnson announced that he would not run for reelection. The thing he feared most from the first day of his presidency had come true. Bobby Kennedy had openly announced his intention to reclaim the throne in memory of his brother.

Four days later Martin Luther King was murdered in Memphis. On that night Bobby broke the news to his supporters at a rally in Indianapolis. He told the crowd: "What we need in the United States is not division; what we need in the United States is not hatred; what we need in the United States is not violence or lawlessness, but love and wisdom, and compassion toward one another, and a feeling of justice toward those who still suffer within our country, whether they be white or black."

BOBBY: "FOR GOD'S SAKE, JACKIE, [YOU] COULD COST ME FIVE STATES."

In the years since her husband's assassination, Jackie had been seen publicly with a number of admirers including historian Arthur Schlesinger, Jr., and director Mike Nichols. Privately, she often entertained Aristotle Onassis at her apartment. He courted her with diamond bracelets tucked inside floral bouquets.

In May 1968 Jackie was a guest on a five-day cruise in the Caribbean aboard Onassis's yacht the *Christina*. During the cruise Onassis proposed. Returning to the states, she immediately consulted with Bobby. His reaction was shock and outrage. "For God's sake, Jackie, a thing like that could cost me five states," he declared. The rest of the family was equally appalled.

For Bobby's sake, Jackie agreed to postpone any thoughts of marriage to Onassis until after the presidential election in November.

Rose: "If You Have Money, You Spend It To Win."

When a reporter asked Rose about all the money the Kennedy family was spending on Bobby's campaign, she snapped, "It's our money and we're free to spend it any way we please. It's part of this campaign business. If you have money, you spend it to win. And the more you can afford, the more you'll spend."

On June 4, the day of the California primary, Bobby and Ethel were staying at the Malibu home of director John Frankenheimer. For relaxation, the family went swimming in the ocean where David, weeks away from his thirteenth birthday, swam too far out. A huge wave came and David disappeared beneath it. Bobby immediately dived and for a minute he, too, disappeared, until he bobbed to the surface, holding David. He gently warned his son about the danger of going out of his depth.

Later that afternoon David got into a fight with some of his siblings and stormed out of their bungalow near the hotel where his father's campaign operation was set up. With no other place to go, he checked himself into a hotel room.

That night, after he was declared the winner of the primary, Bobby spoke to cheering supporters in the Embassy Ballroom of the Ambassador Hotel. "What I think is quite clear is that we can work together in the last analysis, and that what has been going on within the United States over a period of the last three years—the division, the violence, the disenchantment with our society; the divisions, whether it's between blacks and whites, between the poor and the more affluent, or between age groups or on the war in Vietnam—is that we can start to work together," he told them. "We are a great country, an unselfish country and a compassionate country. I intend to make that my basis for running."

After his victory address Bobby left the stage from the rear, and took a shortcut through the pantry to the Colonial Room, where newspeople were waiting for his press conference. He had only gone a few feet when Sirhan Bishara Sirhan, a twenty-four-year-old Jordanian, fired eight shots from a .22-caliber Iver-Johnson revolver from a distance of four feet. Three bullets struck Bobby, one in his armpit, another in his neck, the third tearing through the right mastoid bone behind the ear, scattering bone fragments throughout the lower part of his brain. While Bobby was rushed to the hospital, Stephen Smith took the microphone on the ballroom podium and quietly asked the crowd to leave. Gradually, word spread among them about what had happened.

Teddy learned the news in San Francisco, where he was campaigning for his brother, and immediately flew to Los Angeles. Unable to get a private plane, the operations officer at Hamilton AFB in Marin, twenty miles north, made a military jet fighter available.

Bobby's oldest daughter, Kathleen, just one month short of her seventeenth birthday, was asleep in her dormitory at Putney Preparatory School in Vermont when she was awakened by the school's headmaster who had watched the event on television. Hours later she arrived at Hickory Hill. Joe II, not quite sixteen, was attending Milton Academy in Massachusetts. He, too, headed home to Virginia.

At Hickory Hill, Robert Jr., fourteen, stepped out the door, picked up the newspaper and learned for the first time that his father had been shot. He turned back into the house and fed the paper, crumpled page by crumpled page, into the fireplace.

A few hours later Kathleen, Joe II, and Bobby, Jr., accompanied by Lem Billings, were en route via private jet to their father's bedside.

David Kennedy, isolated in his hotel room, saw the whole tragedy unfold on TV: his father's victory speech, the pandemonium, and the announcement that his father had just been shot. He would never recover from the loss. It was not until dawn that Ethel, from her husband's bedside in the hospital, asked family friends to account for all the children: David, Courtney, Michael, Kerry and Max. After a frantic search they finally located David in his hotel room, staring at the television screen.

President Johnson immediately sent a presidential jet to Los Angeles to bring Bobby's body back, along with members of the Kennedy family, to New York City. Ted selected his brother's coffin and remained with it all during the flight.

Among those in the family delegation were Jacqueline Kennedy, accompanied by her brother-in-law, Prince Radziwill, who had flown to Los Angeles immediately after hearing the news and who had remained at Bobby's bedside in the Good Samaritan Hospital as RFK lay dying.

Teddy delayed calling his parents in Hyannis Port until it was morning there. Rose, who had been rising at six for early mass, got the news from her radio. Joe, helpless in his bed, listened to Ted report to him on the phone.

Senator Robert F. Kennedy lay in state at St. Patrick's Cathedral for two days. A six-man celebrity honor guard kept a vigil around the flag-draped coffin. They included former U.S. secretary of defense Robert McNamara, poet Robert Lowell, former Supreme Court justice and ambassador to the United Nations Arthur Goldberg, Kennedy speechwriter and biographer Ted Sorensen, actor Sidney Poitier, and novelists Budd Schulberg and William Styron.

One unfortunate note: Peter Lawford, invited to the funeral as a single, showed up at St. Patrick's with a young woman he had just met. Clad in black microminiskirt, black hat and black gloves, clinging to his arm, she was impossible to miss. Thereafter, he was cut out of the Kennedy family completely.

Joe II and Robert, Jr., served as altar boys at the funeral mass on June 8. Ted insisted on giving the eulogy. With the assistance of Adam Walinsky, one of Robert's speechwriters, and Milton Gwirtzman, an aide, he spent most of the day preparing. A few minutes after ten A.M., he spoke from the altar and he spoke with uncharacteristic eloquence:

"My brother need not be idealized, or enlarged in death beyond what he was in life, to be remembered simply as a good and decent man, who saw wrong and tried to right it, saw suffering and tried to heal it, saw war and tried to stop it."

Afterward the coffin was borne down Fifth Avenue to Pennsylvania Station, where a twenty-one-car funeral train took Robert to Washington. They reached Arlington National Cemetery at nightfall, and a parade of mourners carrying candles followed the coffin into the graveyard. In the darkness the pallbearers were not sure where to place the coffin. Averell Harriman finally said to Stephen Smith, "Steve, do you know where you're going?" Smith said, "Well, I'm not sure," then he added, "I distinctly heard a voice coming out of the coffin saying, 'Damn it. If you fellows put me down, I'll show you the way!' "

Bobby was buried twenty feet from Jack.

The surviving Kennedys, schooled in the importance of the dynasty, were already looking to the future. Returning to Hyannis, where the ailing Joe had remained, unable to walk or talk, they rushed to cheer him up.

"Daddy, he's got *it!* You should have seen him," Eunice reported to her father. But she was not talking about her only surviving brother, Teddy, the logical heir. It was Bobby's oldest son, Joe, who had personally greeted all one thousand mourners on the train. "Nobody put him up to it, Daddy, he did it on his own!"

Joe Kennedy's daughters remained trapped in their roles. Eunice, who everyone agreed was the best politician in the family, was never considered as the family's next candidate for public office because she was a woman. She contented herself with her family and her work for the retarded. Jean, too, concentrated on charity and her home. After her divorce, Pat Lawford had some serious involvements, including a State Department lawyer and the bisexual director Roger Edens, but she would never marry again.

But for Jacqueline Kennedy, the death of Robert Kennedy was the last straw. She decided to bolt and pursue life on her own terms. She would no longer be a prisoner of her class, her religion, her marriage or the Kennedy family.

After Bobby's funeral she invited Aristotle Onassis and his daughter to spend the weekend with the Auchincloss family at Hammersmith Farm. Afterward she and her mother received thank-you notes and exquisite reproductions of ancient Macedonian jewelry from Onassis. For the rest of the summer he was a frequent visitor to the Hyannis Port compound, ingratiating himself with the adults and children there. He even charmed Rose, although she did not think he knew how to dress and thought his trousers were too baggy.

By fall an incredible rumor was beginning to spread from Cape Cod to Georgetown. The *Boston Herald-Traveler* broke the story on October 17. On that afternoon Nancy Tuckerman, Jackie's social secretary, released a brief statement: "Mrs. Hugh D. Auchincloss has asked me to tell you that her daughter, Mrs. John F. Kennedy, is planning to marry Mr. Aristotle Onassis sometime next week."

The only comment from the Kennedy camp came from Teddy

who said, "I talked to Jackie several days ago, and she told me of her plans. I gave her my best wishes for their happiness."

The romance, the courtship, and the hard bargaining that preceded the engagement, had all been carried on in the utmost secrecy. Late that August she and Ted secretly flew to Skorpios and while Jackie sunned herself, Ted discussed the matter of money with Onassis. Ted explained that if Jackie remarried, she would no longer receive any income from the Kennedy trusts.

When Jack died she had inherited approximately $70,000 in cash, his personal effects, the Cape Cod house and the income from his trusts which amounted to $200,000 a year. In return for agreeing to marry Onassis, she asked for and received a cash payment of $3 million and $1 million for each of her children. In return, she gave up all claims to Onassis's estate. To seal their engagement, Onassis gave his bride-to-be a $1.25-million engagement ring: a heart-shaped ruby the size of an egg surrounded by one-carat diamonds.

They were married in the tiny chapel of the Little Mother of God on Skorpios on October 20 before twenty-one guests who included Caroline and John, and Ari's grown children, Alexander and Christina. At a lavish wedding dinner that night Ari presented all the women with gold bracelets, the men with gold watches. As a wedding gift for Jackie, Onassis added heart-shaped ruby earrings framed in diamonds to match her engagement ring, and a solid gold bracelet studded with rubies in the shape of a ram's head. When she saw her mother wearing them on her wedding day, Caroline, eleven, exclaimed: "Mommy, Mommy, they're so pretty!"

It was raining on Skorpios on the morning Jackie and Ari exchanged vows. Jackie, thirty-nine, was solemn in a long-sleeved, ivory-lace Valentino dress with a matching ribbon in her long dark hair. Onassis, three inches shorter and twenty-three years older than his bride, wore a dark blue suit, white shirt and red tie. Alexander and Christina made no secret of their disapproval. "It's a perfect match," said Alexander. "My father loves names and Jackie loves money."

The world was shocked by the marriage, but not Jackie's family. According to her cousin, John Davis, "Those of us who had grown up with Jackie, felt that Onassis was precisely the type of man we thought she would marry. She had always liked older men, much older men, even as a teenager. And we all knew that her mother and father had relentlessly coached her to marry a very rich man." Friends were also sympathetic. "Jackie did not marry Ari for his money," insisted her longtime friend Joan Braden. "He was fun and different and felt safe, and she was always looking for protection." If anyone took the marriage lightly, it was Onassis, said Braden: "To him, she was just another bauble, whereas to us she was a great heroine."

Jackie had already taken steps to remove her children from the Catholic schools they had been attending. By marrying a divorced man, she knew she risked excommunication and she did not want them to suffer for it. Caroline moved from Sacred Heart to Brearley. John was transferred to Collegiate, amid news reports that he left St. David's because he had been asked to repeat second grade. St. David's headmaster sent a magazine a letter denying this, but it was never published.

Vatican sources said that "the case of the former Mrs. Jacqueline Kennedy is closed as far as the Roman Catholic Church is concerned. She is barred from the sacraments as long as she remains married to Mr. Onassis."

PART FIVE

THE RISE AND FALL OF CADILLAC EDDIE

The thing about being a Kennedy is that you come to know there's a time for Kennedys. And it's hard to know when that time is, or if it will ever come again. . . . I mean, is the country going to be receptive? Will it be the time? And if it is, is it really the best thing for me to do? And how much of a contribution could I make, even if . . . ?

—Teddy Kennedy, 1969

CHAPTER TWELVE
TEDDY'S TURN

I admit that with Teddy I did things a little differently than I did with the other children. He was my baby and, I think every mother will understand this, I tried to keep him my baby.

—Rose Kennedy

Jack and Bobby were gone. Each cut down in his prime by an assassin's bullet. Now it was Teddy's turn to fulfill his father's dynastic master plan. But Edward M. Kennedy, the last of Rose and Joe's nine children, the last of their sons, had grown up in the shadow of his charismatic older siblings. His life had been one of shortcuts and minor scandals. Now he was alone, without the advice of his brilliant father and older brothers.

If Joe and Jack had been raised to lead, Bobby and Teddy were born to follow. Bobby had done it superbly, learning politics at Jack's side. But Teddy was different. While his older brothers had benefited from the close attention of their father, he had been left to drift. Joe and Rose's oft-stated philosophy relied on the older children to teach the younger ones. But now the older ones were gone. And Teddy was on his own.

Born when his mother was forty-one, shortly after his father had ended his serious love affair with Gloria Swanson, he had been named for his father's trusted confidant Eddie Moore, a man who could keep the secrets and was probably the first of the Kennedy loyalists. His early years had been far from stable. Sent off to boarding school for the first time at age eight, by the time he was thirteen, he had attended ten different boarding and day schools. When he made his First Holy Communion, it was Pope Pius XII who administered the sacrament. There was nothing like the kind of pressure on him to excel that his older brothers had experienced. Only twelve when Joe, Jr., died, he became the joy of his father's life. "Ted was the shining light," said Peter Lawford. "He came of age at a time when the old man wasn't feeling very well. Everyone else would be treading softly. But Teddy would come home after being somewhere and his father's face would light up and his spirits would rise."

As a grown man, Teddy would sail into a room, pick up his mother from behind and twirl her, saying, "How's my girl?" and then look over and say, "Hi, Dad, you having any fun?" He took a joy in life that his workaholic father and rigid mother could only marvel at.

Like Bobby, he was never a scholar. Jack once referred to Teddy as "the gay illiterate" and he made it into Harvard as a legacy, because his father and older brothers had passed through the school with such distinction. In his sophomore year he was expelled for cheating. He had been failing Spanish and feared that it would keep him off the varsity football team. He paid a friend to take an exam for him. They were caught and both of them were expelled. It was a shame and a disgrace, but the family would manage to keep it a secret until Teddy ran for the Senate.

After his expulsion from Harvard, Teddy returned to Hyannis Port where he would sit brooding, sometimes for hours. Finally he enlisted in the Army, but he typically did not bother to read the enlistment papers and signed up for four years instead of two. The Ambassador was horrified at the thought of his youngest son spending four years in the service, with a good chance of being sent into combat in Korea. "Don't you ever look at what you're signing?" he shouted.

With one phone call Joe contacted a friend who managed to get hold of Teddy's enlistment papers. Teddy would only serve two years in the Army and they would be in Europe, not Korea. "I like to think that Teddy was so upset by the Harvard affair that he deliberately signed up for four years with the intention of trying to vindicate his name in Korea," recalled his childhood nurse, Elizabeth Cameron. "Anyway, when the family saw him off, I remember they were all singing, 'Bye, bye, baby, remember you're our baby, when the girls give you the eye.' "

In his two years in the Army, Teddy never rose above the rank of private. He returned to Harvard in the fall of 1953.

VETERAN RUGBY REFEREE: "TEDDY KENNEDY IS THE ONLY PLAYER I EVER THREW OUT OF A GAME."

Once back at Harvard, Teddy made the rugby team. During a 1954 match between Harvard and the New York Rugby Club, he got into three fistfights with opposing players and was finally thrown out of the game. According to referee Frederick Cosstick, Teddy was the only player he had expelled from a game in thirty years of officiating.

Cosstick thought a lot about the games in the years that followed. "Rugby is a character-building sport," he explained. "Players learn how to conduct themselves on the field with the idea that they will learn how to conduct themselves in life. Rugby, like life, can be rough. Knocks are given and taken, but you must play by the rules. When a player loses control of himself three times in a single afternoon, to my mind, that is a sign that, in a crisis, the man is not capable of thinking clearly and acting rationally. Such a man will panic under pressure."

Of course, years later, in the crisis at Chappaquiddick, Teddy would do exactly that.

In 1955, his final year at Harvard, Teddy managed to snare a bit of glory during the Harvard-Yale football game. He caught a pass for Harvard's only touchdown, securing himself the letter which had eluded big brothers Joe, Jr., and Jack.

By the time of his graduation in 1956, he had earned honors in government and history. He was still refused admission to Harvard Law School, and spent the next year at The Hague's international Law Institute in the Netherlands. He also worked briefly in North Africa for Hearst's International News Service, which had also employed Jack after the war.

At Bobby's suggestion, and with help again from family friend James Landis, when Teddy returned to the States in 1957, he en-

tered the University of Virginia Law School and graduated in
1959. He managed Jack's 1958 Senate reelection campaign. Soon
Jack was calling him "the best politician in the family."

But the warning signs of trouble continued. While in law
school, "Cadillac Eddie," as he was called, was cited four times
for reckless driving (three times in 1958 and once in 1959). These
violations included running red lights and driving with his lights
off at ninety miles per hour in a suburban area. Teddy was convicted of three violations and fined, but for some reason his
driver's license was never revoked.

According to psychohistorian Clinch, Teddy's repeated driving
through red lights at night at ninety miles an hour was clearly
compulsive behavior, with overtones of rebellion, hostility and
self-destructiveness. Such actions endangered other lives as well,
but this probably scarcely occurred to him. Clinch concluded that:
"A person caught in the grip of unconscious self-hate and rage is
too obsessed with the expression of his own needs to be able to
empathize satisfactorily with others."

In 1957, at the start of his second year of law school, Teddy visited Manhattanville College of the Sacred Heart for the dedication
of the new Kennedy Physical Education Building. There his sister
Jean introduced him to twenty-year-old Virginia Joan Bennett.
The tall, blond Manhattanville senior was an occasional model
and the 1955 Miss College Week in Bermuda and the 1956 Queen
of the Bermuda Floral Pageant.

OLD FRIEND: "TEDDY WAS PHILANDERING FROM THE MOMENT HE WAS MARRIED."

When Joan graduated the following June, Teddy formally
asked her father for her hand in marriage. Their engagement was
announced in September, and Joan and Ted were married on November 29, 1958, in St. Joseph's Roman Catholic Church in Bronxville. Joan and Teddy had wanted their friend Father James
Cavanaugh of Notre Dame to officiate, but the Ambassador insisted on a cardinal, Francis Cardinal Spellman.

Jack was best man for his brother, Bobby an usher. There was a
reception at the Siwanoy Country Club. All the Kennedys were

there, "and there were lots of them," Joan laughed later. "I had no idea what I was getting into. I was just a nice young girl marrying a nice young man."

The couple barely had time for a three-day honeymoon at Lord Beaverbrook's estate in Nassau, before they had to return to their rented three-bedroom apartment in Charlottesville for Teddy's final year.

Ted received his law degree in 1959 and after a delayed honeymoon in South America, he and Joan spent the rest of the summer at Hyannis Port, where plans were first made for Jack's run for the presidency. Pregnant, Joan went to stay with her parents in Bronxville until their daughter Kara was born on February 27, 1960. A month later she joined Ted on the campaign trail.

Joan would soon discover that she had married into a family whose men lived by a unique set of rules. For the next two decades her husband would engage in numerous extramarital affairs.

"He was philandering from the moment he was married," recalled Dick Tuck, an old family friend. "Not one-night stands, but not much more than that. Kind of affairs of convenience. . . . I think most normal people might have more than one affair but not every week, like Teddy. He was always chasing, looking for the conquest."

Then there was the yachting incident. Family friend David Hacket recalled a pre-White House cruise with Teddy from Cape Cod to Maine when Teddy became so enraged at the taunts from a nearby luxury yacht that he boarded the craft and tossed eight men into the water while their terrified wives looked on. These men were complete strangers and he tossed them overboard without knowing if any of them could swim.

Assigned to campaign for Jack in the eleven Western states, Teddy barnstormed in a partially self-piloted plane, in spite of the fact that he had little flying experience; rode a bucking bronco in a Montana rodeo; and made a first ski jump on a dangerous slope, somehow managing to land on his feet. In spite of such stunts on Teddy's part, Jack only carried three of the states.

After Jack was elected President, Teddy made some noises about moving out West and perhaps buying a small newspaper. Joe wouldn't hear of it.

On February 7, 1961, shortly after Jack's inauguration, Teddy was sworn in as an assistant district attorney of Massachusetts Suffolk county. He was merely killing time until he was eligible to run for Jack's vacant seat in the Senate, currently being held by a family friend.

Teddy did not impress his colleagues in the district attorney's office. "He had no feeling for the job, none whatever, and he didn't try to develop any," one recalled. "He wouldn't work; he was listless and uninterested, and he tried cases only when he felt like it, which was seldom. I think he had certain natural talents, especially when it came to arguing cases. He could convince a jury, sway a jury, especially if there were women on it, but the pick and shovel work on the law he never bothered to learn."

Joan loved Boston from the beginning. She and Ted moved into their first home, a red brick town house on Beacon Hill. The living room had huge plate-glass windows overlooking the Charles River. Soon after, they bought a house on the Cape, on Squaw Island, a short distance from Hyannis Port. Their second child, Edward Moore, Jr., was born on September 26, 1961.

But Teddy's legacy as a Kennedy man decreed that he get into politics, and so, he arrived in Washington in January 1963, one of the youngest senators in history, and Joan one of the youngest senatorial wives. Joan and Ted immediately moved to a house in Georgetown, renting a red brick place at 1336 Thirty-first Street.

TEDDY'S PLANE CRASH

On June 16, 1964, Teddy was on his way to the Massachusetts Democratic state convention, where he expected to be nominated for his second term in the Senate, when he was severely injured in the crash of a private plane. With him in the six-seater were fellow Democratic senator Birch Bayh of Indiana, who was to deliver the keynote address, his wife Marvella, and Edward S. Moss, Teddy's administrative aide. Teddy was the only passenger who had not buckled his seat belt. As the twin-engine Aero Commander 680 neared Barnes airport in a heavy fog, the veteran pilot, Ed Zimny, crashed into a hillside. The Bayhs were thrown clear and escaped serious injury. Zimny, the pilot, was killed. Moss suffered massive brain injuries and died within hours. Teddy had six spinal fractures and two broken ribs. He was listed in critical condition and remained in the hospital for six months. "It's amazing he is alive," said a doctor.

Teddy spent several of those months immobilized in a metal frame, unable to move anything but his head, hands and feet. During that time he produced *The Fruitful Bough*, reminiscences by the Kennedy family and friends.

The state convention nominated Teddy in absentia, and Joan did the campaigning for him. She thrived on it. But after his recovery, their marriage stalled. At parties he was known to ignore Joan all evening while he danced with other women, humiliating her and outraging her friends.

Joan was somewhat overwhelmed by the Kennedy style. "The house was always full of cooks, baby nurses, and staff," she told her friend Marcia Chellis. "I felt extra, no good. When I said I didn't want a baby nurse, we had a baby nurse. Everything was done and taken care of and I didn't do it. I was nobody, nothing, not needed." Angry, unhappy, she would appear at dinner parties drunk and tell all within earshot that her marriage was in trouble.

In 1966 Teddy was said to be seeing attractive, blond Countess Llana Campbell, whom he brought up from New York to rented cottages on Martha's Vineyard for long weekend parties.

In July 1967 their third child Patrick was born, and the following year, Joan and Ted were swept up in Bobby's presidential campaign. After Bobby's assassination Joan was so distraught that she was unable to accompany the funeral party to Arlington. She disappeared and no one knew where she had gone.

At the tumultuous Chicago Democratic convention in 1968, the consensus was that the presidential nomination was Teddy's for the asking. But he and his advisors believed that although he could win the nomination, he could not win the election. It was too soon and he was too young. He was also still recovering from Bobby's death and not in any mental shape to campaign. He declined to be a candidate and when Hubert Humphrey was nominated he declined Humphrey's invitation to run as his vice president.

Strains were beginning to show in his marriage. Joan was discovering that her husband was a typical Kennedy male, meaning he had indiscriminate affairs. The summer of 1968 he was seen in the company of a lovely blonde on Aristotle Onassis's yacht.

Joan's drinking escalated. "It wasn't my personality to make a lot of noise," she said, "or to yell or scream or do anything. My personality was more shy and retiring. And so rather than get mad, or ask questions concerning the rumors about Ted and his girlfriends, or really stand up for myself at all, it was easier for me to just go and have a few drinks and calm myself down as if I weren't hurt or angry. I didn't know how to deal with it. And unfortunately, I found out that alcohol could sedate me. So I didn't care as much. And things didn't hurt so much."

Teddy seemed most in control on the floor of the Senate. In January 1969 he won a tough fight for assistant majority leader, or majority whip, the second most important position in the Senate. He defeated Louisiana's veteran senator Russell Long, becoming at thirty-seven, the youngest whip in the Senate's history.

TEDDY: "THEY'RE GOING TO SHOOT MY ASS OFF."

By spring 1969 the stress of being the surviving son was beginning to take a toll on Ted. He was drinking heavily, and on an April trip to Alaska, concerned aides noted him sipping often from a small silver hip flask. Once, a slightly inebriated Ted announced, "They're going to shoot my ass off the way they shot Bobby's."

On the plane home from Fairbanks, he roamed the aisle roaring "Eskimo Pow-er, Es-ki-mo Pow-eer" while spilling his drinks on other passengers. When an aide brought hot coffee, Teddy splashed it, nearly scalding a baby until someone took the cup away.

Yet the media continued to protect Teddy as it had protected his father and brothers. *Time, Newsweek,* and *Life* were all informed of his behavior on the Alaska flight by their correspondents, but declined to run the story. The *Life* reporter, Sylvia Wright, memoed her editors: "He's living by his gut; something bad is going to happen."

That April, Ted also visited Las Vegas where the nervous local sheriff assigned eight deputies to watch him night and day. "One evening," a guard recalls, "Ted said good night to his guards, telling them that he was turning in. But instead of going to bed, he slipped out of his room at the Sahara Hotel and went to the Sands. Two of the deputies, following him secretly, saw him enter a room on the 18th floor. Shortly thereafter, they saw a blond showgirl enter the room. The deputies maintained an all-night vigil, staying at their post despite pleas from Ted's cousin, Joe Gargan, that they leave Ted in peace. Nobody, they say, emerged from the room until morning."

Many of these episodes were fueled by alcohol. It takes a lot of drinking to attract attention in Washington, but Teddy's consumption was becoming the stuff of cocktail party conversations.

"He's the least discreet guy on the Hill," said one old congressional friend. "I have told him ten times, 'Ted, you're acting like a fool. Everybody knows you wherever you go.' " Other senators could get away with it, the friend said. "Jack could smuggle girls up the back way . . . But you're not nearly as discreet as you should be. He looks down with a faint smile and says, 'Yeah, I guess you're right.' But he never listens."

His escapades with women from the Vineyard to Vegas were still known only to insiders, journalists and some law enforcement officials. To the voting public, Teddy Kennedy was still the last of a great family, and as such the strong favorite for the Democratic presidential nomination in 1972.

The night of July 18, 1969, changed all that, when, in a series of events that have never been adequately explained, the Senator became the first driver in forty years to go off the Dike Bridge, and his passenger, twenty-eight-year-old Mary Jo Kopechne, was killed. Ted's name would be forever linked with the scandal of Chappaquiddick.

CHAPTER THIRTEEN

CHAPPAQUIDDICK

I regard as indefensible the fact that I did not report the accident immediately.

—Teddy Kennedy, 1969

I ask you to consider what would happen to a private citizen who, heading 'out to the dunes' after a party with a girl in his car, drove off the road and killed the girl—and then crept quietly away from the scene without saying anything to anyone, leaving car and corpse to be discovered the next day without his assistance. The laws covering a situation like this are stringent—nay, merciless. Such a private citizen would pay a very stiff price indeed for his irresponsible behavior. Yet it seems that Edward Kennedy intends to pay no price at all.

—Gordon N. Walker, Letter to *Time* magazine, 8/15/69

Do we operate under a system of equal justice under law? Or is there one system for the average citizen and another for the high and mighty?

—Teddy Kennedy, 1973

The weekend of July 18–19, 1969, was planned as a reunion of the young women who had worked on Bobby Kennedy's 1968 presidential campaign. Affectionately known as "the boiler-room girls" for the tough, backroom work they did, the get together was a thanks for their role in Bobby's campaign. It would coincide with the Edgartown Yacht Club Regatta in which both Teddy and Joe II would compete.

Kennedys had been coming to the regatta for years and their celebrations were the stuff of legend. According to Leo Damore, author of *Senatorial Privilege*, their 1966 regatta party had been "riotous," and 1967 equally festive, leaving a rented cottage in shambles. The assassination of Robert F. Kennedy had kept the family away in 1968, but in the spring of 1969 Kennedy cousin Joe Gargan began planning a resumption of the festivities.

Gargan reserved rooms for the women at the Katama Shores Inn near Edgartown on Martha's Vineyard. Teddy and the men would be put up at the Shiretown Inn in Edgartown. Gargan also rented a small cottage, gray shingled with yellow shutters, on Chappaquiddick Island, across the channel from Edgartown for a cookout and party after the races. Chappaquiddick was barely five miles long and three miles wide, and at the height of the summer season the population did not amount to five hundred people. It was accessible from Edgartown only by a ferry, which was really a small, flat barge with room for two cars and twenty people. The boat operated between 7:30 A.M. and midnight and made the crossing in four minutes.

The women were Susan Tannenbaum; Esther Newberg, twenty-six; Rosemary Keough; Anne "Nance" Lyons, twenty-six; her sister Maryellen, twenty-seven; and Mary Jo Kopechne, twenty-eight. The men were Joe Gargan; Paul Markham, a former United States attorney from Massachusetts; Charles C. Tretter, an attorney; John B. Crimmins, Kennedy's part-time chauffeur. After a day of swimming and watching Teddy compete, at 8:30 P.M. the group gathered at the cottage on Chappaquiddick for an outdoor barbecue and drinking.

According to Ted, it was around 11:15 or 11:30 P.M. that he glanced at his watch and remarked that he was tired. He was going to catch the ferry and return to his motel. Mary Jo asked for a lift. Teddy got his car keys from Crimmins and the two climbed into the Oldsmobile and took off along the island's one paved road.

About a half-mile away, Teddy took a wrong turn and instead of heading for the ferry, ended up on a dirt-and-sand road that led to Dike Bridge. That's where he went off the bridge and into Pou-cha Pond. Teddy survived. Mary Jo Kopechne did not.

Teddy would later testify under oath that he remembered the Oldsmobile going off Dike Bridge and the next thing he recalled was Mary Jo's movement beside him, "struggling, perhaps hitting or kicking me, and I, at this time, opened my eyes and realized I was upside-down, that water was crashing in on me, that it was pitch-black."

Teddy went on to recall that, "There was complete blackness. Water seemed to rush in from every point, from the windshield, from underneath me, above me. It almost seemed like you couldn't hold the water back even with your hands. What I was conscious of was the rushing of the water, the blackness, the fact that it was impossible even to hold it back . . . I was sure that I was going to drown."

According to Ted, the strong current swept him to the bank, where he called Mary Jo's name several times. Not getting any re-sponse, he swam back to the submerged car and tried "seven or eight" times to reach her.

"I would come back again and again," he told the inquest panel. "Until the very end when I couldn't hold my breath any longer. I was breathing so heavily it was down to just a matter of seconds. I would hold my breath and I could barely get under-neath the water. I was just able to hold on to the metal undercar-riage here, and the water itself came right out to where I was breathing and I could hold, I knew that I could not get under water anymore.

"I was fully aware that I was trying to get the girl out of that car, and I was fully aware that I was doing everything that I possibly could to get her out of that car, and I was fully aware at that time that my head was throbbing and my neck was aching and I was breathless, and at that time, the last, hopelessly exhausted."

Giving up, Teddy managed to walk back to the cottage more than a mile away. That took him about fifteen to twenty minutes, he claimed, and he saw no people, houses or lights along the way.

Outside the cottage he encountered Ray LaRosa, who had crewed for him in the race, and asked him to get Gargan and Markham. "There's been a terrible accident," he told the two men. "We've got to go."

Gargan drove them to Dike Bridge where, he later testified, he and Markham stripped and dove repeatedly into the water to try to reach Mary Jo. They, too, gave up and told Teddy that they would have to report the accident.

According to Teddy's later testimony, a lot of different thoughts came into his mind at that time, about how he was going to call Mrs. Kopechne and tell her that her daughter was drowned, and that he would tell his parents and his wife. Although his thoughts were with them, however, his dime was not. He would not telephone any of them until more than eight hours after the accident.

Kennedy testified that he told the two men, "You take care of the other girls and I will take care of the accident." He then swam across the five-hundred-foot-wide Martha's Vineyard Channel to the mainland, making his way through the deserted streets to the Shiretown Inn at two A.M., where he removed his wet clothing and fell asleep on the bed.

"SENATOR, DO YOU KNOW THERE'S A GIRL FOUND DEAD IN YOUR CAR?"

A half hour later Teddy appeared in the lobby, dressed in blazer and slacks, and spoke to Russell G. Peachey, co-owner of the inn, to ask about the time and to complain about the noise from a party at the motel next door. Peachey would later recall that he noticed nothing unusual about Teddy's behavior.

The manager told him it was 2:25 A.M.

Teddy thanked him and went back upstairs to his room.

"He didn't look to me like a man who had come downstairs to complain about the noise," the manager said later. "Usually a man who just wants to complain about noise doesn't get up and get fully dressed to do it. Especially at 2:25 in the morning."

Around seven A.M. Teddy reappeared in the lobby, freshly shaven and wearing "yachting clothes." To the clerk he "appeared normal in every way."

He asked for a dime to make a phone call, explaining, "I seem to have left my wallet upstairs."

The clerk gave him a dime and he walked to the outside porch to use the inn's pay phone to place a collect call to Helga Wagner, a longtime girlfriend in Key Biscayne, Florida. He had met the stunning blond jewelry designer in 1967 at a cocktail party at the Palm Bay Club in Palm Beach. [At the time she was married to Robert Wagner, vice president of American Eastern Company. They divorced in 1970.]

Teddy told her that "something very serious" had happened and he needed a phone number where he could reach Stephen Smith, who was vacationing with Jean in Spain. After getting the number, he returned the dime to the desk clerk.

When Gargan and Markham got to the Shiretown Inn the next morning, they learned that Teddy had still not reported the accident. They again advised him to call the authorities, but he wanted to contact Burke Marshall, an attorney who had formerly headed the civil-rights division of the Justice Department. He could not reach him.

By nine A.M. the three men were on the ferry back to Chappaquiddick. On arrival they proceeded immediately to a shack about a hundred feet from the dock where Teddy, using his credit card, began a series of long-distance calls from the pay phone inside. He would eventually make a total of seventeen telephone calls before reporting the accident to the police.

At 9:30 A.M. Teddy had finished his calls and was standing outside when Tony Bettencourt, a year-round resident of the island, approached him. "Senator," said Bettencourt, "do you know there's a girl found dead in your car?"

The Senator stared at him and said nothing. Bettencourt offered him a ride to the bridge, but the senator told him he was going over to town.

This puzzled Bettencourt, who had been sent by the Edgartown police chief to await the arrival of the medical examiner on the ferry. Police Chief Dominick J. Arena had been summoned to Chappaquiddick earlier that morning by a phone call reporting that two fishermen had seen the overturned Oldsmobile submerged in about six feet of water near the narrow wooden bridge that led to the private beach.

At the scene at 8:25 A.M., Arena radioed the Edgartown Fire Department to send a diver down into the pond. John Farrar, captain of the department's Scuba Search and Rescue Division, arrived twenty minutes later, donned scuba gear, and descended into the water. Farrar found the body of Mary Jo in the overturned car, her hands clasping the backseat, her face turned upward to the foot-well above her.

"It looked as if she were holding herself up to get a last breath of air," Farrar, manager of a burglar-alarm store, told *People*. "It was a consciously assumed position." Farrar believed the car had contained an air pocket, and that Mary Jo "lived for at least two hours down there." Tying a rope around her waist, he and Arena hauled her body to the surface.

While in the water, Arena had obtained the car's license number L78207, Massachusetts. He had the ownership checked and found it was registered in Senator Kennedy's name. Chief Arena asked that a radio call be dispatched to find him.

Finally Kennedy and his two companions ferried back to Edgartown where Teddy headed for the police station and, saying nothing about the accident involving his car, asked the officer on duty if he might use the telephone. Recognizing him and wanting to treat him with appropriate respect, she directed him to the chief's office where he could make his calls in privacy. Markham asked her to place some calls for him, several to Washington, one to New York, one to Pennsylvania and one inside Massachusetts.

When Chief Arena learned Teddy was at the station, he returned there, still in the wet bathing suit and T-shirt he'd been wearing while diving into the water to see if there was a body in the submerged car.

"The Senator was in clean, dry clothes," Arena recalled. "Poised, confident, and in control. Using my office and telephone. And I'm standing in a puddle of water in a state of confusion."

Arena found it hard to believe that the Senator had been in a major automobile accident. His face bore no marks. He never indicated any physical discomfort. "If he had been injured, or in shock, or confused, nothing of it lingered in our meeting, to my observation," said Arena.

Meanwhile, Gargan and Markham had returned to the cottage where the party guests, having missed the last ferry, had made makeshift sleeping arrangements. They told the others nothing about the accident. The next day, the boiler-room girls went back to their hotel, still unaware of what had happened. "We were fully expecting to find Miss Kopechne there," Nancy Lyons later testified, "but she wasn't, and we waited."

TED: "DAD, I'M IN SOME TROUBLE."

One call Teddy made from the police station was to Mary Jo's parents in Berkeley Heights, New Jersey. "I was alone," Gwen Kopechne said later. "I think he said something about her being in an accident. 'Is she dead?' I screamed. He hesitated but he had to say yes. From then on I don't remember anything." Neighbors rushed to the house after hearing Gwen Kopechne's anguished cries.

Next, Teddy called his own mother, who was about to leave for a fund-raising party at the St. Francis Xavier Church, where she was to autograph books about her sons. Rose canceled the appearance.

He called Joan last.

Then he had to tell his father. He headed for Hyannis Port. Rita Dallas, Joe's nurse after his stroke, recalled that day when the Senator came to his father's bedside, he appeared "drawn, downcast."

Placing a hand on the old man's shoulder, he said, "Dad, I'm in some trouble. There's been an accident, and you're going to hear all sorts of things about me from now on. Terrible things. But, Dad, I want you to know that they're not true. It was an accident. I'm telling you the truth, Dad. It was an accident."

Bedridden since his stroke, unable to speak or advise his only surviving son, Joe Kennedy closed his eyes as Ted explained how he left the scene of an accident and left a girl to drown. Four months later, Joe was dead.

Stephen and Jean Smith were in Spain. Eunice was in Paris. They all returned to Hyannis. Even Jackie from Greece.

Rita Dallas, Joe's nurse and an eyewitness at the gathering, recalls that Rose was so upset that she could not speak. She took Teddy outside near the flagpole, so they could have absolute privacy.

Rose, of all of them, must have recognized the death of her dream.

CBS News reporter Ed Joyce happened to be on nearby Martha's Vineyard and planning to watch the first manned spacecraft land on the moon the following Sunday, when he received a call from the news desk of WCBS Radio in New York that the Senator had been in some sort of automobile accident and a girl in the car had been killed. Joyce took the ferry to Chappaquiddick, drove to Dyke bridge and parked his car, noting skid and splinter marks on the bridge. On foot, he began knocking on the doors of the two houses on Dyke Road that led to the bridge. From these neighbors he learned about the party and was directed to the house. He moved on to the Edgartown police station and Chief Arena, who had been telling reporters all day that he was convinced that "the accident was strictly accidental" and that "there doesn't appear from the principal evidence to be any excessive speed here."

After a short conference with Joyce, however, Arena began to have doubts about the Senator's explanation of the nearly eight-hour time lag between the accident and the time it was reported to the police. He also wanted to know more about the party that the Senator and Mary Jo had attended.

In his report to CBS News, Joyce listed a number of questions that remained to be answered: "How was the Senator able to mistake a dirt road for the continuing pavement of the main road on the way to the ferry he says they were trying to reach?" Joyce had measured the distance between the scene of the accident and the cottage as a mile and two-tenths and noted it would have taken the Senator past several houses, one of whose occupants told Joyce that her lights had been on at the time of the accident.

Joyce went on to ask: "Who were the friends still there at the party and then able to assist Kennedy when he returned? Were they aware of what had happened to Mary Jo Kopechne? And how was Senator Kennedy able to recross the eighth of a mile of water from Chappaquiddick to Edgartown in the late hours of the night when the ferry was not running and return to his hotel room?" Arena, Joyce said, did not yet have the answers. Only the dozen people who attended the party could know, and except for Ted, none of them had yet been questioned.

Joyce's prodding encouraged Chief Arena to reexamine the Senator's story and acknowledge that there were serious gaps. The following morning, Sunday, Arena filed a citation against the Senator for leaving the scene of the accident. "Look, when you're a small-town cop and a United States Senator walks into your office, you snap to attention, right?" he told Joyce. "But I realize he didn't give me a satisfactory explanation of the eight-hour time lag between the time of the accident and the time he walked into my office to report it."

Joyce was the only reporter who had located the cottage or suggested that there were holes in Teddy's story. Most of the others, including the *New York Times*, relied almost completely on the statement Teddy had given to the police in the early morning. It had always been that way for the Kennedy men. The media accepted their version of the wildly inflated heroism of Jack's *PT-109*, of Rosemary's disability, Jack's health, the philandering of all the Kennedy men. When Phil Graham broke ranks, he was carried away in a straitjacket. When Marilyn Monroe threatened a press conference, she died mysteriously. Naturally, Teddy assumed the media would once again fall into line on this one. And for a time they did. One of the few who did not was Ed Joyce.

Sunday morning, Joyce returned to the cottage to have a closer look. The entire area, from the interior of the cottage to the garbage cans outside, had been sanitized.

Joyce also spoke to the cottage caretaker who lived next door with his family. They told him that although they did not see the party goers, they had certainly heard them. Their dogs had barked all night because of the singing and laughter that came from the house next door.

"The party wasn't wild with any riotous goings-on," the caretaker told Joyce. "But they were very loud, and if they had kept it up, I would have called the police. At one o'clock I was pretty fed up with the whole thing, but sometime between one-thirty and two the noise suddenly died down."

More than two hours after Ted said he had left for the ferry, the party suddenly ended.

JOAN: "I PICKED UP THE PHONE AND HEARD TED TALKING TO HELGA—NOTHING WAS EVER THE SAME."

The Kennedy machine went to work. By morning the old all-white, all-male brain trust had gathered at Hyannis Port. Former secretary of defense Robert S. McNamara, Ted Sorensen, Burke Marshall, Steve Smith, Dave Burke, Paul Markham, Joe Gargan, Milton Gwirtzman, Richard Goodwin, and Arthur M. Schlesinger, Jr., John Kenneth Galbraith, Jack Kennedy's Ambassador to India, gave advice by phone.

Together Teddy and his advisors moved into damage control. Yes, a young woman was dead. But all present agreed that the most important thing was to salvage Teddy's political career.

No Kennedy woman was included in these intense sessions, not even Teddy's wife. According to her friend Marcia Chellis, "Joan stayed upstairs in her bedroom almost the entire time, again excluded from taking any part in decisions that would shape the future course of her marriage and the rest of her life."

"No one told me anything," Joan told Chellis years later. "Probably because I was pregnant. I was told to stay upstairs in my bedroom. Downstairs the house was full of people, aides, friends, lawyers. Ted called his girlfriend Helga before he or anyone even told me what was going on. It was the worst experience of my life. I couldn't talk to anyone about it. No one told me anything. I had to stay upstairs, and when I picked up the extension phone, I could hear Ted talking to Helga. Nothing ever seemed the same after that."

Teddy's brain trust concluded that his first step must be to appear on television and get the Kennedy version out as quickly as possible. Thus, ten hours after he told the Ambassador what he had done, a well-coached Teddy appeared on national television from his father's home in Hyannis Port to give his prepared version of what had happened. He spoke for seventeen minutes, explaining that he could not discuss the events of the night until after the matter had been settled in court.

He denied the "widely circulated suspicions of immoral conduct that have been leveled at my behavior and hers regarding that evening." He also denied that he had been drinking heavily that night and apologized for his failure to report the accident.

"I regard as indefensible," he said, "the fact that I did not report the accident to the police immediately."

Teddy concluded by asking Massachusetts voters whether they thought he should resign from the Senate. The next morning, 7,500 telegrams arrived at his home; another 7,500 were still in the Western Union office. "They're calling by the millions," said the editor of the *Boston Globe*. Sacks of mail came to the Hyannis Port compound and, within a week, there were more than one hundred thousand letters, cards, and calls, most of them telling Kennedy to keep his senate seat.

The following Friday, Teddy flew to Plymouth, Pennsylvania, for Mary Jo's funeral. He was wearing a neck brace and flanked by Joan and Ethel. It had been decided that Joan should accompany him, to play the role of loyal Kennedy wife, standing at Ted's side across the aisle from Mary Jo's mother and father.

For Joan, "it was a terrible experience, one of the worst in my life. And it was the beginning of the end for Ted and me."

Teddy then returned to Edgartown to plead guilty to leaving the scene of an accident. Judge Boyle gave him a two-month suspended sentence.

At the height of the publicity surrounding Chappaquiddick, Countess Llana Campbell told the *New York Post* about their 1966 tryst and revealed that three weeks after the accident she met secretly with Teddy in McLean where she told him that because of publicity they would have to end their affair.

VERDICT: "NEGLIGENT DRIVING APPEARS TO HAVE CONTRIBUTED TO THE DEATH OF MARY JO KOPECHNE."

The following January, the inquest was held in Edgartown. A total of twenty-eight witnesses were heard during the four-day proceedings, which were closed at the request of the Kennedy lawyers. John Farrar testified at the inquest that he could have had

Mary Jo out of the car alive in twenty-five minutes if he had been called immediately.

Four months later the 763-page transcript was released. It included a twelve-page summation by District Court justice James A. Boyle that concluded that "negligent driving appears to have contributed to the death of Mary Jo Kopechne."

Pointing out that Mary Jo had told no one she was going and had left her pocketbook at the cottage, and that Kennedy, who was usually driven by a chauffeur, had requested the car keys, the judge wrote: "I infer a reasonable explanation . . . is that Kennedy and Kopechne did not intend to return to Edgartown at that time; that Kennedy did not intend to drive to the ferry slip, and his turn onto Dike Road was intentional."

Under Massachusetts inquest law, Judge Boyle could have ordered Senator Kennedy's arrest, but he chose not to do so. And Dukes County District Attorney Edmund S. Dinis chose not to seek the manslaughter indictment such a finding might have supported. The next day Judge Boyle retired from the bench.

THE COVER-UP

"I know she suffocated when her oxygen ran out," Farrar later told Leo Damore. "She didn't drown."

The Senator's chief counsel at the inquest, Edward P. Hanify, purchased Kennedy's Oldsmobile from the insurance company that had impounded it immediately after the accident and had the car crushed in a compactor, destroying all evidence.

In the immediate aftermath Joan Kennedy suffered her third miscarriage. In the following months Old Joe sank rapidly. By late fall it was clear the end was near. The family gathered around him and on the evening of November 8, 1969, the Ambassador passed away at eighty-one, his dynastic dream in ruins.

At the funeral Teddy read a tribute that had been written by his brother Bobby in 1965, which said in part: "He has called on the best that was in us. There was no such thing as half-trying. Whether it was running a race or catching a football, competing in school—we were to try. And we were to try harder than anyone else. We might not be the best, and none of us were, but we were to make the effort to be the best. 'After you have done the best you can,' he used to say, 'the hell with it.' "

GRAND JURY MEMBER: "THERE WAS DEFINITELY A COVER-UP."

At least one member of the Dukes County grand jury was left with a feeling that justice had not been done. Lester Leland, a local pharmacist and the foreman of the grand jury, believed that its members were pressured by the judge and the prosecutor to drop the case.

"I think we were manipulated," he said. "And I think that we were blocked from doing our job, and if you want to use the word 'cover-up,' then okay, that's what it was."

Leland requested that the grand jury be convened to investigate Mary Jo's death. "We weren't out to get Kennedy," he said. "We just wanted to get to the truth." But no such investigation was ever commissioned.

The grand jury sought to subpoena key witnesses including the women who attended the party, but District Attorney Dinis "told us that we couldn't subpoena them because they'd already testified at the inquest," Leland recalled. The truth is that a grand jury is legally empowered to subpoena anyone it wants. The grand jury was not even permitted to see the transcript of the witnesses' testimony at the inquest. With no evidence and no witnesses, the jury could take no action. "I felt I had been set up by the D.A. so that they could claim there was a grand jury investigation," said Leland. "We had been used. It was a cover-up," he said. "All [the authorities] were concerned with was protecting the Kennedys."

"There was definitely a cover-up," agreed Lloyd Mayhew, another member of the grand jury. "We were all madder than hell that we couldn't subpoena anyone we wanted—our hands were tied." Lloyd, a retired employee of New England Telephone Company, told *People*: "So many things bothered me; they still do. One of them is that within 100 yards of the Dike Bridge is a summer cottage. The lights were on, and there was a phone. Kennedy walked right by it. I don't know what kind of a man would do that."

There is little doubt that Teddy's failure to seek help immediately cost Mary Jo Kopechne her life. If he had reported the accident at once, instead of waiting ten hours, Mary Jo might still be alive.

Not even John Farrar was given a chance to tell the grand jury what he saw when he dived into Poucha Pond and found her body in the car. "I was told outright by the D.A.'s Office that I would not be allowed to testify on how long Kopechne was alive in the car. They were not interested in the least in anything that would hurt Ted Kennedy."

For the six months following the accident, Gwen Kopechne submerged her pain in Valium. It was years before she could even speak about the tragedy. "I was completely out of it," she said in a 1989 interview. "My husband was the one who had to cope." They remain bitter about Teddy's failure to report the accident immediately. "He was worried about himself, not about Mary Jo," Joe Kopechne said angrily. Equally hurtful and confusing is the fact that no one else who was at the party has said anything to explain how their only daughter died.

"I'm angry at every one of those girls," Mrs. Kopechne said. "They should try to explain. Somebody is hiding something. I think all of them were shut up. I think there was a big cover-up and that everybody was paid off. The hearing, the inquest—it was all a farce. The Kennedys had the upper hand, and it's been that way ever since."

The Kopechnes refused to allow an autopsy and brought no legal action against Ted for the death of their only child. "We figured people would think we were looking for blood money," Joseph Kopechne said. They did receive $90,904 from Teddy as a settlement and another $50,000 from his insurance company. They used part of the money to build a hilltop house in Pennsylvania, not far from where their daughter is buried. They frequently visit her grave to leave flowers.

They remained unsatisfied about the case. "I don't believe anything I've heard so far," she said. "I want *him* to tell me what happened. Can't he relieve us of this? Isn't there something he could tell me that would lift this heavy, heavy burden from my heart?"

Most telling were the little things about the Senator. "I don't think he seemed upset either time we saw him," said Mrs. Ko-pechne. "And I don't remember him saying he was sorry."

MARY JO'S MOM: "DID YOU GO UP TO MY DAUGHTER'S GRAVE?"

In the years since the drowning death of Mary Jo, her parents have heard almost nothing from the Senator. "The only time we hear from him is if something's going to happen with him," Gwen Kopechne said. "We get a phone call just to find out how bitter we are and whether we're going to be cooperative."

So they were not entirely surprised when during his 1980 campaign, the presidential candidate called to let them know he was in the area and that Joan was with him. "That's nice," said a stunned Gwen. Later she wished she had confronted him.

"If I wasn't in shock when he called," she said softly, "I would have said to him, 'Did you go up to my daughter's grave?' "

Neither of the Kopechnes doubted that their daughter's death had kept the Senator from ever becoming President.

And still the questions linger. Why was the Senator driving at midnight with a young single woman? Was he drunk? Was he speeding? Why didn't he call the police immediately?

The Senator has never explained how he could have mistakenly taken a sharp right turn off the island's only paved road onto a dirt road. He has never explained why he walked past four houses without bothering to call for help. He has never explained why he put on dry clothes and chatted with the clerk at his Edgartown motel at two in the morning.

If, at this point in his life, Teddy considered giving up the fight, it was not to be. With Joe gone, it was up to Rose to salvage their dynastic dream and she was determined to do so. "Mother put her foot down—hard!" Eunice told a reporter, and Teddy was told that he was to carry on, like it or not.

The important thing, for Kennedy loyalists, was that the dynasty had been saved.

CHAPTER FOURTEEN
TEDDY'S POWER FADES

Oh, Teddy and his girls . . . what can a mother do?

—Rose Kennedy, circa 1973

By the dawn of the 1970s, war, assassination and sheer reckless-ness had wrought havoc with Joseph Kennedy's carefully planned dynastic dream. The mantle had fallen to Teddy by de-fault, and at Chappaquiddick he had proven that he was not capa-ble of carrying it. But like his mother, Rose, he was at heart a stoic, and he pressed on.

The first sign that Teddy's career had lost its luster came on Jan-uary 21, 1970, when he was ousted as Democratic party whip. His fellow senators elected West Virginia's Robert C. Byrd to the post of assistant majority leader.

In the aftermath Teddy continued with the same recklessness and disregard for the consequences that had always characterized his behavior. He became less and less discreet about his relation-ships with other women.

Long considered the front runner for the presidency in 1972, he was suddenly out of the running entirely.

That summer, after Teddy made it clear he was not available for the nomination, the Democratic party nominated George McGov-ern and Kennedy brother-in-law Sargent Shriver.

In the early 1970s Joan and Ted moved to 636 Chain Bridge Road in McLean, Virginia, a rambling house on six acres, with a brilliant view of the Potomac. One wing was reserved for their three children, Kara, Edward, Jr., and Patrick, and a governess. Patrick suffered from asthma so severe he sometimes had to be given direct oxygen and a regimen of steroids.

They filled the house with Sheraton and Hepplewhite antiques. The household also included a live-in cook who had once worked in France for the Rothschilds. There was an office space for the Senator, Joan's secretary, Rosalie Helms, and Teddy's major-domo, George Dalton.

Joan herself struggled to carve out a separate identity while battling a drinking problem. In October 1970 she made her concert debut at the Academy of Music in Philadelphia with sixty members of the Philadelphia Orchestra. The event was a fund-raiser for Pennsylvania's governor Milton Shapp. She played the second movement of Mozart's Piano Concerto No. 21 in C and Debussy's Arabesque No. 1 in G, and received a standing ovation. Ted went backstage afterward: "Well done, Mommy, well done."

It seemed that the only area in which Joan was not overshadowed by her husband and his family was music, and Ted encouraged her to pursue her interest in it. She became a member of the board of the National Symphony Orchestra and made appearances narrating *Peter and the Wolf*, usually under the direction of Boston Pops conductor Arthur Fiedler. "I got some comfort from my music," she told Marcia Chellis. "It would keep me involved for a time."

But the recognition did not help. Joan's drinking increased. Her life was beginning to spin out of control. She was seen often, her makeup "theatrically thick," drunk and disheveled. Another observed, "She looked like she had been dragged through a rathole. She doesn't seem to give a damn anymore."

According to Joan, the Kennedy family treated her alcoholism like a shameful secret. "I tried to talk about it," she said later, "but I was embarrassed by it and Ted was embarrassed by it. Everybody was embarrassed by it, but nobody would really talk about it."

She would dry out in Santa Monica, but when she went back to drinking, her appearance, always her greatest asset, slipped.

Teddy's longtime aide Richard Burke recalls that Joan Kennedy did not even know how to turn on her gas range to boil water for her instant coffee.

TEDDY: "THE PRESS WILL NEVER TOUCH ME."

Teddy continued to follow the Kennedy rules established by his father. In Paris for the 1970 funeral of Charles de Gaulle, he danced until five A.M. in Il Club Privato on the Champs Élysées, with thirty-five-year-old Princess Maria Pia de Savoy, eldest daughter of former king of Italy, Humbert.

Joe, Joe, Jr., Jack and Bobby had all romanced beautiful movie stars, and so, maintaining the family tradition, Teddy targeted Candice Bergen who was making a splash in the sexy *Carnal Knowledge*. Her father, the popular ventriloquist Edgar Bergen, complained to a friend, "That dirty S.O.B. Ted Kennedy is trying to get into my daughter's panties! I have warned her all about him. But she's smart and knows he's just a no-good skirt chaser." Undiscouraged, Teddy continued to phone Candice frequently during the early 1970s to invite her to political rallies or charity functions. She always politely declined to join him.

In his published diaries, H.R. Haldeman recalled that then-secretary of state Henry Kissinger told President Richard Nixon that "Teddy Kennedy is now in the position of being a total animal. . . . At the opening of the Kennedy Center, he went to work on socialite Cristina Ford. He said he wanted her. She said they couldn't because of the press, and he said that 'the press will never touch me.' "

Some people tried to talk to Teddy about his drinking. John Culver, a former senator from Iowa, who had played football with Teddy at Harvard, warned him about it in 1970. Ted's angry reaction was to stop speaking to Culver for four years.

The former First Lady was the only Kennedy woman who had managed to break away from the role imposed on her, but unfortunately, Jackie's marriage to Aristotle Onassis was not a happy one. "They started with separate beds in the same bedroom," said an associate of the tycoon, "and ended with separate beds on separate continents."

At first Onassis had been so pleased with his beautiful acquisition he had showered her with jewels. Once he left a flawless string of cultured pearls on her breakfast tray. On her fortieth birthday he gave her a 40.42-carat Van Cleef & Arpels diamond ring worth $1 million, plus a matching diamond bracelet and necklace worth another $1 million. To commemorate the Apollo 11 space mission, he commissioned a special set of earrings: a sapphire-studded earth and a large ruby moon with an Apollo spaceship attached by a thin gold thread.

But by 1970 Onassis had decided that his trophy bride was cold-hearted and shallow, and resumed seeing his longtime mistress, the soprano Maria Callas. In May he was photographed dining with Callas in Maxim's in Paris. Ever conscious of appearances, Jackie flew there immediately and dined with him at the same restaurant the next night. Yet, when Ari came to New York, there was never enough room for him to stay at Jackie's Fifth Avenue apartment. He was confined to his permanent suite at the Pierre.

The suspicion persisted that she had used him. When a $9,000 bill came from Valentino, he slashed her $30,000 monthly allowance by a third and moved its control from New York to his Monte Carlo headquarters. "The marriage," he would later complain to his lawyer, "has gotten down to a monthly presentation of bills."

The last straw came in 1972 when Jackie sued photographer Ron Galella to restrain him from taking pictures of her and her children. She won a court order restricting Galella from coming closer than fifty yards of her and one hundred yards of her apartment. (Later the court of appeals cut the distance to twenty-five feet.) But when her law firm presented a bill of $400,000 to Onassis, he was furious. With advice from Bobby's old adversary, Roy Cohn, Onassis succeeded in negotiating the lawyers' fees down to $235,000.

JACKIE: "KENNEDY MEN WILL GO AFTER ANYTHING IN SKIRTS. IT DOESN'T MEAN A THING."

In 1972 Teddy's name was linked with Amanda Burden, the twenty-eight-year-old daughter of influential socialite Babe Paley and stepdaughter of William S. Paley, then chairman of the board of the Columbia Broadcasting System.

During this affair a deeply wounded Joan sought advice from

her sister-in-law. "Kennedy men are like that," Jackie told her. "They'll go after anything in skirts. It doesn't mean a thing."

But Joan was no Jackie, and her husband's flagrant infidelity hit at the core of her self-esteem.

On September 3 reporter Arthur C. Egan filed the following story with the *New Hampshire Sunday News*: "Two high-stepping playboy U.S. senators, taking advantage of a Congressional recess, spent a pre-Labor Day holiday sailing around Penobscot Bay with 'two lovely females' who were definitely not their wives."

Egan identified the senators as Teddy and his old friend John V. Tunney of California. (Tunney's wife, Mieke, had filed for divorce the previous May.) The foursome sailed for at least four days aboard Kennedy's sloop, the *Curragh*. The only other person aboard was a crewman who acted as captain.

As soon as the story appeared, both Teddy and Tunney issued denials, insisting that the cruise was a "family affair." Ted claimed that John had joined him for several days and then left, adding, "The rest of the time I was stuck with my two sisters [Pat and Jean]. Can you imagine anything worse than being stuck off the coast of Maine with those two?"

But Egan insisted to Lester David: "I stake my life and reputation on the accuracy of that story. I've been in this business a long time, and I would rather kill a story than write one I wasn't sure was true."

There were other stories that reinforced Teddy's image as an aging playboy who had never gotten in step with the times. According to Dominick Dunne, young guests at a Manhattan debutante party were appalled by Teddy's "tit-and-fanny pinching" and his drinking.

On January 3, 1973, Alexander Onassis had dinner with his father in Paris. Ari confided that he had decided to divorce Jackie. Alexander was delighted, telling his girlfriend, "He's seeing sense at last." But three weeks later Alexander himself was dead at twenty-four, killed in the crash of his small private plane. Ari was devastated. He spent most of the year in mourning for his son.

AIDE: "I SAW TEDDY ON THE FLOOR, ATOP SEXY SINGER."

Steve and Jean Smith celebrated Teddy's forty-first birthday with a "barn dance" at their New York apartment. They rolled back the rugs, spread sawdust on the floor and brought in a genuine donkey. Ted had come to regard Steve Smith as a brother.

Smith had no trouble keeping up with his notorious brother-in-law. During the 1970s Smith had kept two mistresses in New York, one Jewish, the other Irish Catholic. "He juggled his mistresses so well that none of them seemed to be aware of the others," said a friend of one. "Of course he was also spending vast sums on them. He used to make appearances at Halston's shows with various girls, buying them very expensive dresses. Like all Kennedy men, he thought he was irresistible and having mistresses was the norm."

Former Kennedy aide Richard Burke recalls attending a 1973 party given by Joan and Ted for a staff member at their McLean home. They even had a Greek band and a female singer. Joan's condition led to her early exit. Soon, to Burke's surprise, the Senator, fueled by his special blend of daiquiris, was dancing intimately with the singer. "It was a slow number," Burke recalls, "and the Senator leaned his body against the woman, pressing her crotch into his." The guests were soon dismissed.

Later on, Burke returned to "make sure everything was in order. The library had been closed off for the party but now, as I approached, I saw that one of the double doors was ajar. I caught my breath as I saw the Senator on the floor of the library, lying atop the sexy Greek singer. My heart skipped a beat. Instantly I backed away, sure that neither of them had noticed me."

A friend, seeing Burke's distress, spoke frankly to him. "Rick, you know, the Senator really likes you," he said. "The family likes you. You can go far here." Finally he added, "You have to grow up. You can't be—judging, you can't say anything to anybody. If you want to be part of the team, you just have to shut up and go along with it."

But the image of the Senator being intimate with a woman while his wife slept in the same house, continued to bother Burke. He would come to believe that the Kennedy men had developed "an aura of moral invincibility."

Burke soon became office manager, but discovered that juggling the Senator's personal life was one of his key jobs, "and certainly the hardest one." It became even more demanding as the Senator's womanizing increased. Like his brother Jack, he seemed to like women in pairs. "The Senator appeared to be assembling a harem," wrote Burke, "besides his increasing penchant for three-ways." On a trip to Aspen he had discovered the joys of a hot tub and had one installed at McLean.

Not all Teddy's girlfriends enjoyed the three-ways. According to Burke, one summer intern from the South fell head over heels for the Senator and was jealous of his other relationships. "She turned to me as a confidant," Burke recalled, freely admitting that she and the Senator slept together and detailing how the Senator had turned her on to coke and the joys of poppers. The only time she balked was when he tried to get her into bed with himself and another woman at the same time."

It was also in 1973 that Teddy was linked with Suzy Chaffee, three-time world freestyle ski champion and star of chapstick commercials, who had met him the year before.

As Teddy's life deteriorated and Jackie's marriage unraveled, another tragedy was unfolding at Hickory Hill where the loss of Robert F. Kennedy was still deeply felt. Determined to outdo his father in all things, Bobby had always been closely involved with his children, spending time with each one and urging them on to excellence. Ethel, in spite of her willingness to bear his ten children, was not gifted with the qualities that make a good mother. She had her mother-in-law's fertility but she also had her distance. And without her beloved Bobby around, she had developed a volatile temper and a habit of retiring for the night with wine and sleeping pills.

Robert's young sons were bringing that sense of moral invincibility to the third generation. A member of the staff told Burke that two of the brothers "even tried to hit on me."

"What did you do?" Burke asked.

The woman smiled. "Told Joe to grow up, and David I slapped the daylights out of—how's that?"

That summer, Joan made feeble attempts at living her own life. She traveled to Europe on her own, and was photographed dancing in a Paris disco, "makeup askew and noticeably unkempt." Like Rose, she had decided the only way to survive was to get away from her husband and children. "I was so unhappy I escaped for days at a time without telling anyone," she recalled. "Not even Rosalie, my secretary." According to Marcia Chellis, "Joan's pattern was to take an airplane somewhere, anywhere. And when she was discovered missing, a friend of the family would be dispatched to find out where she had gone and bring her back."

CHRIS LAWFORD: "WE'D SIT IN THE DARKNESS TALKING ABOUT WHAT AN INCREDIBLE ASSHOLE TEDDY WAS."

At Hickory Hill things were even worse. To help him recover from the loss of his father, Ethel had packed her son David and his equally troubled cousin Christopher Lawford to spend the summer of 1968 in a ski and tennis camp in Austria. At Camp Meyerhoff they discovered sex and being true Kennedy men, shared their women.

"David and I sort of decided together that there really wasn't any reason to try to be good anymore, so we might as well try to be bad," recalls Christopher.

And bad they were. Rose took to warning her household staff not to leave money or valuables where her grandchildren could get to them, because they would steal whatever was lying around.

In March 1969 Bobby, Jr., was expelled from the Millbrook School because of poor grades and behavior. Joe II was still at Milton, but getting terrible grades and high on pot most of the time.

Teddy was the sole male adult in their lives now and he lacked the self-discipline or desire to seriously parent. "We all felt a lot of bitterness toward him," said Christopher Lawford. "It was probably unfair. There was no real reason for it except that he couldn't fill Uncle Bobby's shoes and didn't try."

One of the first signs of trouble in the third generation was the 1970 arrests of Robert F. Kennedy, Jr., (center) and his cousin, Robert Shriver, in a summer drug raid on Cape Cod. (*UPI/Bettmann*)

Joe II, oldest son of Robert and Ethel Kennedy, grimaces as he watches his brother David being placed in an ambulance. Joe's Jeep, loaded with seven passengers, overturned on Nantucket Island in 1973. (*UPI/Bettmann*)

Joe II shows up in court with his widowed mother, Ethel Kennedy, and his uncle, the Senator. He was convicted on a negligent driving charge resulting from the Nantucket Island accident. (*UPI/Bettmann*)

Pamela Kelley, who was left paralyzed from the waist down after the accident. She was the most seriously injured of the five friends hurt when Joe II's Jeep flipped over. (*UPI/Bettmann*)

For a time in the 1970s, Robert and Ethel's third son, David Kennedy, was a fixture at glittering Manhattan discos. Shown here at Xenon in 1979 with film star Rachel Ward, he was said to have suffered the broken leg in a football game. Months later, he was mugged in a Harlem hotel while trying to buy heroin. *(UPI/Bettmann)*

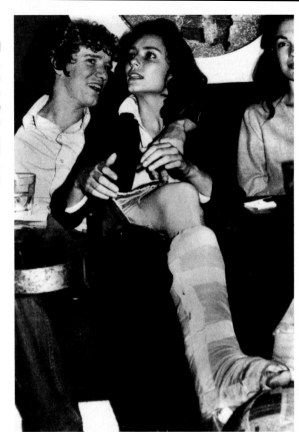

avid Kennedy while under drug ehabilitation treatment by on Juhl in 1980. *Harlin Smith/AP/Wide World)*

Christopher Kennedy Lawford, son of Patricia Kennedy and Peter Lawford, with his attorney at his December 15, 1980 arraignment. He pleaded innocent to charges of possession of heroin and the case was continued. (*AP/Wide World*)

Robert F. Kennedy, Jr., (in overc
is escorted by big brother Joe I
he enters a Rapid city courthous
February 1984 to answer c
charges. Bobby Jr. pleaded g
and was sentenced on March
(*Bettm*

uglas Kennedy was handcuffed
d arrested, along with sister Rory,
picketing outside the South
rican embassy in 1984.
n Hubbard/UPI/Bettmann)

Congressman Joe II is arrested for
demonstrating without a permit
in front of the White House
in 1994, protesting the Clinton
administration's policy on Haiti.
(Mannie Garcia/Reuters/Bettmann)

An outraged William Kennedy Smith speaks to reporters outside his December 1991 rape trial, calling his accuser's testimony a "damnable lie." (*Marc Pesetsky/Reuters/Bettmann*)

atty Bowman testifies in the William Kennedy Smith rape trial in Palm Beach, December 1991. She was the only victim in a rape case ever identified by name in the *New York Times* and on the *NBC Evening News*. Both claimed that such exposure was appropriate since her name had already been printed in a supermarket tabloid. (*AP/Wide World*)

Michele Cassone, another guest at the Palm Beach compound the night of the alleged rape, told reporters about Senator Teddy wearing only an oxford-cloth shirt. (*Reuters/Bettmann*)

Multi-talented Madonna, who conquered stage, screen, and the recording industry, and still found time for John. (*Mike Guastella/Star File*)

John Jr. and Sharon Stone also reportedly had a brief romance. (*Vinnie Zuffante/Star File*)

n's most-publicized relationship
s with Daryl Hannah, but by the
e they attended his cousin
dy Jr.'s 1993 wedding, they
re already drifting apart.
urg/Bettmann)

These days, John is seen with
Carolyn Bessette, a publicist for the
designer Calvin Klein.
(© Laura Cavanaugh/Globe)

Joe II's political ambitions were blamed for the break-up of his first marriage. Here he is shown campaigning for Congress in January 1986, while his wife Sheila holds their five-year-old twin boys. (*Bettmann*)

Joe II took his second bride, Beth Kelly, in a ceremony at his Boston home. Although married outside the Catholic Church, the newlyweds were blessed by Haitian President Bertrand Aristide, a Catholic priest. *(Jim Bourg/Reuters/Bettmann)*

Doug Kennedy. In September 1995, Doug was arrested in Nantucket for trespassing and disorderly conduct after he refused to leave his fishing spot on the rocks at Jetties Beach. He was fined $500.
(*AP/Wide World*)

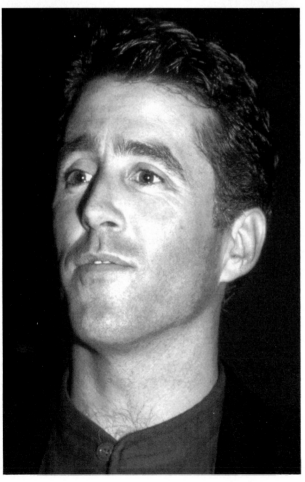

After conquering his heroin problem, Christopher Lawford is now happily married, father of two children, and a regular on television's *All My Children*. (*Jonathan Green/Globe*)

Unable to attend his grandmother Rose's funeral because he was in an alcohol treatment center, Michael Kennedy is still considered one of the most politically gifted of the third generation, and is now back at work at Citizens Energy Corporation. (Issaris/Gamma-Liaison)

Early treatment in a cocaine rehabilitation program helped Patrick Kennedy get his life on track. His political career has even survived his presence in Palm Beach the night of the alleged Good Friday rape. (Porter Gifford/Gamma-Liaison)

Robert F. Kennedy, Jr.'s political ambitions were severely damaged by his heroin problems, but his life seems to be back on track. He is now married to his second wife, has started a second family, and is active in environmental causes. (*Craig Filipacchi/Gamma-Liaison*)

Teddy Kennedy, Jr., survived cancer, the amputation of his leg at the age of 11, and a stint in alcohol rehabilitation. He is now happily married and a new father and is said to entertain political ambitions. (*J. Chiasson/Gamma-Liaison*)

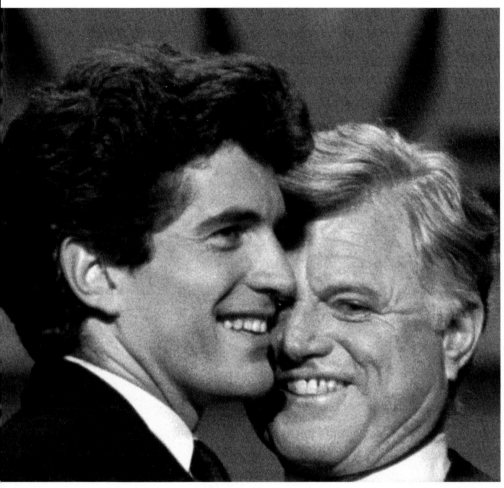

The torch passes. The years have not been kind to Senator Teddy and the Kennedy legend, but the greatest hope for any return to its glory days seems to lie with John F. Kennedy, Jr. The Senator introduced his nephew to the Democratic National Convention in 1988. *(UPI/Bettmann)*

The last hope? John Fitzgerald Kennedy, Jr., rises from the sea and carries with him the
hopes of Kennedy loyalists everywhere, a burden he seems to wear lightly.
(© *Laura Cavanaugh/Globe*)

A disastrous (for the children) rafting trip on the July 4 weekend along Green River in Utah crystalized the new family. According to Chris Lawford, Teddy, Ethel and other adults spent four days drinking and talking among themselves, ignoring them. When Bobby, Jr., and David tried to get them interested in a water fight, they were indifferent. Finally the boys set up their own campsite.

"We'd sit in the darkness," recalled Chris, "talking about what a drag the family was, what an incredible asshole Teddy was to let it happen, how it was never like this when Bobby was alive."

1970 signaled the beginning of the serious drug problems that would wreak havoc in the third generation and unravel Joe Kennedy's dynastic dream.

"Trust no one but family," had been one of his Kennedy rules, but that summer a friend, a Hyannis Port cabdriver, allegedly paid Bobby Shriver ten dollars for a joint. He turned out to be an undercover narcotics officer.

A few days later Bobby Shriver and Bobby Kennedy, Jr., both sixteen, were arrested while at dinner at the Shriver house. A month later, on August 6, Ethel, Ted and Sargent Shriver accompanied the boys to Barnstable District Court to answer their summons. Judge Henry L. Murphy continued the case without finding. Both boys denied the possession charge. The judge said that "unless they get into trouble again," they would not be subject to legal proceedings on the marijuana charge.

Burke recalls that David was growing marijuana on the grounds of Hickory Hill. His younger brother Michael was known to answer the phone there by saying "Confusion here."

Even the Hyannis Port compound was changing. Rose still occupied the rambling big house at the edge of a cul-de-sac. Jean and Stephen Smith had sold their house across the street to non-Kennedys years earlier. Jackie still owned the house she inherited from Jack, next to Ethel's, but she had her own house on Martha's Vineyard and was rarely there. The Shrivers had once owned the house next to the Smiths, but they, too, had sold out and bought another house nearby. The Senator's home was across a bridge on Squaw Island.

While Ted and his nephews floundered, a new generation of Kennedy women was beginning to break away from the restrictions once imposed by Joe and Rose. If the third generation of Kennedy men was shaping up as a pack of pot-smoking slackers, their sisters and female cousins were demonstrating seriousness and independence. Bobby's oldest daughter, Kathleen, was the first to set her own rules. Fittingly, she had been named for Bobby's rebellious and ultimately tragic sister Kick. After graduating from Putney, Kathleen had gone on to Radcliffe College where she fell in love with David Townsend, one of her instructors. They were married in November 1973. Her bridesmaids gave her a potter's wheel for a wedding present and David made her wedding band. The newlyweds moved to Santa Fe, New Mexico, where David got a job teaching English at St. John's College, and Kathleen attended the University of New Mexico Law School in Albuquerque.

Earlier that month, while Joan was secretly in an alcohol rehabilitation clinic in Switzerland, Ted called to tell her that a lump on twelve-year-old Teddy, Jr.'s, leg had been diagnosed as a rare form of fast-growing cancer, and their son would need immediate surgery to save his life. The boy was admitted to Georgetown University Hospital. Ted took a room next to him. Joan flew back, Rose up from Palm Beach.

Teddy, Jr.'s, leg was amputated on November 17.

The Senator took time out to give Kathleen away at her wedding, then returned to his son's bedside.

A rigorous regimen of chemotherapy followed. But more attention to Teddy, Jr., meant less to his siblings. Kara, chubby and insecure, experimented with marijuana and hashish and began running away from home, showing up at halfway houses, where her father would be called to come and pick her up.

JFK'S SECRET MARILYN TAPES ERASED

Richard Burke recalls that during the summer of 1973 a trusted longtime Kennedy friend was preparing materials for the John F. Kennedy Library. Burke was shocked to learn that the aide's main chore was "erasing the tapes." Burke became the first outsider to learn that President Kennedy had taped conversations in the Oval Office. "There is highly sensitive security stuff that we have to erase," the aide informed Burke. "You can never really tell anyone about this, but I'm going through the tapes and erasing anything that shouldn't be heard. There are conversations with some people that we don't want to be on the tapes." Included in the erased material were intimate conversations with Marilyn Monroe and Judith Campbell.

Burke was "shocked and embarrassed." He recalls: "Many of these conversations were very soulful and very erotic. These tapes were the very proof of an affair the family was interested in erasing from history, and this was graphic proof indeed."

JOE'S ACCIDENT

Little media attention was paid to Joe II's tragic accident that summer of 1973. Bobby and Ethel's oldest son was driving on a beach on Nantucket Island when he lost control of his Jeep. The car flipped over. Several passengers were injured, including his brother David and a young woman, Pamela Kelley, who was left paralyzed from the waist down. Ted's press secretary Dick Drayne took the lead in the damage control department, while Steve Smith quietly arranged a generous cash settlement for Pamela.

Joe II subsequently appeared before the Nantucket District Court where he was charged with reckless driving. He was lectured by Judge George Anastas: "You had a great father and you have a great mother. Use your illustrious name as an asset instead of coming into court like this."

Onassis and Jackie welcomed 1974 in Acapulco, and during their return flight to New York on January 3, the tension between them was palpable. During the flight Onassis began drafting his last will and testament. Jackie was bequeathed a lifetime income of $200,000 a year, plus a twenty-five percent share in Skorpios and the *Christina*. Caroline and John would each receive $25,000 a year until they were twenty-one. If Jackie challenged the will, she would immediately forfeit her annuity, and his executors and heirs were instructed to fight her "through all legal means."

Several months later Onassis was told that he was suffering from myasthenia gravis, a progressive neuromuscular disease. It was incurable, but he was optimistic.

By the end of the year, driven in part by his daughter Christina's hatred of Jackie, Onassis was consulting with lawyer Roy Cohn about a divorce.

Loyalists continued to urge Teddy to consider a run for President. Few of them considered Chappaquiddick more than a bump in Teddy's road to the White House, a mere bridge to cross, as it were. Arthur Schlesinger, who had been called to Hyannis to plan strategy immediately after the accident, believed that the experience had made Teddy a stronger man, "iron had gone into Edward Kennedy's soul."

On August 4 Richard Nixon resigned from the office of President, and was succeeded by Vice President Gerald R. Ford. Almost immediately pressure grew on Ted to announce that he would run for the Democratic nomination in 1976.

One concern: Ted's Senate term would be up that year and he could not run for both offices.

On September 23 Teddy withdrew his name for consideration for the 1976 presidential nomination. Sargent Shriver soon launched his own doomed bid, which wasn't helped by Teddy's decision to stay neutral.

The curse of Chappaquiddick had still not lifted. That spring of 1974 Joan signed into Silver Hill Foundation in New Canaan, Connecticut, a small private hospital known for its clinical work with alcoholic patients. After three weeks she went home to McLean in mid-June. Two weeks later she was back at Silver Hill for a much longer stay. On October 9 she was arrested for drunk driving in McLean after a minor car accident. She pleaded not guilty, her driver's license was suspended for one year and she was fined $200. Her sad cycle continued. She spent almost a month in an alcohol rehab unit at a New York City hospital. "It was awful," she told Marcia Chellis. "I had three roommates, all women on welfare. They wouldn't let me leave for twenty-eight days. There were people there off the streets. One woman had gone from a hundred dollars a night to doing the same things for a bottle of wine. I was so upset that as soon as I got out of there and went home, I drank again."

AIDE: "TEDDY'S KIDS WERE CAPTIVE TO THEIR FATHER'S SEXUAL FLINGS."

During the summer of 1975 Ted arranged a trip for Teddy, Jr., and three school friends from St Alban's. Their chaperon was Richard Burke, who usually supervised the mailroom of Ted's Senate office and had only just graduated from Georgetown himself. They drove through Colorado and Utah. Occasionally Ted and his great friend John V. Tunney would join them as they did in Lake Tahoe, entertaining two new female acquaintances.

Burke's heart went out to all three of Ted's children. "They were captive to their mother's alcoholism and continual absences, captive to their father's sexual flings, and most of all, captive to their name."

Teddy and Joan tried marriage counseling, but he sought companionship elsewhere, most notably in the Georgetown home of twenty-seven-year-old Page Lee Hufty, a beautiful, blond Standard Oil heiress.

According to Barbara Gibson, Rose Kennedy's longtime secretary, the Senator would show up in Palm Beach on Friday with Hufty, "his girlfriend of the moment," and be joined by Christopher Lawford and Joe II, each with a date of his own. "They would all dance around, trading girlfriends among themselves as they did," Gibson recalled. "Later the Senator might go off with his girlfriend or the girlfriend of one of his nephews."

Many other nameless women passed through the hot tub at McLean. According to Richard Burke, Teddy freely indulged in amyl nitrite or "poppers," and snorted cocaine with him and women in McLean.

Aristotle Onassis's health had begun to fail. On February 3, 1975, Jackie received a call from Athens to say that Ari had collapsed with severe abdominal pain. His doctors diagnosed a case of gallstones and stressed that he was in an "extremely vulnerable" state. Jackie left for Greece immediately. Christina, also informed of her father's condition, flew back from Gstaad, the Swiss ski resort where she had been holidaying. Three days later Ari made the decision to have his gallbladder removed at American Hospital in Neuilly-sur-Seine, near Paris.

Jackie and Christina visited him there, but, told he was in no immediate danger, Jackie returned to New York. On February 8 he was dead. Notified in New York, Jackie immediately flew back to Paris. Ted followed a day later.

Jackie issued a statement: "Aristotle Onassis rescued me at a moment when my life was engulfed in shadows. He meant a lot to me. He brought me into a world where one could find both happiness and love. We lived through many beautiful experiences together which cannot be forgotten and for which I will be eternally grateful."

Ted was at Jackie's side on the Boeing 727 that carried Ari's body to its burial on Skorpios. Caroline, John and Jackie's stepfather, Hugh Auchincloss, were already waiting for them at the airport.

After a short, simple Greek Orthodox ceremony, Onassis was buried outside the chapel.

As they headed away, Christina rode in the backseat of a limousine with Jackie and Ted. Ted chose this moment to lean across to Christina and say, "Now it's time to take care of Jackie."

"Stop the car!" Christina demanded. She got out and joined her grieving aunts in another limousine.

One of Christina's oldest friends said, "Christina knew that Teddy wasn't there to share her grief, to hold Jackie's hand. He was there for a specific purpose; he was going to want to discuss business sooner or later."

In the end Jackie challenged the prenuptial agreement she had made with Onassis, and after lengthy negotiations she received a $20 million settlement, plus an extra $6 million to pay the taxes on her inheritance. In return, she gave up her share of Skorpios and the *Christina*, which Onassis had left her.

Even as Jackie's claims against the estate were being negotiated, she accepted a $200-a-week editing job at Viking Press.

On April 18 the *New York Times* broke the story that Ari had been planning to divorce Jackie and that, shortly before he died, he had asked lawyer Roy Cohn to begin proceedings. "Several friends of the Onassis family have said Mrs. Onassis wants more money," the front-page story announced. "Christina," it continued, "is said to be bitterly hostile to Mrs. Onassis."

Jackie was deeply disturbed by the story. She called Christina in Monte Carlo after the story appeared, threatening that unless Christina put out a statement saying that everything had been wonderful between her father and Jackie, she was going to make no end of trouble over the estate.

Four days later the *New York Times* ran a story headlined: MISS ONASSIS DENIES HER FATHER PLANNED DIVORCE. "These stories are totally untrue," she insisted, adding that her own relations with her stepmother were based on friendship and respect, and there were "no financial or other disputes separating" them.

On April 24 Jackie and Christina flew separately to Skorpios for the religious service marking the fortieth day after Ari's death.

In the 1970s Jackie distanced herself from the Kennedy family. She could not bear Ethel's children, especially David and Bobby, or Pat's son Christopher Lawford and their drug problems. Even the Shrivers attempted to keep their children away from the troubled boys. Nevertheless, Jackie allowed Caroline to intern in Ted's Senate office the summer of 1975.

Later that year Caroline went to London to study art history at Sotheby's, the venerable auction house. During her stay she was shocked when a bomb planted under a car she was about to enter exploded and killed a passerby. Police theorized that the bomb, planted by Irish terrorists, was not meant for Caroline, but for the British M.P. Hugh Fraser, a longtime Kennedy family friend at whose home she was staying. Fraser had received threats from Irish terrorists.

JUDY CAMPBELL: "THE KENNEDY MEN WERE MORALLY BANKRUPT."

In December, Judith Campbell stepped out of the past and into the glare of the spotlight. Recently married to golf pro Dan Exner, she had been living in fear since the previous June when her old friend Sam Giancana was murdered in the basement kitchen of his

Oak Park home. He had been preparing to meet with a representative of a senate committee.

When Jack Kennedy's ex-mistress called a press conference, suddenly all the rumors and innuendo about Jack's Oval Office romances turned out to be justified. Judith Campbell Exner had places and dates. A distressed Eunice Shriver was especially troubled by Exner's charges. She asked her brother if there was any truth to the rumors. Teddy assured her they were not true. Loyalists would be further troubled when Exner published her memoir, *My Story*, the following year.

Angered at the secrecy surrounding Judy Campbell's testimony, columnist William Safire demanded to know why the senate committee had not questioned Frank Sinatra about his role in "the first penetration of the White House by organized crime," nor investigated "the first murder of a prospective senate witness" (Giancana).

In summing up the Kennedy dynasty from her own unique perspective, Ms. Exner has said: "The father really set the pace for the boys. I used to say that the Kennedy men were morally bankrupt. And I still feel that way."

In 1976 Jackie's stepfather Hughdie died, nearly broke, having lost most of his personal fortune trying to keep his brokerage afloat. Her mother Janet would be forced to sell Hammersmith Farm and move into a smaller house and servants' quarters on the grounds.

Having shelved any presidential plans to concentrate on his senate reelection campaign, Ted named his nephew, Joe II, his campaign manager. It had become a family tradition that working in an older Kennedy's campaign initiated the younger generation. As the oldest of the third generation, it should have rightfully gone to Kathleen Kennedy Townsend, but instead the job went to Joe. In the Kennedy family the men still ran things.

Many regarded Joe II as brusque, but more settled and responsible since the 1973 accident. Possibly dyslexic, Joe had dropped out of prep school three times, college twice. In 1976 he had just graduated from the University of Massachusetts and a stint as a volunteer at the Daniel Marr Boys Center in South Boston where he taught sailing to the underprivileged.

Cardinal Cushing lauded Joe II's appointment as "a most powerful vote of confidence."

Ted's campaign was a success, and he returned to office with
nearly seventy-five percent of the vote. Joe II briefly considered a
run for Congress himself.

Despite Teddy's disavowals of any interest in the presidency,
that February when he took Joan, their children and a large contingent of nieces and nephews on a skiing holiday in the Berkshires, he was at pains to include a reporter and press
photographers in the party.

Many family members had come to regard Joan as the greatest
impediment to his political future. Teddy himself resented taking
the blame for his wife's worsening alcohol problem.

Her mother had recently died of alcoholism and, determined to
break the cycle, Joan enrolled in an alcoholism treatment program
at McLean Hospital outside Boston. An apartment on Beacon
Street was purchased for her and just after the 1976 Christmas
holidays she moved in.

"When Joan left Washington, her home, her children, her husband, and all the reminders of her painful past, it was in a way, an
admission of defeat," said her friend Marcia Chellis. "Yet it was
also her only hope."

Boston marked a new beginning for Joan. But she was still a
Kennedy: She depended entirely on Ted for financial support and
on his staffs in Boston and Washington for everything she needed,
including her treatment. According to Chellis, "Joan still lived like
a Kennedy."

In late fall, Teddy visited Athens, Greece, accompanied by a
large contingent of aides and his nephew Joe II. Teddy had been
invited by former prime minister Constantine Karamanlis. The
group was housed as guests of the Greek government at Grande
Bretagne Hotel. Taki Theodoracopulos, a UPI reporter and legendary playboy, recalls getting a call from a member of Teddy's
staff, who asked him to "round up two dates, American girls pref-
erably," for the Senator and his nephew.

Knowing the tastes of the Kennedy men, Taki took three girls,
all American students, with him to the hotel. "Teddy was pretty
much drunk," he recalled. "In fact, he was really out of it."

After some time Joe and Taki and two of the girls went to

a nightclub. Teddy stayed behind in his suite with a third girl, a proper young Connecticut woman who was "very, very impressed with the Kennedy," Taki recalled.

"The next thing I knew, a hysterical [name deleted] came over to my house accusing Kennedy of having offered her drugs while trying to win her favor," said Taki. "Although I was very leery at first, when [she] continued to be hysterical and rang her parents and asked them to get her out of Greece, I became convinced that she was telling the truth. In fact, three years later, I wrote about the incident in *Private Eye* and some newspapers over here picked it up as well." Taki believes that the story was squashed in the United States, and that "the only good thing that emerged from it was that Bobby Kennedy, Jr., stopped speaking to me."

While some Kennedys reveled in drugs as recreation, others were becoming casualties of the drug holocaust. David Kennedy had dropped out of Harvard and spent most of his time stoned, shifting between friends in New York and Cambridge and Hickory Hill.

Back at Hickory Hill his mother refused to let him use any of the family cars, or give him cash. He would borrow cars and money from the servants and drive into Washington or up to New York to score heroin. Sometimes he would disappear for days.

On February 26, 1977, Rose celebrated Teddy's forty-fifth birthday with a small luncheon in New York. Guests included artist Jamie Wyeth.

For a while Caroline was a copy girl at the *New York Daily News*. Once she stopped at a nearby deli for lunch and was chagrined when pictures of her, taken by a lurking photographer and released via UPI, made their way back to the newsroom moments before she did. Coworkers there remembered her as bright, amiable and friendly. But she was also frustrated and alert to anyone who tried to take advantage of her name. Discussing a future reporting assignment from *Rolling Stone*, she told a friend, "They want me to write it just because my name is Kennedy. I really haven't done anything with my life yet."

After getting her fine arts degree from Radcliffe College, Caroline shared an apartment on Manhattan's West Side with three roommates (two male, one female). She got a job as a researcher in the Film and Television Development Office at the Metropolitan Museum of Art. She partied, but not as heartily as her male cousins.

On June 12 ground was broken for the John F. Kennedy Memorial Library. Ted, Rose, Jackie, Caroline and John, Jr., attended the ceremony in the run-down Dorchester section of Boston.

By that summer, Ted had banked enough seniority to gain one of the Capitol building's coveted private offices just off the Senate rotunda. According to Richard Burke, Ted's office was equipped with a comfortable sofa and bar, where he entertained several romantic conquests. But his time management was fueled by an escalating use of cocaine.

Helga Wagner was still in the picture. Burke recalls her as "one of the most consistent but least demanding of his girlfriends."

That August 1977 Caroline covered the Memphis funeral of Elvis Presley for *Rolling Stone*. Some felt she was too hard on the locals, but Andy Warhol defended her: "Caroline's really intelligent and the people down there really *were* dumb."

When Ted was invited to visit the People's Republic of China for Christmas, 1977, it was one of the first official visits since Richard Nixon had reopened relations between the two countries. Besides Joan and their three children, the Kennedys were accompanied by Eunice, Pat, Jean, Caroline and Michael.

Joan's drinking problems continued, although she was seeing a therapist, Dr. Hawthorne, regularly in Boston. Sometimes Ted joined her, but he resented attempts in the press to blame him for her alcoholism. She had been dealing with the problem since high school.

Joan saw little of her children—Ted, Jr., Kara and Patrick, who were living with Ted in Washington. According to Chellis, the only Kennedy who appeared to care about her was Eunice.

In January 1978 Teddy became chairman of the powerful Senate Judiciary Committee.

Bobby Kennedy, Jr., had graduated from Harvard in 1977, and like his uncle before him, he sought to turn his Harvard senior thesis into a book. His well-publicized biography of maverick Alabama judge Frank Johnson, who had fought the Ku Klux Klan and whom he admired for his courageous compassion (and who taught Bobby, Jr., to chew tobacco), was published in 1978, and reviews were mixed.

DAVID KENNEDY: "MY UNCLE TEDDY'S AS BAD AS I AM!"

David's drug problems were worsening. That summer, while Ethel was up in Hyannis Port where David was no longer welcome, Senator Teddy had agreed to keep an eye on his troubled nephew. David was supposed to stay with him at McLean, where he would be watched twenty-four hours a day by Teddy's crusty majordomo, George Dalton. But the day before David was supposed to move in, he pleaded with his uncle to let him spend a few more days at Hickory Hill. "I promise to be a good boy," he told his uncle. "I promise I won't get into any trouble."

David telephoned some family friends, Supreme Court justice William O. Douglas and Gertrude Ball, an executive with the Park Agency, to report a burglary at Hickory Hill.

According to David, he had surprised a burglar who had smashed his way through a third-floor window, and the two of them had struggled before the intruder fled. Douglas and Ball were ready to notify the police, but Noelle Fell, Ethel's assistant, was more familiar with David and insisted that first they check out his story.

Upstairs they found the window broken and the room in shambles, with blood, needles and vials on the floor. David and his girlfriend were asleep and no one could wake them. Fell told Douglas and Ball that there was no burglary. David had been looking for drugs, or shooting drugs, or had simply freaked out.

He was sent back to Teddy's house in McLean, but lasted two days before he returned to Hickory Hill, swiped one of his mother's credit cards and headed for New York, telling the staff: "My uncle's as bad as I am; he can't do anything for me."

That summer, buoyed by Lou Harris's polls that indicated voters were fed up with Jimmy Carter and saw Ted Kennedy as a caring leader and considered Chappaquiddick old news, Ted began to seriously consider challenging Carter for the Democratic nomination.

A sober Joan gave interviews to *McCall's* and *People* in which she talked candidly about her drinking problem. Both magazines featured her on the cover, *McCall's* with an awkward-looking Ted beside her. Some were surprised by her claims that she had been sober a year and was attending Alcoholics Anonymous, since one of the basic tenets of AA is that the affiliation is never discussed in public.

Another critical step in making Teddy campaign-ready came when Stephen Smith cut a deal with the *National Enquirer*. The Smith office would feed Kennedy family stories to the tabloid as long as the paper stayed from the more lurid stuff, especially stories about David. For a while it was Richard Burke's job to provide such stories and review them before they were printed.

Joan's sobriety was short-lived and by Christmas, 1978, she was drinking again. She opted not to join Ted and their children in Aspen for the holidays and stayed instead in her Boston apartment. Chellis recalls that Joan's deep despair, intensified by drinking, "led to liaisons with men whom she ordinarily would not have seen."

In spring 1979 she entered the resident program at Appleton House, the alcohol treatment center at McLean. Soon she moved to a small halfway house on the grounds of the hospital. By June she was allowed to return briefly to her Boston apartment.

Still determined to challenge President Jimmy Carter, Ted met with his family and staff at Hyannis Port in August to consider another run. Joan attended these discussions, commuting from Boston.

Although he had refused to run in 1972 and 1976, the time now seemed right for Ted. Polls indicated Democratic voters preferred him to Carter and that the general public had forgiven him for Chappaquiddick.

Caroline was seeing thirty-one-year-old Tom Carney, a Yale graduate and author. Carney often joined Jackie and Maurice

Tempelsman on Cape Cod and on a Caribbean vacation in St. Maarten. But the romance ended in 1980 after two and a half years. Carney married someone else.

Maurice Tempelsman had become the most significant man in Jackie's life, and he had little in common with the Kennedy men. A partner of his family's firm, Leon Tempelsman & Son, his own American Coldset Corporation (a Dallas-based manufacturer of diamond drill bits) and a host of diversified European holdings in African mining and manufacturing, he was considered one of the top power brokers in the international diamond market.

Jackie first met Tempelsman in 1962, when he and his wife, Lily, were invited to a White House dinner party. But they barely exchanged greetings at the time. Years later a mutual friend brought them together, with the idea that Tempelsman could replace Jackie's longtime financial advisor, Andre Meyer, who had just died. She liked him immediately and asked him to handle her finances. Soon their professional relationship became a social one as well. "Jackie relies on him in some of the same ways she relied on Onassis," said a relative. "He's a rock and has a kind of level-headedness that she deeply appreciates."

Tempelsman advised her on her children, on the menus for dinner parties, and on her finances, reportedly quadrupling her $26 million settlement from the Onassis estate. "It's probably the happiest relationship she's ever had in her life," said a former colleague. "She looks to him for support and companionship. She looks to him to make decisions."

They shared a love of culture and the outdoors. They spent many long summer weekends on his seventy-foot yacht, the *Relemar*, named for his three grown children, Rena, Leon and Marcee. They would often sail from Martha's Vineyard to the nearby Elizabeth Islands, where they would enjoy a picnic on the beach.

In 1979, ten years after her husband's murder, Ethel Kennedy remained obsessed with his memory. Hickory Hill had become a shrine to Bobby. "Pictures of Bobby were everywhere," recalls Noelle Fell. "Even in the closets. You'd open a door and there was a life-size photo. It was spooky. Ethel was still obsessed with her husband so long after his death." The only man who had captured her attention at all was Frank Gifford. "Frank Gifford was the only other man I ever saw Ethel get excited about, besides her husband, Bobby," recalls Fell.

Joe II made another break with Kennedy family tradition when he chose a Protestant bride, Sheila Rauch, daughter of a prominent banker from Main Line Philadelphia, whom he had known since 1970. They married on February 3, 1979, in a joint Episcopal-Catholic ceremony and soon moved to a large farmhouse on Boston's South Shore.

DAVID KENNEDY: "I'M A STONED-OUT JUNKIE."

Early in 1979, using money from his trust fund, David rented a penthouse apartment on East Seventy-second Street in Manhattan, and became a regular fixture at trendy discos and clubs. His name was linked with the beautiful young actress Rachel Ward. "Rachel wanted to get an apartment with me and settle down," he said. "But I knew I was too fucked up. I was back on smack. She had no idea what I was up to."

One night at Xenon, David got into a fistfight with Philippe Junot, the playboy husband of Princess Caroline of Monaco.

Like most of the women in David's life, Rachel Ward was unaware of his serious drug problem. "We smoked joints now and then," she recalled, "but there was no suggestion of heroin. He ate like a pig and didn't take very good care of himself, but he was crazy, with a wonderful sense of humor, and he was always very merry."

In truth, David had never fully recovered from the 1973 accident in which Pamela Kelley was crippled for life. Although the driver, big brother Joe II, had gone on to a promising career in Congress, David had been hospitalized with a back injury. In the course of treatment for chronic pain, he had become addicted to such prescription drugs as painkillers Demerol and Percodan, and the sedative Mellaril.

On September 5, in the late afternoon, David was beaten and robbed of $30 in a seedy Harlem hotel. He told police that he had been driving in the neighborhood in his $16,000 BMW when he was waved down by two men who forced him into the hotel where a third assailant took his money at knifepoint.

The Kennedy machine moved into spin mode. Ted's office issued a statement that David, on leave from Harvard, was simply visiting friends in New York, but reports soon emerged about the real nature of the hotel. The Shelton Plaza was a well-known shooting gallery where David was known variously as White James and Sweetwater. He had gone there to score heroin.

Although David was driving with expired Virginia tags and a stack of unpaid parking tickets in his glove compartment, and at first lied to police about the circumstances of the beating, he was never charged with any crime and was listed as a crime victim.

Stephen Smith, appointed David's legal guardian, arranged for family members to gather for a Kennedy powwow in his New York office. Teddy, Ethel, David's brothers Joe II and Bobby, Jean and Steve Smith, all carefully rehearsed how they would bring up the subject of therapy with David.

But David didn't want to hear it. He accused them of conspiring to get him out of the way so he would not be an embarrassment during his uncle's upcoming presidential campaign. "We love you," said Bobby. "You're killing yourself, and it's killing us to see you doing this to yourself!"

"You oughta know!" David shouted. He was probably the only other person in the room who knew that Bobby was as deep into drugs as he was.

David was admitted to the drug rehabilitation program at McLean Hospital. A few weeks later he was moved to Massachusetts General, where he was found to be suffering from bacterial endocarditis, a heart disease usually contracted by use of contaminated hypodermic needles.

Later, with Teddy's campaign for the Democratic presidential nomination coming up, David was banished to California. He was enrolled in a yearlong drug rehabilitation program in Sacramento. The Aquarian Effort was run by Don Juhl, forty-one, who had treated such celebrities as Beach Boy Dennis Wilson (who eventually died of drug overdose) and actor Jan-Michael Vincent, who continues to provide tabloid fodder. The $100,000 tab was paid out of David's trust fund.

"I agreed to take it because my Uncle Ted told me to get my act together or I'd wind up in an institution for the rest of my life like his sister Rosemary," David told a friend.

In therapy sessions and among friends, David raged at his family, especially his mother. Ethel made secret visits to her troubled son, but their sessions usually left him more angry and depressed than ever.

Immediately after his treatment in Sacramento ended, David was arrested for drunk driving, pleaded guilty and paid a $380 fine.

"As far as the problems of the past go, they're all over," said his therapist. "He is in no kind of trouble."

Joe II made his first move to be an official Kennedy candidate by polishing up his public image. With the help of longtime family advisor, Richard Goodwin, he developed the idea for Citizens Energy Corporation (CEC), a nonprofit oil company that, operating worldwide, eliminated middlemen and supplied heating oil to the poor and elderly at greatly reduced prices. CEC gave Joe a power base, an image and high visibility. His name appeared on billboards throughout Massachusetts below the slogan, "No One Should be Left out in the Cold, Phone Joe Kennedy."

CEC bought crude oil in bulk, refined it and provided heating oil to the underprivileged at thirty to forty percent below market price. It paid for the operation by selling gasoline and other by-products of the refining process to commercial customers.

On October 21 the family gathered for the dedication of the John F. Kennedy Library, the air electric with the expectation that Teddy was about to announce his candidacy for the 1980 Democratic nomination. Even President Jimmy Carter, the man he planned to challenge, was on hand, bravely shaking hands with all assembled, except for Jackie, who seemed to shrink when he approached her.

No one in media seemed to doubt that Teddy would sweep the country if he only chose to run. Former Iowa Democratic chairman Tom Whitney, in whose state the first caucus was scheduled, said, "The heart of the Democratic Party in Iowa belongs to Ted Kennedy. It is his for the asking."

JIMMY CARTER: "I'LL WHIP TEDDY'S ASS."

In the White House a beleaguered President Jimmy Carter watched the Kennedy buildup. When asked what would happen if Teddy Kennedy decided to run, Carter snapped, "If Kennedy runs, I'll whip his ass." Ted soon responded: "I always knew the White House stood behind me, but I didn't realize how close they would be."

No one seemed to notice the date of this new campaign, for 1979 would mark an important anniversary: It was ten years since Chappaquiddick.

ROGER MUDD: "DO YOU THINK, SENATOR, THAT ANYBODY WILL EVER BELIEVE YOUR EXPLANATION FOR CHAPPAQUIDDICK?"

Although he had been pursued for years by Barbara Walters, Ted opted to give his first big interview to Roger Mudd. Their ties went way back and the Team Ted considered Mudd safe and Kennedy-friendly. Mudd had been at Ethel's side in Los Angeles as she made her way to her fallen husband, and his son had served as a summer intern in Ted's office. Mudd was a neighbor in McLean and a regular participant in the Robert F. Kennedy Tennis Tournament. It was a typical cozy relationship between the Kennedy family and the media.

At the taping Mudd's scripted questions seemed pointed, but Ted left sure that Mudd and his editors would come up with a friendly picture. That's what the media was for—to serve the interests of the Kennedy family, especially when one of them was running for president.

Ted was so confident, in fact, that when Mudd asked to visit him at Squaw Island with a crew to get some added footage, he readily agreed. According to Marcia Chellis, Ted's staff had called each of the children and Joan to ensure that every member of the family would be there. "But Joan didn't feel up to the immense preparation required for a 'casual' weekend in front of TV cameras," Chellis recalled. Kara and Teddy, Jr., turned out to have other plans and didn't appear, either. The TV crews arrived, the senator and his staff arrived, but with no touch football or family fun to capture on camera, Roger Mudd sat down with the Senator in captain's chairs on the lawn overlooking the ocean for the interview.

When the edited interview aired on November 4, it started to go wrong early on when Roger Mudd asked, "What is the present state of your marriage, Senator?" Teddy hemmed and hawed, and it was downhill from there.

Soon Mudd moved on, asking: "Do you think, Senator, that anybody will ever fully believe your explanation of the Chappaquiddick . . . ?"

A stunned Kennedy could only ramble incoherently, repeating "that happens to be the way it was" three times.

Worse, when Mudd asked Kennedy why he wanted to be President, Teddy was literally speechless, groping painfully to produce phrases like "It's imperative for this country to either move forward, that it can't stand still, or otherwise it moves back."

The one-on-one interview was interrupted in order to allow CBS cameras, with a voice-over by Mudd, to re-create the nighttime ride on Chappaquiddick. Mudd explained that he and a camera crew had gone to the island, and Mudd himself drove the car repeatedly over the route to relive as driver the actual road and light conditions Ted would have experienced. Then the camera crew had attached a camera to the car's left front fender and with only the car's headlights to light the way, retraced the route that Kennedy and Mary Jo had taken on the night of July 18, 1969.

Teddy had claimed at the time of the accident that he had not realized he had gone off the macadam surface and onto a dirt road that led to the water. But the re-creation clearly contradicted him: The camera showed graphically how the car began bouncing when it hit the rougher surface.

The attention returned to Ted, with Mudd asking if he wanted to "say something more to illuminate in people's minds what indeed went on that night, other than saying it's all in the record?" He stuttered and rambled incoherently.

Afterward Teddy's reaction was shock and anger. "The son of a bitch ambushed me, cornered me with the worst questions! I should've known it, damn it." But it was too late. The damage had been done.

Even the Kennedy campaign luck ran out, as international events conspired against him.

Three days before Teddy announced his candidacy, Iranian revolutionaries took a group of Americans hostage in the American embassy in Teheran. In spite of the disastrous Mudd interview and the hostage crisis, on Wednesday, November 7, at Faneuil Hall in Boston, Teddy announced that he was a candidate for the Democratic nomination, and named the trusted Stephen Smith to serve as campaign manager. On December 28 Soviet troops invaded Afghanistan.

President Jimmy Carter was suddenly concerned with two high-visibility international crises. Instead of meeting Teddy's campaign challenge, he chose to stay near the White House Rose Garden and look presidential.

But Thanksgiving weekend found the Kennedy family in Palm Beach full of confidence. "I'm very happy about everything," Rose said as she handed out "Kennedy '80" buttons. "I've always been behind my sons when they wanted to do something. And I believe Teddy will make a good president."

TEDDY'S WOMEN PROBLEM/ WOMEN'S TEDDY PROBLEM

The Kennedy magic still had a powerful hold on the media. Take the case of Suzannah Lessard's devastating article about Teddy's womanizing. Pundit Michael Kinsley, then editor of the *New Republic*, wanted to run the piece, but, according to another pundit, Richard Brookhiser, the publisher, Martin Peretz, said no.

After a number of other magazines refused to touch it, the article finally appeared under the title "Teddy's Women Problem/ Women's Teddy Problem" that December in the *Washington Monthly*. Without naming names, Lessard described Teddy's philandering in great detail:

"The type of womanizing that Kennedy is associated with is a series of short involvements—if they can be called that—after which he drops the lady. Sometimes he hasn't even met the woman previously. She has been picked out by one of his cohorts as the type of woman who appeals to him, and asked if she would like to have a date with the senator. . . . The picture does not exclude longer relationships, but the short-term pattern evidently is a deep part of Kennedy's nature, as well as an image that Kennedy seems in some way to enjoy. . . .

"But if a man of middle age acts this way, and over a long period of time, over decades, then the behavior becomes quite unsettling. What it suggests is a case of arrested development, a kind of narcissistic intemperance, a huge, babyish ego that must be constantly fed . . . Certainly it suggests an old-fashioned, male-chauvinist, exploitive view of women as primarily objects of pleasure . . ."

All of Washington was soon talking about the story and the Senator's sex life. By declaring himself a presidential candidate, he had given the town license to discuss in the open what had only been rumored before.

Writer Henry Fairlie claimed he attended one dinner party where "for a full hour and a half, 14 talented and interesting men and women talked of nothing but the sexual activities of Edward Kennedy."

Suddenly, character had become the issue of the campaign. When the issue became character, not charisma, Teddy Kennedy was at a distinct disadvantage. Tip O'Neill had warned him that he could never be President, because of "the morality issue."

Kennedy and his brain trust dealt with the character issue by working overtime on Teddy's image. Joan was to be at his side as much as possible. The children were taken out of school to support the effort. Niece Maria Shriver took a leave of absence from her job as hostess of *PM Magazine*. Eunice and Jean, Sydney Lawford, Bobby Shriver and Joe II all pitched in. Jackie, Caroline and John, Jr., were reserved for the most critical occasions.

PART SIX

THE LEGACY

CHAPTER FIFTEEN
COLLAPSE OF THE DREAM

We must face the problems we are facing as we have always faced
the problems we have faced.

—Statements made by Senator Edward M. Kennedy
during his 1980 presidential campaign

In January 1980 a rumor circulated that Joan Kennedy had slipped
off for a face-lift in late January at Hahnemann Hospital in Brighton, Massachusetts. The scrub nurses were said to have been secretly flown in from New York to keep it quiet. It was all part of
the campaign buildup.

In Boston, advisors, including historian Doris Kearns Goodwin,
would gather to rehearse Joan for her public appearances. It
seemed to work. In subsequent appearances reporters noted her
new poise and self-assurance. They also noted that she was not
wearing a wedding ring.

But the 1980 campaign was a new game and neither Teddy nor
surviving Kennedy courtiers were equipped to play it. Not even
Jackie could help. She was involved with her own problems, including sister Lee's growing alcoholism. (In 1981 she would personally bring Lee to East Hampton AA meetings.)

And the strain of the marriage charade was already starting to
take a toll on fragile Joan. "She was realistic enough to know that
things were not going well between her and Ted, and it made her
feel uncomfortable to pretend otherwise," recalled Marcia Chellis,

who feared that the stress of deceiving the press and the public might endanger Joan's sobriety.

The first important primary was in Iowa on January 21. In spite of appearances by Joe II, Rose and Joan, et al., Teddy lost, drawing only 31% to Carter's 59%. No one in the campaign had foreseen a defeat like this. New Hampshire was another disaster.

Unfortunately, on the heels of the disastrous Mudd interview, the increased public scrutiny revealed Ted to be an inarticulate bumbler. Devoted aides like Richard Burke watched in agony as the Senator committed one verbal gaff after another on the campaign trail:

"We should expedite the synfuels program through the process of expediting," he boldly declared at one stop.

"We must face the problems we are facing as we have always faced the problems we have faced," he proclaimed on another occassion.

A TelePrompTer was introduced and Stephen Smith brought in Norman Lear as a consultant. Burke also suspected Smith played a key role in the removal of CBS's Phil Jones from the Kennedy beat, and the assignment of Jed Duval in his place.

Then came the February *Reader's Digest* major feature, "Chappaquiddick: Shocking New Facts," (a condensation from a new book, *Death at Chappaquiddick* by Richard and Thomas Tedrow). Publication coincided with the New Hampshire primary. This was the magazine that had put JFK's *PT-109* adventure into mass circulation. Now it was turning on the last of the Kennedy brothers. The revelations were devastating.

Still more primary disasters followed: in Florida in March; in Illinois; a narrow victory in New York didn't keep him from faltering again in Virginia, Kansas and Wisconsin. He squeaked through in Michigan and Pennsylvania.

Forced by new campaign funding laws to employ more innovative techniques to raise money, the campaign enlisted a dozen contemporary artists—including Andy Warhol, Robert Rauschenberg, Robert Morris, Richard Serra and Jamie Wyeth—to donate to the campaign original lithographs that could then be sold.

On March 3, as part of the poster project, Warhol attended a poster signing at the Brewster Gallery on Madison Avenue. Warhol spent the afternoon signing and he reported that all the other Kennedys were there, except for Teddy, who was in Massachusetts, and they all posed together for photographers. "[Pat Law-ford] was nervous so she was drinking," Warhol reported, "and she gave a speech. It was hard work. Kerry went around selling the posters. They were $750 and $2,000."

Even Stephen Smith grew disgusted with his brother-in-law's womanizing and drugging on the campaign trail. Coke, booze and women, and a venereal-disease scare were all recalled by Burke in his memoir of life with Ted. After a key meeting had to be delayed while the senator and a female were locked away in the master bedroom at McLean, Smith spent most of his time in New York, away from Washington, the campaign and Teddy himself.

The image of the campaign was not helped by the drug prob-lems of the third generation of Kennedy men.

Nephew Christopher Lawford was arrested for impersonating a physician in order to buy a prescription painkiller at an Aspen, Colorado, pharmacy while working for the campaign. Charges were later dropped after he completed probation, but his drug use continued.

Christopher had never really recovered from the collapse of his parents' marriage in 1964. He saw little of his father after the breakup. "I had a lot of resentment that I didn't have a father growing up," he recalled. When they did get together, "we were more friends than father-son. I loved my father, but it was weird. He went out with women who were my age. Then I had my own insanity which prevented me from being there for him later on."

Pat Lawford sent Chris to Middlesex prep school in Concord, Massachusetts, where he experimented with drugs for the first time and was ultimately expelled for drug use. After his mother found him behind a couch with a needle in his arm, she sent him to stay with his father in Los Angeles for a while. This was, per-haps, not wise.

David Kennedy visited Chris there in the summer of 1971, and recalled: "I knocked on the door and there's Peter Lawford. I hadn't seen him for years. The first thing he does after saying hello is offer me a pipe full of hash."

In October 1971, when Chris's forty-seven-year-old father mar-ried twenty-one-year-old Mary Rowan in Puerta Vallerta, Chris was his best man. Everyone in the wedding party wore jeans, and the ceremony was aboard a yacht. Two years later Peter and Mary separated, and she divorced him in January 1975. By then, Peter Lawford had become dependent on drugs of every variety, from Quaaludes and marijuana to cocaine and more.

Chris came to stay with his father again in January 1973, and the father and son shared drugs. "Peter and I would stay up all night doing dope together and talking about family problems," Chris recalled. "We'd have what seemed a breakthrough—saying we loved each other and hugging and all that. But the next morning it would be all gone. He'd snap at me and absolutely cringe if I called him 'Dad' instead of 'Peter.' "

Chris was best man again on June 25, 1976, when his father married twenty-five-year-old Deborah Gould, an aspiring actress he'd known three weeks, at a friend's home in Arlington, Virginia. Although no other Kennedys were able to make it, Senator Teddy did call with his good wishes.

The marriage was shaky from the beginning. A few months after the wedding, Deborah moved in with Henry Wynberg, a good friend, former used-car salesman and photographer, best known for his romance with Elizabeth Taylor. Wynberg's Beverly Hills home was always full of beautiful young women and while visiting his estranged wife there, Peter met seventeen-year-old Patty Seaton, who was wearing a gold-plated Quaalude around her neck. He left with her. Soon, Deborah had gone home to Miami, and Patty had moved in.

Chris managed to graduate from Tufts University in 1977 and enrolled in Fordham Law School in New York, but his growing heroin habit forced him to drop out after only a few months. Often his partner in heroin shooting was his cousin David.

TEDDY: "THE DREAM SHALL NEVER DIE."

On June 14 Teddy took time out to give his niece Courtney away at her wedding to Jeffrey Ruhe.

After attending the University of California, Courtney had become the first in the family since Jack to show a serious interest in their Irish heritage. She studied history and literature at Trinity College in Dublin, then worked as a production assistant at Children's Television Workshop, where she met her husband. Ruhe was an assistant to Roone Arledge, president of ABC-TV News and Sports and a longtime friend of the Kennedy family.

A week later the Kennedy family celebrated Rose's ninetieth birthday with a giant fund-raiser at Hyannis Port to pay off Teddy's campaign debt. They still hoped to salvage the nomination at the national convention.

The convention opened on August 11 in New York. Team Kennedy rented the entire sixteenth floor of the Waldorf-Astoria. Joan stayed first at Rose's three-bedroom apartment on Central Park South, but soon changed her mind and moved into the Waldorf, next to Ted's suite. As a young girl, Joan had made her debut in the grand ballroom of the same hotel.

But the Joan strategy was beginning to backfire. Observers could not help noticing that offstage the senator and his wife had nothing to say to each other and went their separate ways.

In spite of Teddy's flagrant womanizing, his treatment of his wife and his part in the death of Mary Jo Kopechne, he had been endorsed by the most visible of the women's activists including Barbara Mikulski, Bella Abzug and Gloria Steinem. But when it became clear to him and his supporters that they would be unable to change the rules on voting, Kennedy withdrew his nomination.

Showing perhaps a rare flash of his old man in him, Teddy agreed to campaign for Carter in return for the Carter forces' agreement to pay off some of his campaign debt.

With the help of longtime aides Bob Shrum and Carey Parker, he crafted a concession speech that challenged the Democratic Party. "For me, a few hours ago, this campaign came to an end," he told the crowd in Madison Square Garden. "For all those whose cares have been our concern, the work goes on, the cause endures, the hope still lives, and the dream shall never die." Many regarded it as his finest public performance.

Carter was defeated in the election. Teddy talked privately of quitting the Senate, perhaps to succeed Kurt Waldheim as Secretary General of the United Nations.

On September 13 the family gathered at New York's exclusive Le Club to celebrate Michael Kennedy's engagement to Vicky Gifford, daughter of football great Frank Gifford. Caroline, John,

Eunice and Ethel were there. The only adults missing were Jackie, Ted and Jean.

During the evening Eunice confided to Andy Warhol that her own taste in art ran to madonnas. Michael, who had graduated from Harvard that June, gave a speech about how he loved Frank Gifford and it was like having a new father.

"The little ten-year-old gave a speech about how when Michael was in a car and had to go to the bathroom he pissed in a beer bottle and they were all telling him to shut up but he wouldn't," Warhol reported. "Robert, Jr., gave the best speech, he'll probably be better than Teddy, he'll probably be the one. But the funniest Kennedy was [David] who was dancing with his girlfriend's purse and being like a fairy. They all dance pretty good. Kerry wrote some songs and they all sang them."

TEDDY'S CLOSE CALL

Teddy lived with the specter of assassination. At the 1978 convention every policeman carried a Polaroid picture of an armed man said to be out to get him.

In November 1979 a deranged woman with a knife had run into his Senate office. She was caught, but not before she wounded a security guard.

In December, John W. Hinckley, Jr., twenty-five, of Evergreen, Colorado, lingered in the office reception room. The busy staff was unaware that in his pocket he carried a loaded pistol that he intended to use to kill the Senator.

Senate business kept Teddy away, and after waiting more than three hours, young Hinckley left. Three months later, on March 31, Hinckley would fire on President Ronald Reagan and his press secretary, James Brady.

On December 20, 1980, Andy Warhol attended a Christmas party in New York. He never went anywhere without his Polaroid camera and this night was no exception. "I was taking pictures of this handsome kid I thought was a model and then I was embarrassed because it turned out to be John-John Kennedy."

Joan knew her life was changing. "I spent four hours talking to Jackie," she told Marcia Chellis. "She said she's crazy about Ted, but she's known for years that I should have done it fifteen years ago. She was so supportive. She even suggested I use her New York lawyer." Jackie also offered to introduce her to eligible men. The Christmas holiday was clouded by the pending divorce announcement. Nevertheless, Joan went to their McLean home and to Lift One in Aspen for the family's traditional ski vacation.

On their return in January 1981, Ted and Joan decided to make their split official. Teddy's Washington office issued their joint statement, a statement Joan said she had never seen:

"With regret, yet with respect and consideration for each other, we have agreed to terminate our marriage. We have reached this decision together, with the understanding of our children, and after pastoral counseling. Appropriate legal proceedings will be commenced in due course, and we intend to resolve as friends all matters relating to the dissolution of our marriage.

"In the interests of our children and other members of our family, we hope that the press and the public will understand our wish to decline further comment on this family matter."

Father James English, pastor of Holy Trinity Church in Georgetown, revealed that he had discussed the split with Ted and Joan. "They're very fine and mature people and when they came to the decision . . . I said it was the best thing." He added: "They understand the Church won't recognize this."

Now free to date openly, Teddy was often linked in the media with British debutante Louise Steel and West German princess Angela Wepper, as well as longtime pals Amanda Burden, Suzy Chaffee and Helga Wagner.

Joan had begun dating a handsome Boston psychiatrist, Dr. Gerald Aranoff, whom she had discovered on a TV program speaking about the problems of treating pain in America. He was the Director of the Pain Unit at the Massachusetts Rehabilitation Hospital in Boston.

On March 14 Michael Kennedy and Vicky Gifford were married in St. Ignatius Loyola church in Manhattan. The streets outside were mobbed with TV crews and police. Inside, the aisle was lined with flowers. The bridesmaids, including Kerry Kennedy, wore purple gowns made for them in Switzerland and pink slippers. "She was the prettiest bride I've ever seen in my life," Andy Warhol reported. "Really the best-looking bride. It made you want to get married, it really did."

In November Jackie gave a twenty-first birthday party for John. Caroline was now often seen with Edwin Schlossberg. "Caroline likes funny people," Warhol observed when told of the relationship. "He probably was babbling intellectually and she got fascinated, he was probably saying strange peculiar quotations or something." He spotted them in Aspen during the Christmas holidays. "They're madly in love," he reported, "and they were going off to parties."

A month later, at her annual Christmas party, Jackie took the tall, reserved Schlossberg by the hand to personally introduce him to her friends.

Schlossberg, author, artist, poet, philosopher, grew up on Park Avenue and attended the Birch Wathen School. The son of a prosperous textile company owner, he had earned his Ph.D. from Columbia University by writing a dissertation in the form of an imaginary conversation between Albert Einstein and playwright Samuel Beckett. By the time he met Caroline, he had formed his own company that designed projects and exhibitions for educational institutions, the entertainment industry and museums. Described as a Renaissance man, he was the author of nine books, including a computer handbook and a limited edition of poetry written on Plexiglas, aluminum and black cloth.

Schlossberg was as different from Kennedy men as it was possible to imagine.

TEDDY STROLLS NAKED ON PUBLIC BEACH AND IS NAMED IN WASHINGTON DRUG INVESTIGATION

Early in 1982 photographers for a German news magazine were in Palm Beach, stalking Tatum O'Neal. The star was said to be involved with one of the Shriver boys. The paparazzi had rented a boat and were anchored offshore, but instead of catching Tatum in a clinch with Tony Shriver, their telephoto lenses caught a fat, naked Teddy Kennedy, strolling the public beach in clear view of several elderly ladies.

In April the Washington police completed a yearlong under-cover investigation of a narcotics ring operating among congressional aides. That month, according to Taki, "a raid landed an alleged supplier, Douglas Marshall, the son of a diplomat, who sang like the proverbial canary. Marshall was charged but after one month he fled to Australia." Marshall soon returned to the United States. According to Taki, "Among the names he and one of his alleged confederates gave the police was that of the senior Senator from Massachusetts." Teddy was the only Senator named in the investigation.

In the aftermath of the election, Teddy seemed to abandon all restrictions on his cocaine consumption. "In the past he had used cocaine almost exclusively on weekends," Burke recalled. But now he was showing up at his Senate office with "watery eyes and sore nostrils." Observers sometimes noted white powder clinging to his nose.

It was also in 1982 that Ted met socialite Lacey Thompson Neuhaus, beautiful blond daughter of a wealthy Houston investment banker. They would continue to date for the next few years. A "sweet" Catholic former model, she was described as "the most like Joan."

Kathleen Kennedy Townsend, who had written position papers and campaigned for her uncle Ted during his brief 1980 presidential bid, still had to fight for the plum assignment she yearned for: managing his 1982 senate reelection effort.

Bobby, Jr., had graduated from Harvard with a degree in history and literature in 1977, and he earned a law degree at the University of Virginia in 1982. The summer of 1987 he married Emily Black, a fellow law school graduate and a Phi Beta Kappa graduate of the University of Indiana. Bobby went to work in the Manhattan district attorney's office while Emily went to work for Legal Aid.

In the fall, David left Sacramento with plans to return to Harvard and become a lawyer or a journalist. He took an apartment with a girlfriend on Beacon Hill and briefly worked as an intern at the *Atlantic Monthly*. He returned to Harvard, but lasted a semester before dropping out again.

At a Thanksgiving gathering at Hyannis, Teddy sought the family's support for the 1984 presidential bid he was strongly considering. It was not to be. The reaction was firm, especially from Steve Smith, who finally suggested they take a vote. The poll was unanimous, except for an outside guest, writer Dotson Rader. No one in the family wanted to go through another presidential campaign.

On December 6 Teddy and Joan met at Barnstable Probate Court on the Cape and filed for divorce citing an "irretrievable breakdown" of their marriage. They sought a no-fault separation agreement. Joan was accompanied by one lawyer, Teddy by three. After asking each a few questions, probate judge Shirley Lewis granted the decree, which would become final in one year.

Under the divorce agreement Joan received $5 million in cash, as well as the Boston condo, the house on Squaw Island, plus child support payments and annual alimony of $175,000. She and Teddy shared joint custody of Patrick, fourteen, who was living with Teddy in McLean.

On December 18 young Ted, Jr., was arrested on his way home from Wesleyan University. He was stopped by a New Jersey state trooper and charged with driving his Jeep sixty-four miles per hour in a fifty-miles-per-hour zone. The trooper noticed an open box of pot in the car. Young Ted was released in time to spend Christmas with the family in Aspen. He eventually paid $30 in fines and court costs.

In 1983 Ted would bring the same commitment and dedication to his officially single lifestyle as he had brought to his work in the Senate. He was seen at a political fund-raiser at the Helmsley Palace and dancing the night away at a hot downtown club, with yet another beautiful blonde, Helena LeHane, who often sat on his lap. He was also linked to Cynthia Sikes, twenty-nine, a star on television's St. Elsewhere series, and he was still seeing Lacey Neuhaus and Helga Wagner.

One female power in the Democratic party told journalist Lally Weymouth that if Ted was serious about becoming President, "I think he's got to put his private house in order and has to stop with Miss X, Y, and Z. I believe if he really wanted to be President he would get a serious, really bright woman to live with."

It did seem that Teddy was eager to clean up his act. The big question was: Had he entirely given up on the 1984 election? Or was he secretly hoping for a convention deadlock in San Francisco from which he could emerge as a compromise candidate? Weymouth spent a great deal of time with Teddy in the spring of 1983 in hopes of finding the answer to that question. She had already heard from his boosters. John Kenneth Galbraith told her that Teddy was "bright, well informed and secure in what he knows. I think he's a better legislator than either of his brothers and would be an excellent president." Another associate assured her: "He's actually finishing sentences and getting into playing the kingpin role." But in spite of such kudos from his staff and media friends, Weymouth reported that "I found a Kennedy with few if any original thoughts or ideas on the wide range of subjects we covered—from the Chicago mayoral election to El Salvador."

He was, in fact, as inarticulate and muddled as he had been when he sat down for his disastrous interview with Roger Mudd. "I had always assumed that Kennedy's performance was either a dreadful aberration or a result of trying to deal with Chappaquiddick on the air," Weymouth said. "We weren't talking about Chappaquiddick, however, but about issues, his hopes, his dreams, and his vision of the future of the country and the Democratic party."

To Weymouth, the most interesting thing Kennedy had to say was that he still harbored presidential ambitions. "I've always said I'd like to be President," he admitted, adding quickly, "I'm comfortable with this decision. No one will work harder for a Democratic President in 1984 than I will, and no one will work harder for their reelection in 1988."

Other political veterans were skeptical. "I don't think Teddy can be elected president," said Senator Barry Goldwater. "People are not going to forget Chappaquiddick, not just that a woman died, but that he lied. Let's say he'd said, 'I was having a party. I had a few drinks.' It would have been forgotten. Honesty is the only thing in politics."

Even more alarming, exit polls at his recent senate race in Massachusetts revealed that even many of those who voted for him for Senator would not vote for him for President.

That February, Ted celebrated his fifty-first birthday with a party for his staff at his McLean home. In the living room, aides had positioned a large photograph of a football player in a jersey bearing the number "88." On the dining room table, waiting to be cut, was a cake with George Washington's name, the date of the birthday they shared, and the year in which he became President printed in icing on one side. On the other side were written Teddy's initials, his birthday, and the word "President," followed by a big question mark.

"EVERYONE KNEW LEM WAS QUEER."

When David Kennedy was released from his Massachusetts hospital, Teddy, deep into his campaign for the presidential nomination, delegated Lem Billings to look after him. This was an interesting choice, since in recent years Jack's former roommate had embraced the counterculture. His hair had grown long, his clothes disheveled and his drug use extensive. He was already a surrogate father to Bobby, Jr., and, in the tradition of Kennedy rules, had smoked marijuana, snorted cocaine and shot speed and heroin with his young charge.

Although Billings had no interest in women himself, he encouraged Bobby to bring women back to the apartment they shared. He seemed to get a vicarious thrill from Bobby's conquests, the same way he used to from his beloved Jack's exploits.

"Everyone knew Lem was queer—the Kennedys, the Skakels, everyone," Ethel's brother-in-law George Terrien told journalist Jerry Oppenheimer. "I never could figure out why Ethel would let Lem have such an intimate relationship with the boys. She always remained blind to what he really was."

BOBBY KENNEDY, JR., ARRESTED

That August, in an eerie warning of trouble to come, the Coast Guard found Robert F. Kennedy, Jr., twenty-nine, aboard a small boat that had been adrift for some twenty hours about a mile off the coast of Hyannis. Bobby, Jr., was cited for operating the sixteen-foot Boston Whaler without registration, life jackets and distress signals.

A month later he was arrested on a far more serious charge. He was deep in the grip of heroin addiction.

On Sunday night, September 11, Bobby collapsed on a plane, apparently from drug withdrawal. He was traveling alone from Minneapolis to Rapid City en route to the Deadwood, South Dakota, home of friend Bill Walsh, a former Catholic priest, who was helping him kick his drug habit. Suddenly, passengers heard a commotion in the rear of the plane. One of them walked to the rest room and found Bobby, sitting on the toilet, incoherent, cold and clammy.

According to journalist Jerry Oppenheimer, "It took five minutes for two passengers and the stewardess to coax him out of the rest room and get him to lie down in a pair of vacant seats. They covered him with a blanket and administered oxygen; Bobby had lost muscle control, his eyes were dilated, his pulse weak." Still, when they asked him for his name, he had the presence of mind to say Bobby Francis.

The pilot radioed ahead to request that a paramedic and ambulance be on hand to meet the flight. When the plane landed, Bobby, Jr., was helped down the steps, but declined medical assistance.

This caught the attention of local police. It would take them two days to get a search warrant to search Bobby's bag for drugs, but when they did, they found two-tenths of a gram of heroin. Four days later Pennington County state's attorney Rod Lefholz ordered him arrested for possession of heroin, a felony carrying a maximum penalty of two years in jail and a $2,000 fine.

Meanwhile, Team Kennedy, headed by Stephen Smith, had moved into crisis mode. By Tuesday, accompanied by hastily summoned drug counselor Don Juhl; Bobby flew by private jet to Summit, New Jersey.

There he was admitted to Fair Oaks, a drug treatment center whose patients have included rock star John Phillips and his daughter, MacKenzie.

Before more details came to light, Bobby announced that he had admitted himself for treatment of drug abuse. "With the best medical help I can find, I am determined to beat this problem," he said in a statement released by the Senator's Washington office. "I deeply regret the pain which this situation will bring to my family and to so many Americans who admire my parents and the Kennedy family."

Frequently touted as a promising campaigner, "the one to watch" among Bobby's eleven children, Bobby, Jr., had become better known in private for traveling in the fast lane.

According to family insiders, Bobby, Jr., planned to work for a while as a lawyer, then possibly run for office from New York, as his father had. But it's hard to work as a lawyer when you can't pass the bar. Bobby failed the bar exam in July 1982 and walked out without completing a second exam the following February. More and more, he was said to slip away alone, sometimes by bicycle, sometimes in his car, to Harlem to purchase drugs. "He would go to 116th Street," an acquaintance told *People* magazine, citing a block where suburbanites often came to buy drugs. "You pay $10 or $30 at one end of the block and get your drugs at the other end of the block. Sometimes he would visit a 'shooting gallery' and be the only white person there. He's the bravest person I've ever met."

Bobby, Jr.'s, marriage had not stabilized him. "Kennedy seemed to founder in the Manhattan D.A.'s office," *Newsweek* reported, "while prosecuting one assault case, a colleague recalls, he nodded off in court."

Another observer reported to *People* that Bobby was almost unable to function while handling routine arraignments. "He wasn't really coherent," the observer said. "His line of reasoning was impossible to follow. He kept talking about how people in jail try to change their names, and it had nothing to do with what was going on."

In May he took a leave from the $20,000-a-year post to prepare for the bar exam again. Then in July he resigned from the job, and began a two-month stay with Bill Walsh in Deadwood.

"We started out at about 11 A.M.," said Walsh of their daily regimen. "We ran four or five miles together in the hills, then we'd lift weights for about 20 minutes, followed by a swim at the Deadwood recreation center. After our workout," Walsh added, "Bobby spent most of his time studying. Then, late at night, he would come down and have a few beers at the bar and throw darts."

Bobby's binge began on September 9 when he joined other young members of the Kennedy family at a Manhattan nightspot to mark cousin William Kennedy Smith's twenty-third birthday. The next night, a bachelor party to celebrate the upcoming wedding of Peter McKelvy to Sydney Lawford. By the time of the September 17 nuptials, however, Bobby was in Fair Oaks. The following March [1984] he would be convicted, given a suspended sentence and put on two years' probation.

Peter Lawford had grown estranged from his daughters because they did not share his involvement with drugs. They reached out to him, but he was unable or unwilling to accept their love. Sick and reclusive, he now spent most of his time alone in his Los Angeles apartment, ignoring visitors like Elizabeth Taylor who banged on his door.

Sydney Lawford, educated at Foxcroft School in Virginia, the University of Miami, and Franklin College in Lugano, Switzerland, and Tobe-Coburn School in New York, had briefly considered a career in fashion. When she married on September 17 at Hyannis Port, the Kennedy family had urged her not to invite her father and to let Uncle Teddy give her away. She insisted that he be there, even paying for his airfare.

Lawford was drunk throughout the rehearsal, stumbled as he escorted Sydney down the aisle, and got even drunker at the reception. The only Kennedy who spoke to him was Jacqueline Onassis, who joined him when he was sitting alone and engaged him in a half-hour conversation.

By now Lawford was living with Patty Seaton in a tiny apartment in West Hollywood. His old friend Elizabeth Taylor, just out of Betty Ford, had reached out to him there and convinced him to enter Betty Ford Center in December 1983. Although he remained alcohol-free for the five weeks he was there, he was regularly meeting a helicopter that brought him cocaine in the nearby desert. As soon as he got home he started drinking again.

That June, Teddy traveled to Tufts University to speak at his daughter Kara's graduation. A few days later he spoke at son Patrick's commencement at Fessenden School. He put in an appearance at John Kennedy, Jr.'s, graduation from Brown and spoke at Moses Brown prep school where Max Kennedy, Robert's son, was graduating.

"Will Kennedy grow old gracefully in the Senate or will he go for the White House once more?" Lally Weymouth asked in a lengthy *New York* magazine profile of Teddy. "He's well positioned now to hang back, make noble speeches, pay attention to his kids, avoid the media—and, if a candidate fails to emerge during the primaries, come forward at the convention in a draft." But, of course, things didn't turn out quite that way.

Joe Rauh, a Washington lawyer and prominent Democrat, told Weymouth that he believed Kennedy was aiming at 1988, but worried that he might have miscalculated. "God knows what will happen," Rauh said.

Jackie had found a new life as an editor for a New York book publisher. At Doubleday the former First Lady arrived at her midtown offices by taxi, liked to be called Jackie by associates, kept her office door open, stood in line at the coffee machine and even operated the copying machine herself. Her manuscripts went with her to her hairdresser, she carried them in a Hermes book bag, poring over them as she had her hair blow-dried in a private room. At first she was assigned a windowless cubicle. John Sargent, the company's chairman and a close friend, apologized for the room. "Oh, that's all right, John," she assured him. "I've lots of windows in my home."

Her biggest coup, so far, had been snaring Michael Jackson to write his autobiography for a $400,000 advance.

When she wasn't in New York, Jackie might unwind at her secluded 356-acre Martha's Vineyard spread, or her estate in Bernardsville, New Jersey horse country. She sailed, rode and read voraciously. She had managed to build a life for herself, completely independent of Kennedy men and Kennedy rules.

The family was to suddenly experience a betrayal from within its own ranks. When the May 1984 issue of *Playboy* magazine appeared early that April, it contained highly touted excerpts from a new book, *The Kennedys: An American Drama*, by Peter Collier and David Horowitz. It promised to be a no-holds-barred examination of the Kennedy family, especially the highly dysfunctional third generation. And David, glad to unload his anger, had talked to the authors freely. He was quoted extensively in the *Playboy* article.

"David was bitterly criticized for breaching the family faith," the authors wrote in an afterword to the book when it was published. "The word used in condemning him was *treason*." Publicly, the family dismissed the excerpts as "absolutely inaccurate, the lowest form of journalism except to call it journalism dignifies it."

A friend said that David was devastated when the article appeared. He knew he had made another mistake in a life full of mistakes. He would never measure up to his father and uncles.

He immediately went back on drugs, and spent a month at St. Mary's Rehabilitation center in Minneapolis, where he registered under the name "David Kilroy."

On April 19 he was released. The next day he flew to Palm Beach to a traditional Easter weekend.

DAVID KENNEDY FOUND DEAD

David checked into the $292-a-night two-room suite at the Brazilian Court Hotel in Palm Beach. He had been banned from the North Ocean Boulevard mansion because of his drug problems.

For the next five days, according to hotel staff, David drank and drugged heavily. He was in the hotel bar by eight A.M., downing double vodkas and grapefruit juice. His brother Doug, a senior at Georgetown Prep, stayed across the hall.

Word drifted back to a worried Ethel that David, days out of rehab, was on another bender.

On Monday night David met Marion Neimann, a forty-year-old German woman, at a local bar and invited her to join him for dinner. At her estimate he put away at least seven vodkas at dinner, then invited her back to his hotel room.

It was 10:30 P.M. by then and mostly they talked. David left the room briefly and returned with cocaine. Things turned maudlin as he spoke about his problems, seeing his father die on television and being in constant pain. After Marion Neimann left around 11:30 P.M., David went out to the Kenya Club for more drinking and, possibly, more cocaine.

In any case, he was losing it when he asked another female friend to get him back to his hotel. Once safe in his room, he took the phone off the hook.

On Tuesday, David was allowed to visit his grandmother. Ethel called Palm Beach attorney Howel Van Gerbig for advice. A drug counselor spoke to David that night and David admitted he had consumed nine to ten drinks and a lot of cocaine.

At nine A.M., Wednesday, April 26, David telephoned his girl-friend in Boston and advised her that he was planning to fly home that day with his cousin Sydney Lawford. The friend later claimed he sounded normal and sober.

Just before 11:30 A.M., Ethel called the hotel. She had been un-able to reach David and did not know if he had made his flight back to Boston. Would someone check on her son? While she stayed on the line, a desk clerk and a porter went to David's room. When he did not answer their knock, they opened the door with a passkey.

They found David on the floor, on his back, fully clothed, be-tween two beds. There were no signs of violence or robbery. No drug paraphernalia was found, but a half-empty bottle of pre-scription pills was beside the body. A search of the room yielded 1.3 grams of cocaine, and signs that more had been flushed down the toilet. Just who had flushed it down became something of a mystery.

The desk clerk returned to the phone and told Ethel that they had called the paramedics. Ten minutes later he called her back.

"We have found your son and the paramedics have arrived," he said.

"He's dead, isn't he?" Ethel replied.

"I'm sorry, yes," the clerk answered.

Ethel gasped and hung up. Soon Caroline and Sydney arrived and identified the body. There has been some speculation that these two young women participated in a traditional Kennedy cover-up by removing David's drugs.

The Florida state attorney of Palm Beach County investigated the death. A report was released that October, minus over a thou-sand pages of testimony including the toxicologist's report. But evidence indicated that there was cocaine and Demerol in his bloodstream.

In the excitement surrounding David's tragedy, few reporters noted that Rose had suffered a severe stroke on Easter Sunday and received the last rites of the Catholic Church. She was in-capacitated after that.

In mid-October two former bellhops were charged with selling cocaine to David. One of the hotel employees who found the body testified that Caroline Kennedy had come to the hotel that morning with another woman, possibly her cousin Sydney Lawford. An hour after he discovered the body, he saw Caroline heading toward David's suite, having been unable to reach him on the phone.

On October 17 Caroline publicly denied that she ever entered David's room. She repeated this denial in a sworn statement released by Palm Beach County state attorney David Bludworth on January 14.

In July, while hospitalized for bleeding ulcers, Peter Lawford had married his longtime companion Patty Seaton. He was in and out of hospitals for the rest of the year. On Christmas Eve he died at sixty-one.

Senator Kennedy released a tribute: "The death of Peter Lawford is a special loss to all of us in the Kennedy family, and my heart goes out to his children, Christopher, Sydney, Victoria, and Robin. We take comfort from the fact that we know he will also be missed by all of the people who enjoyed his many roles in films and on television. He was a dedicated and creative actor as well as a loving father and loyal friend to all of us, especially in the challenging days of the New Frontier."

Lawford was cremated on Christmas Day and the following evening a small group of family and friends attended the funeral at Westwood Village Mortuary. Joining his four children were Caroline Kennedy and Bobby Kennedy, Jr. After the service his ashes were entombed in a double crypt fifty yards from Marilyn Monroe's.

In 1988 Lawford would return to the news again when his widow, after a spat with his four children, accepted their check for $430, paid the past-due bill for his funeral expenses and had his ashes removed from the crypt. Accompanied by a photographer from the *National Enquirer*, she traveled to Marina del Rey, boarded a boat and scattered the star's ashes into the Pacific.

In June, Teddy, Jr., graduated from Wesleyan University and moved back to Boston. A month later he made his national political debut with a speech before the Democratic convention.

On another happy note, David's younger brother Michael had graduated from the University of Virginia Law School that year.

In December Rory Kennedy, born six months after her father's death, and her brother Douglas were arrested for protesting apartheid in front of the South African embassy in Washington. (The charges were later dropped.)

Like so many of the skeletons in the Kennedy closet—the lies about Rosemary, the lies about Jack's health, the unanswered questions about Chappaquiddick—the mysterious death of Marilyn Monroe and its connection to the Kennedy brothers would not go away.

The question of a Kennedy cover-up of the Marilyn Monroe affair was back in the news in 1985, when Roone Arledge, president of the ABC Network news division, suddenly killed a 20/20 segment that explored the relationship between the Kennedy brothers and Marilyn, much of it based on research by Anthony Summers. The journalist was convinced that there had been a relationship between Marilyn and Robert Kennedy. Arledge was not convinced, killing the segment because "it did not live up to its billing" and labeling the piece "gossip-column stuff." Arledge claimed that the fact that Ethel's son-in-law Jeffrey Ruhe was Arledge's assistant, had nothing to do with it.

Geraldo Rivera complained bitterly about management's decision and was fired after fifteen years at ABC.

Veteran Hugh Downs, coanchor of 20/20, stated "that the segment was 'more thoroughly documented than network coverage of Watergate at its height.' "

TEDDY'S "TABLETOP CONSUMMATION"

By now Teddy's attentions had turned to Cindy Pace, another beautiful blonde who at twenty-six was two years older than his daughter, and he continued to blaze new trails in Washington fun-making. There was the night at La Colline, a French restaurant near Teddy's office, that Teddy and another Senator staged a mock duel, fencing with gladiola swords. And it was at the same restaurant that Teddy and his great friend Senator Christopher Dodd of Connecticut performed "a Mexican hat dance" on their own framed photographs. According to *The Washingtonian* magazine, which broke the story, "Kennedy spotted Dodd's framed photo [on the wall] and shouted 'Who's this guy?' Laughing, he grabbed the photo from the wall and threw it on the ground, breaking the glass in the frame. Dodd, not to be outdone, located Kennedy's photo and returned the favor." Kennedy's photo was quickly replaced, this time inscribed with the Mardis Gras motto: "*Laissez les bons temps rouler*—Let the good times roll."

And it was in December 1985 that the famous "tabletop consummation" occurred. According to Michael Kelly of *GQ*, Ted and Senator Dodd were having dinner with two very young blondes in a private dining room at La Brasserie, another chic Washington restaurant. When their dates retired to the powder room, Ted summoned a waitress. "The two of them were three sheets to the wind," recalled an observer. "Teddy was all bloated and puffed up."

When the 5'3" waitress entered, the 6'2", 225-plus-pound Teddy grabbed her and threw her on the table. She landed on her back, sending crystal, plates, cutlery and lit candles all over the floor. Then Teddy picked her up and threw her on Senator Dodd, who was sprawled in a chair. With the waitress on Dodd's lap, Teddy jumped on top and began rubbing his genital area against hers, supporting his weight on the arms of the chair. As he was doing this, another waitress entered the room. Both women screamed, drawing one or two dishwashers. Startled, Teddy leaped up and laughed.

"He got this goofy grin on his face," said the observer.

Bruised, shaken and angry over what she considered a sexual assault, the waitress ran from the room.

To the second waitress, the two men "looked like they got caught." Dodd said "it's not my fault." Teddy said something similar, adding, "Makes you wonder about the leaders of this country." The Senators and their dates left shortly thereafter.

JOE II: "THE ONLY THING I MISSED BY NOT GOING TO HARVARD WAS A QUICK PREP-SCHOOL WIT—AND I'M GLAD."

Joe II finally decided to fulfill that legend and join the family business of politics. His six-year-old CEC had branched into en-

ergy conservation and health care, logging $1 billion in sales in
1985 and providing a springboard for Joe's leap into public service. Some critics questioned how much CEC had actually done
for the poor. "Citizens Energy Corporation is a brilliant vehicle to
launch a political career," said one observer. "It did much more
for Joe than for anyone else."

Massachusetts governor Michael Dukakis had recently dis-
couraged him from running for the mostly ceremonial post of
lieutenant governor. It was said that Dukakis was not enthusiastic
about being overshadowed by the Kennedy magic. Instead, like
his uncle Jack, young Joe targeted a safe congressional seat.

Thomas P. O'Neill, Jr., (Tip) the Speaker of the House of Representatives, planned to retire in November 1986, creating the opening. That December, Joe announced that he would run for the
congressional seat once held by his uncle Jack.

Coincidentally, in the six weeks before Joe announced his candidacy, local TV stations ran "public service announcements" for
CEC. These slickly produced commercials were broadcast about
forty times a week on five local stations, promoting Joe as a local
Robin Hood who would be sure that the poor would not be cold
that winter.

Actually, Joe II was not the first Kennedy to covet this particular
congressional seat. It was said that Teddy, Jr., who had been
working with the handicapped, also expressed interest. But in a
family conference Joe stated his case, making the point that he had
already been active in "public service," that his overtures about
running for lieutenant governor had not been welcomed by Governor Dukakis and besides, he was the oldest of the cousins. The
family support went to Joe. Although Joe has denied this, the
story has the ring of truth.

Joe did not have his father and uncles' impressive education
credentials, but he countered: "The only thing I missed by not
going to Harvard was a quick prep-school wit, and I'm glad."

Joe, with typical Kennedy media savvy, had been preparing for
this moment for years, and the media was soon in lockstep behind
his candidacy. There were a few dissidents, among them *The New
Republic*, which quibbled: "Largely overlooked were the more relevant elements in Joe Kennedy's record: the tragic auto accident
years ago that left a friend paralyzed, an embarrassing academic
history, and an outspoken contempt for liberalism."

Journalists Richard Gaines and Scot Lehigh were particularly bothered by the television appearance of "unregistered Kennedy lobbyists" to boost the candidate. They complained that local Channel 5 had "even let its political 'commentator' Doris Kearns Goodwin, author and wife of longtime Kennedy worshiper and speechwriter Richard Goodwin, apologize for Joe's youthful inexperience with the observation that elective politics ought not to be a system accessible only to seasoned pros."

So close were Goodwin's ties to the family that she had been called in to advise the troubled Joan Kennedy during Teddy's 1980 presidential bid. And in 1987 Goodwin would be given almost complete access to the Kennedy family archives to produce her book *The Fitzgeralds and the Kennedys: An American Saga.*

And on the day Joe announced, *Herald* columnist Howie Carr noted the event in his column: "Here's a man who understands the crisis of education," he wrote. "It's unclear where the hell he got his high-school diploma although he apparently attended Manter Hall, a private school in Harvard Square for rich dummies."

Joe, heir to two great political legacies, operated from an office that overlooked a road named for his great-grandfather, the irrepressible Honey Fitz. Yet he and his family hastened to insist that he was running on his own accomplishments and did not have any special advantage in the campaign.

"In this crowd," explained his sister Kerry, twenty-six, referring to the entire third generation of Kennedys, all twenty-eight of them, "you don't get anything without working for it, earning your keep. He's going to have to earn every vote like everyone else."

"I don't think there was any sense of destiny about him running," said his brother Michael, twenty-seven, "at least not in his own mind. Obviously, growing up in this family, that question is asked of you, and obviously, our family is very interested in politics and always has been. But Joe is not interested in titles and politics as such."

And to mark the occasion, there was, of course, a story in *People*, which described him in the same glowing terms that its parent company, Time, had once used to describe his father and his uncles:

"He seemed to stand above everyone in the restaurant, a handsome man, broad like [his] Uncle Ted, but with finer features, like his father. His left hand kept slipping in and out of the side pocket of his suit jacket, a favorite mannerism of [his] Uncle Jack. Joe even left the reception like a Kennedy: He walked into the bitter New England night without an overcoat."

A sense of entitlement surrounded Joe from the beginning of the campaign. In fact, Joe's announcement that he would run came six months after James Roosevelt, Jr., had announced that he would run for O'Neill's seat. Roosevelt, a grandson of FDR, had lived in the district for twenty-one years, while Joe moved into the district after announcing. He and Sheila gave up their rustic thirteen-acre spread on Boston's South Shore and acquired a 2-1/2 story red-frame house on Bigelow Street in Brighton. Moreover, Roosevelt had been district coordinator for Teddy's 1980 presidential campaign, and went to the convention as a Kennedy delegate. In 1982 he was Teddy's legal counsel for his senate reelection campaign. But loyalty had never been a Kennedy strong point. Media manipulation had, and once again, most of the media was in the family's thrall.

JOHN, JR., MAKES ACTING DEBUT OFF-BROADWAY

During the day John Kennedy, Jr., twenty-four, had been working as a management and planning assistant in New York City's Office of Business Development. On August 4, 1985, he made his New York acting debut before an invitation-only audience at the seventy-five-seat Irish Theater on Manhattan's West Side. Although the run was only six performances, John's acting was praised. "He's one of the best young actors I've seen in years," said Nye Heron, executive director of the Irish Arts Center, where the play was mounted.

In *Winners*, a four-character play by Brian Friel, John played an Irish Catholic youth engaged to marry his pregnant girlfriend, played by real-life girlfriend Christina Haag. At the end of the ninety-minute play, the couple is found drowned.

A serious security guard was posted at the door. Among those who were welcomed, John's cousins Kara Kennedy, Willie Smith, and Tony Radziwill. A fit-looking Robert F. Kennedy, Jr., with his wife, Emily, made one of his rare public appearances since conquering his heroin problem. Jackie and Caroline were both said to be out of town.

"This is definitely not a professional acting debut by any means," John insisted. "It's just a hobby."

That same year, Caroline made an abrupt turn on her career path. She resigned from her job at New York's Metropolitan Museum of Art, where she had worked five years in the film-and-television division, to enroll in the Columbia University School of Law. "I was bored with museum work," she said.

At Columbia she was considered quiet, almost shy, making no friends and leaving the campus as soon as classes were over. Gradually she gained confidence and developed a small circle of acquaintances with whom she would have lunch and chat in the first-floor lounge. At the end of the school year, they gave her a wedding shower in the lounge.

The substance abuse problems that so profoundly affected Bobby, Jr., David Kennedy and Christopher Lawford, now threatened another cousin, Teddy's younger son Patrick. A senior at Philips Andover Academy, nineteen-year-old Patrick checked himself into Spofford Hall, in Spofford, New Hampshire, during the 1986 spring break, to be treated for cocaine addiction. For years his treatment would remain another family secret.

Like her cousin Caroline, Maria Shriver followed her own star. In fact, she became a star on her own.

Two months after graduating from Georgetown University, she met Arnold Schwarzenegger when her brother Bobby brought him to a family tennis tournament. "I thought Arnold was interesting and I was impressed by his sense of humor," she recalled. "But I was starting a TV job in Philadelphia, and I had to block a lot of other stuff out for a time because it was important for me to find something on my own and excel at it. I grew up in a family where everybody excelled in a big way."

The night before his April wedding, Arnold presented Eunice and Sargent Shriver with a portrait of Maria, which he had commissioned from Andy Warhol, joking: "I'm gaining a wife and you're gaining a painting."

During the celebration a friend of Arnold's brought in a sculpture that Kurt Waldheim had sent. "My friends don't want me to mention Kurt's name because of all the recent Nazi stuff and the U.N. controversy," said Arnold, "but I love him and Maria does too and so thank you, Kurt."

Warhol and a cast of hundreds were most definitely invited to the wedding of Maria Shriver to Arnold Shwarzenegger on April 26, 1986. Warhol flew up from New York with entertainer Grace Jones. The crowd outside the church was the largest he had ever seen around a church. Oprah Winfrey gave a speech. Jackie Onassis was there with John, Jr.

The church service was an hour, and the actual wedding ceremony fifteen minutes. A soprano sang "Ave Maria."

On March 2 a forty-one-line announcement on the society page of the *New York Times* informed the world that Jacqueline Kennedy Onassis of New York was pleased to announce that her daughter Caroline Bouvier Kennedy, "the daughter also of the late President John Fitzgerald Kennedy," was engaged to "author and executive" Edwin Arthur Schlossberg, and a summer wedding was planned.

The engaged couple spent that weekend in Hyannis Port where they accompanied a wheelchair-bound Rose on a brief outing near the family compound.

The match was unconventional, especially for a Kennedy woman. Not only was Ed thirteen years older, he was Jewish. But those who knew Caroline knew it was right. "Ed was what Caroline had been looking for in a man, an older person who has acted as a calming influence in her life," said one family member. "He was everything she wanted—a warm, loving human being whose interests matched hers. She couldn't find those qualities in a younger man."

On July 19 Caroline married Schlossberg in the little white pillared church of Our Lady of Victory, in the quaint old town of Centerville. Ed's father, Alfred, told *Long Island Jewish World* that the service was "an accommodation," on the part of both families.

The bride wore a gown of white silk organza with cloverleaf appliques by Carolina Herrera. She arrived in a white limousine with Senator Teddy, who helped her with her train and patted her back encouragingly before they entered the church, walking down an aisle draped with honeysuckle and wild roses. When the onlookers grew noisy, Caroline hushed them with a finger to her lips. Thirty minutes later, they emerged from the church, and Ed's best man, John Kennedy, blew his sister a kiss.

Jackie, in a fitted, pale lime green sheath, bit her lip and struggled to hold back tears as she emerged from the church on the Senator's arm.

Guests included matron of honor Maria Shriver, old New Frontiersmen like John Kenneth Galbraith and Arthur Schlesinger, Jr., columnist Art Buchwald, all the Kennedys, including Ethel, Joan and Eunice, and Jackie's close friend, the singer Carly Simon.

At the bridal dinner John stood up and talked about how pleased he was that Ed had asked him to be his best man. "All of our lives," John said, "there's just been the three of us—Mommy, Caroline and I; now there's a fourth."

The reception at the Hyannis Port compound featured "personalized" fireworks by George Plimpton: a flower for Rose, ninety-six, who could not attend and a chaotically exploding display entitled "What Ed Schlossberg Does."

Unlike the exuberant Shriver-Schwarzenegger nuptials the previous April, Caroline's wedding was as private as a Kennedy family affair could be.

Afterward Doris Kearns Goodwin remarked to Jackie that she must be very proud of creating that bond between her children. "It's the best thing I've ever done," Jackie answered. "Being a mother is what I think has made me the person I am."

"They have a great relationship, and both have a tremendous sense of humor," said Caroline's friend Maura Moynihan. Schlossberg commented about their relationship: "The most remarkable part of it is that we've never had a fight."

Unlike their flamboyant cousins, both Caroline and John were quiet and thoughtful. John, twenty-five, was working for a city redevelopment agency in New York and planning to start New York University Law School in the fall. Barbara Gibson, Rose's former secretary, compared Caroline favorably with the rest of the Kennedy family. "If there was a group of cousins, she'd be in the back. She was very well-mannered, very quiet, cooperative, poised and calm, unlike many of the other children. Caroline was the most trustworthy—I would lend her my car."

That fall, Kathleen Kennedy Townsend made an unsuccessful run for the Maryland State Legislature, losing to the incumbent Republican Helen Delich Bently, 41% to 59%. The first Kennedy woman to seek political office, Kathleen had been an antiwar activist at Harvard, wrote her Yale Law School thesis on Emma Goldman, worked with Navajo tribes and Eskimos, served in the Massachusetts Office on Human Resources, written articles urging a rebirth of voluntarism and managed her uncle Ted's 1982 Senate campaign. A trim, energetic young woman usually clad in a suit and jogging shoes, she recognized the power of the family name.

"Listen," she acknowledged cheerfully, "when you're trying to get votes, I'm not going to dwell on motives, let me tell ya . . . There's certainly a great deal of affection for my family. You can't vote for me only because I'm a Kennedy, but I don't want to pretend I'm not."

The mother of three daughters, Meaghan, ten, Maeve, eight, and Kate, three, Kathleen ran in Maryland's Second District, where her husband David was now a professor at St. John's College in Annapolis.

"Kathleen's strong principles, almost religious in their intensity, have caused her family to sometimes call her 'the nun,' " reported Carol Kramer in *McCall's*. "She is probably the most pious Catholic of the third generation children."

Joe II: "Women Don't Have a Very Good Record of Dealing with the Kennedys, Either."

During the primary campaign, Joe and his staff demonstrated a quick, go-for-the-jugular style. When one of his volunteers was caught tearing down his opponent's campaign signs, Joe called to offer a $100 check, which was accepted. "I hear a couple of my workers got carried away," he told James Roosevelt, Jr., "but it was no big deal." Roosevelt replied: "It might not have been a big deal, but it was a bad way to start a campaign, and I hadn't seen that kind of thing done in all the Kennedy campaigns I worked for. That's when he said he was sorry."

This was a true Kennedy-style campaign in all its expense and sense of entitlement.

There was the June 15 Bunker Hill Day Parade which always brings out Boston's politicians in full force to march through the working-class streets of Charlestown. Governor Michael Dukakis, up for reelection, led, followed by Boston's popular mayor, South Boston's own Raymond Flynn. Behind them followed a phalanx of minor ward healers and functionaries.

Near the rear of the parade, a small band blared, marching with the tall, smiling Joe II. Not only had he had the foresight and resources to bring his own marching band, he was accompanied by two "spotters," who pointed him toward the most adoring spectators. According to Jill Feldman, who covered the event for *GQ*, this moment would be recalled with glee by Kennedy's staff. At the height of Dukakis's "Massachusetts Miracle," their man upstaged the governor by leading a parade from the rear. As usual, a Kennedy man marched to his own drummer.

But Joe bristled at the mention of any sort of Kennedy legacy. "That's a crock of baloney," he snapped at one reporter. "I don't believe there's any kind of mantle. What there are, are certain assets that I can use for positive goals . . . but I'm not carrying around all that baggage."

Joe was a born campaigner, in spite of the occasional slip of the tongue. On one occasion he told a crowd, "Back when my family was in power . . ."

To no one's surprise, Joe won the primary and the general election.

Anyone still not convinced that Joe was the designated heir for the Kennedy dynasty must have missed the barrage of publicity that accompanied his arrival in Congress in January 1987.

After the election Joe and wife Sheila sat for a particularly revealing interview with Maureen Orth. Sheila, now thirty-seven, held a master's degree in city planning from Harvard and worked part-time as a housing consultant. Their twin boys were now six.

Joe, well-coached, praised his wife. "Sheila has more sound judgments than anyone I know on issues you face in life. For me, she's the final word." But his temper flared a bit when Orth noted that Kennedy women had not always been happy in Washington. "Women don't have a very good record of dealing with the Kennedy's either," he snapped.

Sheila attempted to smooth things over. "The Kennedys aren't the only family with a macho tradition in which men get their way," she said. "I know the image is that the men do whatever they want to do and the women are left to pick up the pieces, but that's changing. When we get to Washington I am definitely working, and we are going to live in a situation so that things I want to do get done, even if they aren't visually exciting or newsworthy."

Joe by then had recaptured his composure and was able to close with an appropriate comment: "Sheila's never going to be a political wife. I think it's great that she's got her own independent way of thinking about things."

"That drives him nuts," Sheila whispered.

Joe's siblings were also moving into adulthood and many of them were training for "public service" by working in Joe's campaign. There was Michael, twenty-eight, a vice president of CEC; his sister Kerry, twenty-six, a Boston College law student; Christopher, a 1986 graduate of Boston College where he had majored in political science; Matthew (Max), twenty-one, a junior at Harvard; Douglas, nineteen, who had finished Georgetown Prep that year; and Rory, the youngest, seventeen, was a high-school student in Virginia.

"I never expected to make it to 30," Christopher Lawford said in 1991, but by that time he had not only made it to thirty-one, he had conquered his drug problems. After his 1980 drug arrest in Aspen, he had moved back to Boston. In spite of continued drug use, he managed to earn a law degree from Boston College in 1983. But, he acknowledged, "I was just not a legal beagle." After failing the bar exam, he decided to shelve a legal career.

He had already met Jeannie Olsson, an ad-sales assistant for *New York* magazine, whom he married a month before his father's death. "I couldn't help him because I had the same issues," Jeannie now admits.

The death of his cousin David motivated Chris to finally give up drugs. "David and I were just best buddies," he said, "I don't really want to talk about it. It's really hard when you lose someone you care about." Together Chris and Jeannie finally did overcome their drug use in 1985 by enrolling in an addictive behavior course at Cambridge Hospital in Massachusetts.

Patricia Lawford's three daughters were content to stay out of the limelight. Sydney, twenty-nine, was married, with one child, James Peter McKelvy, Jr. (12/6/85), and living in Baltimore.

Victoria, twenty-seven, worked for a nonprofit arts group for the handicapped, affiliated with the Kennedy Center in Washington. In the summer of 1987 she married Robert B. Pender, Jr., a lawyer in Washington.

Robin, twenty-four, still single, was a stage manager in New York-area theaters.

TEDDY CAUGHT WITH HIS PANTS DOWN

By 1987 Teddy had become so sensitive to rumors about his drinking, that he announced: "I don't have a problem." But that September Teddy and a young blond lobbyist allegedly got carried away over a chardonnay-fueled lunch in a private room at La Brasserie. When a waitress entered expecting to offer them coffee and to ask if they needed anything else, she found the Senator on the floor with his pants down. He was on top of the lobbyist. He and the thunderstruck waitress made eye contact, and she backed out of the room and closed the door. (Author's Note: This was not one of the two waitresses involved in the 1984 Brasserie incident.)

Caroline and Ed Schlossberg spent frequent weekends at their country home in the Berkshires. An old barn set on several acres, Ed had converted it into a two-story residence. Here they could sit before a roaring fire, reading and studying, or walk through the woods.

After a chunky adolescence, Caroline had emerged a slim, pretty young woman with long light-brown hair, bright blue eyes, who was usually clad in sweat pants, loose sweaters and high-top black sneakers or boots.

Once a month she attended meetings in Boston at the John Fitzgerald Kennedy Library where she was the youngest on the twenty-member board of trustees. Her father's former aide, Dave Powers, was now curator of the library's museum section, and praised her contribution: "She has never missed a meeting. She contributes ideas all the time on how to make the museum more appealing to the new generation who never lived through the Kennedy years."

MADONNA: "GOING TO BED WITH JOHN, JR., WAS LIKE GOING TO BED WITH AN INNOCENT."

John, Jr., was distinguishing himself in another Kennedy tradition: romancing women both beautiful and infamous. In time, the list of his lovers would include Daryl Hannah, Sonia Braga, Sarah Jessica Parker and model Julie Baker, but perhaps the most notorious of his conquests was Madonna, who told a friend "going to bed with him was like going to bed with an innocent." The affair was short-lived. "Madonna wasn't right for John," said an observer. "She comes on far too strong for him. Blatant sexuality really embarrasses John." And Madonna's love of the limelight was at odds with John's basic shyness.

John's mother was relieved when the romance fizzled. Jackie had monitored developments closely. Once, when she knew they were on a date, she called his apartment through the night until he picked up the phone at two A.M. Madonna was with him and she listened as Jackie pumped her son for information and said she wanted to meet her.

Although the affair died, John and Madonna remained friends.

THE SHRIVERS AND THE SPECIAL OLYMPICS

Of all the Kennedys, Eunice had managed to have the most successful and long-lasting union, as well as a fulfilling career. She and Sargent Shriver shared a deep commitment to the Catholic faith and attended mass and Communion daily. Their daughter Maria once described their marriage as "a religious union." While her political abilities were ignored in the family, Eunice built up the Special Olympics into an international event and did much to change attitudes toward the mentally retarded. By 1987 Eunice's life's work, the Special Olympics, had come into its own.

That year the Seventh International Summer Special Olympics

Games were held in a flag-bedecked and overflowing Notre Dame Stadium, and kicked off by a star-studded gala televised on ABC, the network which has always had a special relationship with the Kennedy family. Eunice's son Bobby Shriver, thirty-three, was the executive producer. "He was persistent about the show," Eunice told *People*, "I never doubted that he could pull it off, but I didn't see how people would accept seeing a social cause like this combined with entertainment."

The Special Olympics was that year's largest worldwide amateur sports event. Barbara Mandrell, Queen Noor of Jordan, John Denver and Don Johnson were among the celebrities watching as delegates from all fifty states and seventy-two foreign countries marched across the playing field. Whitney Houston and Denver sang. Maria Shriver was also enlisted. "This was an easy show to book," she said. "There was always an instant 'yes' whenever I asked my friends to cooperate."

Maria Shriver had become one of the most successful in breaking away from the Kennedy identification entirely.

"All those commas—the daughter of, the girlfriend of, the granddaughter of, the niece of—I hate them!" she once complained. "What absolutely drives me is to be considered as somebody outside the commas, somebody considered for her work alone."

For that reason she chose a profession no one else in the family had ever considered. "There comes a time for everyone when they have to decide if they are just going to fit in the niche or whether they are going to go out on their own," she said. And Maria went out on her own. After graduating from Georgetown she apprenticed at television stations in Philadelphia, Baltimore and Los Angeles. She studied with coaches, lost weight and approached her career with the same determination that her husband trained for bodybuilding competitions.

After a brief stint on the *CBS Morning News*, coanchoring with Forrest Sawyer, she moved on to NBC, anchoring a new Sunday edition of the *Today* show with Garrick Utley.

Although their sister Maria had become the best-known Shriver, the three Shriver brothers had reached maturity with a healthy combination of their Kennedy and Shriver traits. Bobby Shriver graduated from Yale (1976) and Yale University Law School (1980). He wrote for several newspapers including the *Chi-*

cago Daily News and the *Los Angeles Herald-Examiner*. After putting a few years at an investment banking firm in New York, Bobby Shriver formed his own venture-capital group, demonstrating a most un-Kennedy interest in business. After the success of the televised 1987 Summer Special Olympics, he followed Maria to Los Angeles and took over the direction of Special Olympics Productions, a company that benefits and promotes the organization. He also acquired an interest in the Baltimore Orioles.

Mark Shriver graduated from Holy Cross College in 1986 and used some of his Kennedy trust fund to found Choice, a Baltimore-based social-services program for inner-city teenagers and juvenile offenders. Besides being president of Choice, Mark also served on the board of the Maryland Special Olympics.

Anthony Kennedy Shriver inherited his mother's commitment to the retarded. In 1987, while attending Georgetown University in Washington, D.C., Tony Shriver drew fifty volunteers to the first Best Buddies meeting, pairing them with individuals from group homes and special schools. Enthusiasm for the project continued even after he graduated the following year and was studying for his LSATs. After being constantly interrupted by calls from students at other schools wanting to start their own chapters, Tony says, "I thought I'd just take a couple of months off to get this going at a couple of other colleges. I never stopped."

With $6,000 seed money from the Joseph P. Kennedy, Jr., Foundation, Tony turned his college project into a full-time job.

Joe II was caught in a petty embarrassment regarding an inflated resume. His office had released a biography to the press that stated "1974 Peace Corps volunteer—Kenya (assisted in the development of an agricultural project)." The information appeared as part of a larger resume in the highly influential *Almanac of American Politics*. The only problem was that Joe had never been a Peace Corps volunteer. When the discrepancy showed up in a local Massachusetts newspaper in 1987 and was picked up by a wire service, Joe's office corrected the record to say that while in Kenya roping giraffes for a television program he had helped out on a Peace Corps project. A spokesman called the error unintentional.

Robert Kennedy's other children were coming of age. That August, Christopher married a fellow graduate of Boston College, Sheila Berner, in Winnetka.

Rory, the daughter born after her father's death, had entered Brown University, which her sister Kerry and cousin John Kennedy, Jr., also attended.

Teddy continued his youth outreach. Two sixteen-year-old female pages were descending the Capitol steps late one afternoon when Ted's limo pulled up. The Senator opened the door. In the backseat was a bottle of wine on ice. Teddy asked if one would have dinner with him. When one shook her head, he turned to the other, who also declined. The Senator signaled his driver and took off. "He didn't even know me," one page recalled. "I knew this kind of stuff happened, but I didn't expect it to happen to me."

At one point it was rumored that the Senator had installed his current girlfriend at his house in McLean. Known to his staff as "the T-shirt girl," because she had previously sold T-shirts at a New England beach, she had reportedly met the Senator through his son Teddy, Jr. (another family tradition).

In September, Caroline began her third and final year at Columbia University Law School. At law school Caroline was named a Stone Scholar, a distinction awarded to students who earn a VG (very good) grade average. The award is named for the late Chief Justice Harlan Fiske Stone. Only about ten percent of the class is chosen for the award. That summer, Caroline worked as an intern at Paul Weiss Rifkind Wharton & Garrison.

Ted's daughter, Kara, twenty-seven, worked at Metromedia in New York for a while after graduating from Tufts University, but the fall of 1987 found her taking graduate-level courses in international relations and planning to work in her father's 1988 reelection campaign as a media coordinator.

In April 1988 Ethel Kennedy celebrated her sixtieth birthday with a party for two hundred at Hickory Hill. Guests were asked to wear what they were wearing when they first met her.

Weeks later, friends gathered to mark the twentieth anniversary of Robert F. Kennedy's assassination with a candlelit Mass of

Rememberance and Rededication at Arlington National Cemetery. More than a thousand people attended.

During the ceremony Ethel was flanked by Senator Teddy and
her oldest son, Congressman Joe II. Her old friend Andy Williams
sang "Ave Maria" and "The Battle Hymn of the Republic." John
F. Kennedy, Jr., and Christopher Lawford were among the altar
boys.

All guests received a souvenir program with a reproduction of
Aaron Shikler's 1975 posthumous portrait of Bobby on the cover.

Once again Kennedy rules applied. Journalist Jerry Oppenheimer has revealed that months before the service, Teddy approached his friend Gerald Macantee, international president of
the powerful American Federation of State, County and Munici-
pal Employees (AFSCME), the largest union in the AFL-CIO.
Teddy, like many other legislators, had benefited from AFSCME's
vigorous political action committee. And the organization was delighted to have employees design and produce the program for
free.

There were signs of strain in Joe II's marriage. "There's just not
enough time to be with my family," he often complained. Many
believed that Sheila Rauch was tiring of her role as a political wife.
One observer who met the couple on a plane remembered that
Joe, exuding characteristic charm and energy, launched into an
impassioned discussion with several constituents. "He really
seemed in his element, but Sheila ignored his conversation entirely," she said. "I wondered how could anyone marry a
Kennedy and not expect to be drawn into the people-to-people
campaigning." By early 1988 the couple was on the verge of
breaking up. But they stuck together for the sake of Joe's successful reelection bid that November.

Joe continued to receive favorable publicity, but he had not won
the support or respect of his congressional colleagues, who often
regarded him as arrogant, dim and bad-tempered. This was un-
derscored in December 1988 when he failed to win a seat on the
powerful House Appropriations Committee. Still, there was
much speculation among his supporters that he would run for the
governorship of Massachusetts in 1990.

Since her election defeat two years earlier, Kathleen had become the director of the Maryland Youth Corps Program under which high-school students were enlisted in various types of community service, teaching illiterates to read, working in nursing homes, cleaning up the shore, in return for high-school credits.

By 1988, Bobby Jr., thirty-four, had conquered his heroin addiction, had become a professor of environmental law at Pace University in Westchester, and a staff attorney for the Natural Resources Defense Council and the Hudson River Fishermen's Association. He lived in Mount Kisco, New York, with his wife, Emily, and their two children, Robert F. III (1985) and Kathleen Alexandra (1988).

Brother Michael had succeeded Joe II as president of Citizens Energy Corporation, working in an office that featured a gag gift from his mother: a giant poster of Lenin. "I guess some people might consider Citizens a socialist concept," he acknowledged. By now the nonprofit company had expanded to a sixty-person operation that provided not only inexpensive fuel but also prescription drugs to low-income families. Michael and Vickie now had three children.

After working briefly for Archer-Daniels-Midland Corporation after college, brother Christopher, twenty-four, was employed as a leasing agent at the Merchandise Mart but devoted part of his time to fund-raising for the Greater Chicago Food Depository, a food bank that served as a liaison between bulk suppliers and 495 local soup kitchens. He also raised money for El Valor, a group devoted to helping people in the city's Hispanic community. His wife Sheila was a second-year law student at Northwestern.

Brother Max, twenty-three, a senior at Harvard majoring in American history, was contemplating law school and business school. "I'd like to learn about environmental law," he said. "The environmental problem is not caused by people hunting but by businesses polluting, and they are the most powerful. In order to have any kind of effect on them, you have to know how they work."

Max was closest to his brother Douglas, twenty-one, a sopho-more at Boston College. A member of the Community for Creative Nonviolence, Douglas spent some of the previous Christmas working in a shelter for the homeless in Washington. He was un-certain about what he would do after college. "Definitely not law or politics," he said. "Right now, learning how to write better is the most important thing for me."

After graduating from Brown, their sister Kerry, twenty-eight, had worked with Amnesty International, documenting abuses of Salvadoran refugees by U.S. immigration officials. "That work was the final thing to get me to go into law," she said. "I realized that I needed the professional background to help effect change in that area." After graduating from Boston College Law School, Kerry became executive director of the RFK Memorial Center for Human Rights which supports the work of political activists around the world. The Center is a small organization compared to Amnesty International. There are a couple of staffers and some in-terns, and its funding comes from the memorial's small total en-dowment of $3.5 million. The Center gives a human-rights award each year "to a person who stood up to government repression at great personal risk."

Although living in New York, Courtney, thirty-one, divided her time between Boston where she was treasurer of her brother Joe's 1988 reelection campaign and a member of the JFK Library board, and Washington, where she headed fund-raising for the RFK Me-morial.

In August, Rory, a student at Brown, traveled with her mother to Namibia and Nairobi.

In 1988, after exploring a few acting jobs in Boston, Christopher Lawford decided to follow in his father's footsteps and try Holly-wood. His sisters were also attracted to media. Victoria was work-ing as media coordinator for Very Special Arts. Sydney Lawford McKelvy was married to a television producer in Baltimore and raising two children. Sister Robin was working as a stage manager in New York.

On April 7 Caroline flew to Boston to unveil a three-foot plaster model of Massachusett's official memorial to her father, by Massachusetts sculptor Isabel McIlvain, which would stand on the west front lawn of the gold-domed State House on Beacon Street. The statue, which Caroline had helped select in a competition and which she felt best captured the essence of her father, shows him in a walking pose, elbows bent, left hand tucked characteristically in his jacket pocket. At the unveiling of the model in Nurses Hall inside the State House, Caroline, in a black-and-gold maternity dress, delivered one of the few public addresses she has ever made:

"There are many memorials to my father in this country and around the world," she said. "But of all of them, this one in the state he loved means the most."

On May 17 Caroline was awarded her degree from Columbia Law School. Among the family members who gathered to watch her get her diploma were Ed, Jackie, John and her uncle the Senator. Also there were Nancy Tuckerman, Jackie's longtime friend and White House social secretary, and Martha, Jackie's housekeeper who had known Caroline since she was a little girl. Jackie's longtime companion, Maurice Tempelsman, was also there, but was careful to sit apart from her during the ceremony. They always avoided each other at such functions to evade being photographed together.

Before the year was out, Caroline would give birth to her first child, Rose Kennedy Schlossberg (June 25), and pass the bar exam on her first try.

She was also at work with Ellen Alderman on a book, *In Our Defense: The Bill of Rights in Action.*

In 1988 it was John, Jr.'s, turn to address the Democratic national convention. After graduating from New York University Law School in 1989, he would be appointed an assistant district attorney in the office of Manhattan D.A. Robert M. Morgenthau. In 1990, on his third try, he would finally pass the bar.

TEDDY: "PURSUIT OF THE PRESIDENCY IS NOT MY LIFE. PUBLIC SERVICE IS."

In 1988 Teddy announced he would not run. "I know that this decision means I may never be President. But the pursuit of the presidency is not my life. Public service is."

Coincidentally, that same year, Leo Damore's *Senatorial Privilege: The Chappaquiddick Cover-up* was published, and became a national best-seller. Its devastating revelations still had the power to shock.

PATRICK KENNEDY SPENDS $87,000 CAMPAIGNING FOR $300 A YEAR JOB

Patrick Kennedy had traveled with his father during Teddy's unsuccessful campaign for the presidency in 1980. "That was tough," he would later recall. "I was only 12 and I was very timid." Lanky, red-haired and energetic, he bore little resemblance to his father and older brother.

Nevertheless, after working on his cousin Joe II's 1986 congressional campaign, he was determined to carve a career for himself in the family business. "That was really exciting. I realized it was time for the torch to pass to our generation." Patrick had grown up in McLean, Virginia, prepped at Andover in Massachusetts, and moved to Rhode Island in 1986 to attend Providence College, where he majored in philosophy. There he found a need for "a sense of purpose and direction" in his life, and being a Kennedy he sought it in politics. Since then, he had been elected president of the Young Democrats, become a State House page, running errands and working as a summer legislative researcher, and been a delegate to the Democratic National Convention.

By the summer of 1988, Patrick decided to challenge John Skeffington, a five-term incumbent, for a seat in Rhode Island's House of Representatives.

During the primary campaign Patrick's father, the Senator, and his cousins John F. Kennedy, Jr., and Congressman Joe II, visited the district, shook hands and posed for snapshots outside neighborhood polling places. In the Kennedy tradition, he also laid out the big bucks, estimating that he spent over $87,000 campaigning for the two-year, part-time job that would pay him a mere $300 a year. That figured out to about $66 for each of the 1,324 votes he won.

According to David Grogan of *People* magazine, assistance from the Senator and other family members was not Patrick's only advantage. "With the guidance of some of his family's skillful advisors, Kennedy employed polling, computer-generated direct mail and other sophisticated techniques in the campaign," Grogan reported. "He had a get-out-the-vote system that was much more advanced than we usually see," said House Speaker Joseph De Angelis. "The Kennedys know their business, and their business is politics."

But it was not just about money. There was no way his opponent, undertaker John Skeffington, could match the attention generated when the Senator arrived via helicopter to canvass for his son. "Sometimes I didn't know whether I was running against Patrick or his father," said a rueful Skeffington. He had held the seat for nine years, had lived in the blue-collar district all his life, was backed by the state Democratic party and was a Kennedy supporter as well.

Some critics viewed young Patrick as a carpetbagger for running against a Democratic incumbent, and urged him to wait his turn. Patrick denounced their "arrogance" and suggested they let the voters decide.

"One thing that has always been stressed in my family is that if you've been given a lot, you're expected to give back a lot," he assured voters. "Kennedys have always represented the working class, the interests of labor."

Patrick won the September primary by a margin of 1,324 votes to 1,009. Victory in the heavily Democratic, blue-collar working-class Ninth District was a foregone conclusion.

Young Patrick was frank about his ambitions: "Oh sure, I'm ambitious," he told *People.* "I'd love to hold national office."

In the many glowing stories about the latest Kennedy to seek a career in politics, *Harper's Bazaar* and *People* among them, there was no mention of his 1986 stay in rehab, a story that might truly be inspiring to other families coping with the problem.

TEDDY TO BOUNCER: "GET OUT OF MY FACE!"

Ted was pursuing a new romantic interest and it seemed to be serious: Dragana Lickle, divorced wife of Gary du Pont Lickle. Although, according to Mr. Lickle's attorney, Joseph Farish, the du Pont heir regarded Ted as "a bad influence" on his two young children, Teddy and Dragana continued what Farish characterized as a "slap and tickle relationship for quite a while." She became the only woman Teddy ever took home to his mother.

Teddy remained convinced that he did not have a drinking problem, even when he got into a January 1989 brawl at American Trash, a bar on New York's Upper East Side. According to the bar's bouncer, David Shapp, the Senator entered at one A.M., "absolutely inebriated," and engaged in a political discussion with a group of young people. Another patron, an off-duty bouncer, broke in, shouting, "Why don't politicians do something about drugs?"

The Senator responded, "Get out of my face."

Undeterred, the concerned citizen, possibly intoxicated himself, pressed. "You're nothing like your two brothers." The Senator threw a drink in the man's face. At 4:30 A.M. friends put Ted in a cab and sent him home. The next day his office issued a statement saying that the Senator had stopped at the bar after dropping friends off and before going to his sister Pat's apartment. The incident "was of no consequence and the senator regretted it had occurred."

Concerned observers from Cape Cod to Palm Beach saw a life spinning out of control. "He really will do anything at all," said Washington columnist Diana McLellan. "I think he's mad." Bill Thomas, a columnist for *Roll Call*, said, "He's off the reservation . . . out of control . . . He has no compunctions whatsoever." Thomas likened Teddy and his fellow Senator Christopher Dodd to "two guys in a fraternity who have been let loose upon the world."

Joan's struggle for sobriety also continued. During the summer of 1988, she rammed her car through a fence in Centerville, a few miles from her Squaw Island home.

Early in 1989 Joe II and Sheila acknowledged the obvious and announced that in spite of "long and intense efforts to find another course," they were separating after ten years of marriage. Sheila and the boys moved out of the house in Brighton and settled into a new place in Cambridge. Until now Joe had been the favored candidate for a 1990 race for governor of Massachusetts, but he announced that he would not be entering the race.

Observers speculated that Sheila had left him because of Joe's extramarital flings, but family associates and handlers insisted that it was the irreconcilable differences between a born politician and a woman who loathed the spotlight. One longtime Kennedy supporter told *People:* "Joe is as outgoing as they come—and Sheila is much more reserved."

JOHN, JR., NAMED "SEXIEST MAN ALIVE"

Jackie was amused when John, Jr., was named "the Sexiest Man Alive," in a May 1989 *People* cover story, until the twenty-eight-year-old assistant district attorney failed the July bar exam.

Later that year John was able to indulge his acting ambitions by narrating an audiotape version of *Profiles in Courage*. His father's Pulitzer Prize-winning book had been a major title for Harper & Row, now known as HarperCollins, since the book's original publication in 1954. Now Caedmon, an imprint of Harper Audio, was producing the audio version.

Harper Audio vice president and publisher Susan Knopf told the trade magazine *Publishers Weekly* that the book "has an importance and significance that we hope will open up audio to a wider audience, including a whole new generation of younger listeners." Knopf said that John "does a tremendous job of conveying its message."

John had agreed to read for the tape with the understanding that Harper Audio would make a substantial donation to the John F. Kennedy Presidential Library in Boston. "That was an integral part of the agreement," Knopf said. A trustee of the library, John had also donated his performance fee to the institution. The new release was featured on ABC's *Good Morning America* on Thanksgiving Day, with John introducing his favorite selections from the cassette.

PART SEVEN

WELCOME TO THE NINETIES

CHAPTER SIXTEEN
A New Generation
in the Spotlight

Neither Joe nor Jack was punished by church, state or wife for such behavior and the late-born Teddy, coming into the family when its adult behavior patterns were already mythologized, presumably figured that neither the rules of decency nor of retribution applied to a Kennedy.

—Michael Kelly,
GQ, 1990

As the last decade of this century opened, nothing testified to the tattered state of the Kennedy dynasty more eloquently than the face of Senator Teddy.

There was little trace of the matinee-idol handsomeness that once wowed the girls on the campaign trail. Bloated, mottled, marked by telltale broken capillaries, the once-perfect nose swollen like W.C. Fields, the Irish blue eyes bloodshot and red-rimmed, he looked more like a tired old Boston ward heeler than the flower of America's first family.

His older brothers, Joe, Jack and Bobby, had been cut down in their prime and would be forever enshrined in history as young, virile examples of the best America had to offer. Teddy had outlived them all, and lived hard, and it all showed in his face.

During one 1990 interview, the reporter noted that Teddy's hands tended to shake so violently that he could not manage to drop his contact lens into its case without help.

At fifty-seven he was still a fixture at Washington night spots and exclusive private clubs. In the family tradition, he maintained a catholic and democratic interest in models, congressional pages, T-shirt saleswomen, waitresses and socialites.

While researching a profile on Teddy for *GQ*, Michael Kelly attempted to interview the Senator, but was told by the Senator's press secretary and deputy press secretary that Teddy had a blanket policy of not doing interviews with "life-style magazines." The press secretary explained: "Frankly, he doesn't do interviews with life-style magazines because they tend to ask life-style questions."

Years of neglect had also taken their toll on the former winter White House. Little maintenance had been performed on the Palm Beach mansion since the Ambassador's death, and it had come to resemble the home of Norma Desmond in *Sunset Boulevard*. "The beautiful red tile roof was falling apart," recalled one visitor. "Wooden window frames were rotting. The outdoor glass patio tables were frequently cracked by coconuts that had fallen from the trees. And some of the stone that surrounded the swimming pool had been so rust stained it looked as though a murder had taken place, the blood not completely washed away. Inside was as bad, with threadbare curtains, greasy old linoleum and peeling paint."

Rose refused to make repairs, possibly because it was not her house. Joe left it to the children jointly, with the stipulation that their mother be allowed to remain in it for her lifetime.

Joe's surviving children were also involved in a decade-long dispute with the town of Palm Beach. In 1979 the town had begun a movement to preserve landmarks, beginning with a house where Douglas Fairbanks had lived. Since then at least one hundred houses had been designated as landmarks. But not the onetime home of President John F. Kennedy.

"YOU'VE HEARD OF THE BOOK-OF-THE-MONTH CLUB. TEDDY HAS A BLONDE-OF-THE-WEEK CLUB."

Approaching sixty, Teddy was not ready for landmark status, either. He was known to come on to every attractive woman who caught his eye. His approach was called "crude, unsophisticated, like a teenage boy with raging hormones who wants to have sex." One young woman he approached said, "It was pathetic, very high school, a lot of giggling and heavy breathing."

"Almost every weekend," wrote Norma Nathan in the *Boston Herald*, "there is the Senator schlepping into Hyannis Port with a fresh blonde in tow. You've heard of the Book-of-the-Month Club, Kennedy has a Blonde-of-the-Week Club. They still talk about the time his boat was wedged on rocks in Wood's Hole, on the southwest tip of Cape Cod, and the Senator single-handedly entertained the two blonds aboard."

JOHN, JR.—THE HUNK FLUNKS—AGAIN

John F. Kennedy, Jr., continued to live life on his own terms, as his mother had taught him. Every morning, he left his Upper West Side $1,500-a-month apartment and rode to his office on his black mountain bike, working out after work at Wall Street's Downtown Athletic Club. In off hours he could often be seen on rollerblades in Central Park, or walking with his longtime girlfriend, actress Christina Haag.

"John is a guy's guy," said a friend, explaining that the assistant district attorney put a premium on fun and fitness. That premium included membership in three health clubs, as well as late nights dancing vigorously in downtown clubs.

He was a typical Kennedy man of action. "What really struck me was his restlessness," said one lawyer who had taken a bar review with him the previous summer. "He couldn't sit still for more than ten minutes at a time. The classroom had a door that opened onto a little deck, and every day he'd get up and open the door three and four times for really no reason."

And always, he was haunted by the shadow of his family. At twenty-nine, his father was already a Massachusetts congressman, and his uncle Bobby was chief counsel for a Senate subcommittee. At thirty, Uncle Teddy had won his Senate seat. Even sister Caroline had managed to pass the bar on her first try. His cousins Bobby, Jr., Kathleen, Michael and Kerry Kennedy, and Steve Smith had all managed to be admitted to the bar.

Unfortunately, in May 1990 John, Jr., failed the New York State Bar exam for the second time in seven months. Possibly, he had been spending too much time parachuting at New Jersey's Sky Manor airport. New York tabloids trumpeted the failure with headlines like THE HUNK FLUNKS, and the event prompted another *People* magazine cover story. John bravely faced reporters who appeared outside his office and assured them, "Hopefully, I'll pass it in July," vowing that if he didn't, he would keep trying "until I'm ninety-five." He finished by assuring the press that "I'm clearly not a major legal genius."

On May 5, Caroline gave birth to a second daughter, Tatiana Celia Kennedy Schlossberg.

JOE II TO BRIT SOLDIER: "GO BACK WHERE YOU CAME FROM."

Since entering Congress, Joe II had become a prominent critic of British policies in Ireland. On one visit to Belfast he even challenged a gun-toting British soldier.

"Joe was in a car driven by a priest, and they had to stop at a checkpoint," said Roy O'Hanlon, senior editor of the *Irish Echo*, a New York newspaper. "The soldier wanted to examine the trunk of the car, and Joe objected, saying that the driver was a priest, after all. The soldier told Joe that he should go back home, and Joe told the soldier to do the same. The British press were all over that."

In 1990 Joe convened a congressional hearing to examine British violations of human rights in Northern Ireland. Among those who testified was Paul Michael Hill, thirty-five, one of the notorious Guildford Four, who had just been released from a British prison on appeal. Hill and three others had been convicted of the October 1974 bombing of a pub that left five dead and fifty injured in the town of Guildford, near London.

Hill was still facing a life sentence for another crime, the kidnapping and murder earlier in 1974 of a former British Army soldier. During the police interrogation into the Guildford bombing, Hill had also confessed to the soldier's murder, but later retracted, claiming that the confession had been forced out of him. After Hill was released from prison, he wrote *Stolen Years*, a book about his prison experiences in which he denied any direct IRA involvement and said he had confessed to the Guildford bombing only under duress.

Just before going to prison, Hill fathered a daughter by his childhood sweetheart Gina Clarke. And in a 1988 prison ceremony he married a New Jersey paper mill buyer with whom he had been corresponding since 1985. That marriage ended after two years.

Joe introduced Hill to his mother, who soon became one of Hill's biggest supporters. Ethel went so far as to play matchmaker, suggesting Hill visit her daughter Courtney Ruhe, who was recuperating from a skiing accident. "She was looking rather pathetic and very pitiful surrounded by all these flowers," Hill recalled. "Poor little thing!" Soon the couple was spotted at Irish bars all over New York's Upper East Side, where Courtney, like most of the Kennedys, kept an apartment. Courtney, goodwill ambassador for a Rome-based AIDS pediatric foundation affiliated with the United Nations, was heard telling friends, "I love Paul. He's the most magnetic man I've ever met!"

KENNEDY & CUOMO: A MARRIAGE OF PASSION AND PRAGMATISM

Family historian Arthur Schlesinger, Jr., characterized Kerry Kennedy as "a powerhouse disguised as an ingenue." Even before graduating from Boston University in 1982, she had started work for Amnesty International. Five years later she took her law degree at the Boston College Law School, and in 1988 founded the Robert F. Kennedy Memorial Center for Human Rights. As its executive director, she led or participated in human-rights missions to a dozen countries, from Chile and Kenya to Haiti, Poland and Northern Ireland.

And on June 9, at Washington's St. Matthew's Cathedral, Kerry married housing advocate Andrew Cuomo, son of New York State's governor Mario Cuomo. To Schlesinger, the great dynastic marriage united "two families dedicated to fervent idealism tempered by political realism," combining, in Kerry's words, "passion and pragmatism."

"It's got awful good bloodlines," said Frank Manckiewicz, her father's onetime press secretary. "Like they say in baseball—it's one of those trades that helps both clubs."

Like the guest list, the wedding ceremony was a mix of old and new. Kerry entered the church preceded by bridesmaids, ushers and flower girls, forty-one attendants in all, but at the critical moment she chose to stride down the aisle alone. "She stuck to her guns," said columnist Art Buchwald. "She didn't want anyone to give her away."

After the hour-long ceremony, the three hundred guests adjourned to a reception at Hickory Hill, where they feasted on a buffet of lamb and salmon while dogs wearing white satin bows roamed the green lawns.

Teddy was further reminded of the swift passage of time when he gave away his only daughter, Kara, thirty, to Michael Allen, thirty-three, an architect in Washington, D.C. The September 8 ceremony took place at Our Lady of Victory Church in Centerville, Massachusetts, where her cousin Caroline had married Ed Schlossberg in 1986. Until recently, Kara had been a producer for Boston's *Evening Magazine* news show. Her new husband, a native of Jamestown, Rhode Island, had been a member of the U.S. yachting team when it won the 1980 Sardinia Cup and was a founding director of Newport's Museum of Yachting.

CHAPTER SEVENTEEN
PALM BEACH SCANDAL

I wouldn't trade life with him for ten seconds. I'd rather be poor
and in the condition that I'm in than trade with Ted.

—Orrin Hatch, 1990

By March 1991, Christopher Lawford, now the father of a son,
David Christopher Kennedy (1987) and daughter, Savannah Rose
(1990), was pursuing the same career as his late father: acting. He
had a prominent role in 1991's *Run* and bit parts in such films as
Impulse, *The Russia House* and *The Doors* (in which he made a one-
line appearance as a *New York Times* reporter).

His cousin-in-law Arnold Schwarzenegger directed him in a
small role in the HBO series *Tales from the Crypt*. "I like to work
with people I know," said Arnold, "and with Chris, it's very easy,
because he has the talent."

Chris had also become a regular as sexy Charlie Brent on the
popular ABC soap *All My Children*. "It has been much easier for
me than for anybody else," he acknowledged.

Christopher George Kennedy, twenty-seven, had moved up to
vice president of marketing for the Kennedy-owned Merchandise
Mart Properties, Inc. He seemed to be the only Kennedy showing
a serious interest in the family business and was working toward
an M.B.A. at Northwestern University's Kellogg School. But it remained to be seen whether he had inherited old Joe's drive and
toughness.

Chris's brother Max, twenty-six, who had graduated from Harvard in 1987, married Victoria Anne Strauss on July 13. A second-year law student, he ran a summer camp for homeless children at Hickory Hill. His brother Douglas, twenty-three, who had also worked with the homeless, graduated from Brown.

Sister Kerry was running the RFK Memorial Center for Human Rights in New York City. Rory, the youngest, was concerned about feminist issues and had spent the past summer working for Bella Abzug.

If the women seemed more comfortable with their heritage than the third generation of Kennedy men, it might be because, according to Victoria Lawford, the girls gave up the competition sooner than the boys did. "Sure, Caroline wanted to be prettier than Maria, and Kara wanted to be skinnier than Sydney," she said. "There just wasn't a prize to fight over, and none of the girls was the kind to fight anyway."

Caroline took a brief break from her life as a very private person to go on a nationwide book tour for *In Our Defense: The Bill of Rights in Action*, which she coauthored with Columbia University Law School classmate Ellen Alderman. The book defined each of the ten amendments through a specific court case. "We really did want to show how people use these rights in action," she said. "I wanted to take my experience and the advantages I've had and try to communicate them to other people." She refused to make any publicity appearances without her coauthor. "I hope," she said, "to keep the focus on the book."

On Good Friday, March 29, 1991, some members of the family gathered in Palm Beach for what the Senator would later describe as a "typical Easter weekend." A dinner party with Patrick; Willie; Jean Smith; William Barry, a former FBI agent who had been security chief for Robert Kennedy and had remained a close family friend; his wife; daughter and son-in-law.

Stephen Smith had died only eight months before. Since marrying Jean in 1956, he had made himself indispensable to the family. Like fellow in-law Ethel, he had become more Kennedy than the Kennedys. In his case that meant a life lived according to Kennedy rules.

Smith had become the family's indispensable fixer, appearing in an Aspen court when a disgruntled caterer sued Ethel over an unpaid bill, bailing David out of his many drug arrests and arranging for his hospitalizations, negotiating a settlement with the young girl Joe II crippled, plotting Teddy's Chappaquiddick strategy.

Although he had been a notorious womanizer, Jean, like her mother, chose to ignore her husband's infidelities. "He was God in that family," said a friend. "No one had the nerve to criticize him."

After dinner the older group began to reminisce about Steve Smith. Jean's son, Willie, thirty, a fourth-year medical student at Georgetown University in Washington, D.C., and Teddy's son Patrick, twenty-four, the Rhode Island State congressman, went out to a club with two friends, Brigitte and Cara Rooney. Ted went to bed at 10:30 P.M., but was unable to sleep.

Sometime after, Willie and Patrick returned and went to bed themselves. But at 11:30 P.M., the Senator roused his sleeping son and nephew to go and "have a few beers" at Au Bar, a local nightclub on Royal Poinciana Way.

Soon seated at a prime table near the small dance floor, Teddy and the lads ordered drinks, sipped them and began to unwind. After a while, Willie went to the bar, where he engaged in conversation with a young woman who said her name was Patty Bowman. He asked her to dance.

While they were on the floor, Anne Mercer, Patty's friend, walked by. Patty introduced the thirty-three-year-old blonde to Teddy and Patrick. Mercer made her feeling about the Kennedy family clear, calling Patrick a "bore," adding, "With genes like this, there'll be no more Kennedy dynasty."

Teddy chided her for her rudeness. "How dare you speak in this manner. This young man is a member of the legislature of Rhode Island."

An embarrassed Patrick rose and went to the bar where he and Michelle Cassone, a twenty-six-year-old waitress, began a conversation and soon went to the dance floor. At about 2:30 A.M., Teddy was ready to leave. Willie couldn't be found, so Teddy and Patrick left without him. Patrick invited Michele to join them at the house; she accepted and followed them in her own car.

At closing time, three o'clock, Willie discovered that his uncle had gone, and asked Patty Bowman for a ride home. She agreed;

on arriving, Willie showed her around the mansion, then took her through what three generations of Kennedy men call the Tunnel of Lust, which led from the mansion to the private beach. They walked along the sand and kissed.

Afterward, in another family tradition, Willie took off his clothes and dove into the surf for a brief swim. When he emerged from the water, Patty said she wanted to leave. Followed by Smith, she went back into the grounds of the mansion. By the poolside, she later testified, Willie suddenly wrestled her to the ground and forced her to have sex with him. Willie's account was that Patty permitted him to enter her, even guided him with her hand. Unfortunately, at one point, he called her "Kathy," which upset her.

Patty ran into the house where, in the kitchen, she telephoned her friend Anne Mercer. Meanwhile, Willie cooled off by doing several laps in the pool. About four A.M. Anne Mercer and a friend, Chuck Desiderio, arrived at the mansion and agreed to follow Patty back to her home in Jupiter, about twenty miles north of Palm Beach.

Later that Saturday, Patty Bowman filed rape charges against William Kennedy Smith.

What followed was a classic exercise in Kennedy arrogance.

At 1:30 P.M. on Easter Sunday two detectives called at the mansion and asked to speak to Senator Kennedy. Bill Barry informed them that the Senator had already left town, "but it was possible he may still be around." The truth was that the Senator was inside the mansion, about to have Easter Sunday lunch with his guests.

Teddy did not leave Palm Beach until the next day.

Although he had yet to be charged with any crime, Willie submitted blood and hair samples to police on April 7; the results, expected in six to eight weeks, would help to determine whether charges would be filed.

Without Steve Smith around to control this disaster, the new generation of Kennedy men initially had to depend on second-rate handlers and sycophants. Nevertheless, they managed to score some victories in the press.

The most notorious pro-Kennedy story appeared in the *New York Times* on April 17. It revealed that the hitherto unidentified rape victim was one Patty Bowman, twenty-nine years old, unmarried and the mother of a two-year-old daughter, who lived in an estimated $250,000 three-bedroom house bought for her by her stepfather, Michael G. O'Neil, the retired head of the General Tire and Rubber company.

Patty, whose parents were divorced when she was thirteen, was born in Akron, Ohio, went to high school in Stow, a few miles northeast of the city. She attended college in Ohio for two years, then moved to Florida, where the climate helped ease the pain of arthritis which set in after she was seriously injured in an auto accident at the age of sixteen.

Meanwhile, her mother, Jean, became a top executive of General Tire and eventually married Mr. O'Neil. Patty lived for a while in Orlando, then moved to Palm Beach, where her daughter was born in 1989. After Mr. O'Neil retired, he and her mother moved to an exclusive development in Jupiter.

In a lengthy article, *New York Times* reporter Fox Butterfield further revealed that Ms. Bowman had been fast in high school, and that she liked to cook, and listen to Bruce Springsteen music, that her home had peach-colored walls, everything down to the titles of the books in Bowman's bedroom. Equivalent information about the accused rapist was never provided. But by far the most controversial item in the article was the revelation of the rape victim's name for the first time in a reputable newspaper.

In a note accompanying the article, the *Times* stated that since the name of the victim had already appeared in the *London Sunday Mirror* and the *Globe* and the *NBC Nightly News*, there was no point in continuing to honor press tradition of not releasing the name. Tom Brokaw, on the *NBC News*, had revealed her name, again on the grounds that it had already been published in the *Globe.*

In the weeks following the alleged rape, Willie issued a terse statement through his attorney, calling the news reports "inaccurate," and claiming, "Any suggestion that I was involved in any offense was erroneous."

Teddy, meanwhile, returned to Washington and attempted to resume his senatorial duties. He had sensed for months that he needed to come to grips with himself, and he made it plain that he was open to advice. One person who was willing to give it was Orrin Hatch, the conservative Republican from Utah, who served on Teddy's Labor and Human Resources Committee and was, incongruously, one of Teddy's closest friends in the Senate. Meeting in Hatch's office several weeks after Palm Beach, the two Senators had discussed Teddy's latest crisis, and Hatch laid it out. "You know what you really need to do, don't you?" he said. "You've got to stop drinking." Kennedy lowered his head and said, "I know."

Teddy did not quit drinking, however.

That summer, while the family waited for the trial to begin, disturbing facts about Willie began to emerge. Prosecutor Moira Lasch found three women who claimed they had been victims of Willie Smith and were willing to take the stand and testify to that under oath.

SMITH VICTIM #1: "I WAS GOING STEADY WITH HIS COUSIN—BUT WILLIE STILL TRIED TO RAPE ME!"

The first young woman claimed that in 1983 while she was dating Max Kennedy, she was introduced to Willie Smith at a party in Manhattan. "He was very friendly," Victim #1 told the Palm Beach County State's Attorney's Office. "And he was very interesting. I remember speaking with him for a long time. He was quite charming. I felt completely comfortable with him. I felt he was in no way trying to come on to me."

She had intended to spend the night with friends, but when they left early, Willie invited her to stay at a guest room in his parents' home. Everything seemed fine until they reached the guest room.

"I mean, one moment he was standing in front of me saying good night, and then the next minute he tackled me onto the bed and was trying to kiss me," she told the state's attorney.

"He had his body completely covering mine and pinned on the bed. From there, he continued to try to put his hands on me. He stayed on top of me, put all his weight on me and tried to kiss me. And he put his hands on my breasts and up my dress."

Victim #1 told the District Attorney's Office that Willie fondled her as she tried to push him off. "I was completely surprised," she recalled. "It was completely unwelcome. I wanted it to stop immediately. I said: 'What are you doing? Stop. Willie, get the hell off of me!' "

Once again, she managed to escape his embrace. She told him she was leaving and started down the stairs.

Then, in a frightening foreshadowing of the Good Friday incident, she also told how Willie tried to convince her that nothing had happened. "He told me that he had just gotten a little carried away and made a pass at me," she said.

Willie grabbed her and tried to stop her from leaving, she added, and pinned her up against the wall.

"I remember being really scared and thinking this is a nightmare," she said. "I think I said I was going to tell his cousin. He said: 'Don't—that's not the way it happened.' "

Frightened, she made her way out to the street. Willie followed, trying to convince her it was just a pass. She spent the night at a friend's home.

The next day she called Max Kennedy and told him the story. But Willie had already called his cousin, apologizing for the "pass" and Max dismissed the incident. It was one of the oldest of Joe Kennedy's rules: Kennedy men had to stick together.

SMITH VICTIM #2: "WITHOUT ANY WARNING WILLIE GRABBED ME BY MY WRISTS."

Victim #1 was not the only woman to recall such an ordeal. Victim #2, a doctor, also told the D.A.'s office about an encounter with Smith. In the spring of 1988, she had been in her third year at Georgetown Medical School. Willie Smith was in his second. She met him at a student party. "He seemed quiet, a very gentlemanly young man," she said in a sworn statement to the state's attorney in Palm Beach. Willie invited her and others to a late party at his family's home in Georgetown. He told her to follow him in her car.

Willie and Victim #2 were the first to arrive at the house. He led her to a small apartment set back from the road and made drinks. Willie suggested that the others might have gone to the pool. "I was frightened," she told the state's attorney. "I thought that if I didn't somehow talk this fellow out of it, I was going to be raped."

She recalled, "We arrived at the back entrance to a pool. Soon after we arrived, he began to take off his clothes. Almost immediately after he was nude, he dove into the pool.

"It was very much of a surprise. I was nervous at that point." Willie tried to get her to join him in the water, but she refused. He got out, put on his clothes and walked her back to the apartment. She went inside to get her purse.

That's when Willie made his move. From being a "reserved, quiet, gentlemanly type at the party, here I saw a complete change in character," Victim #2 said. "Without any warning, he grabbed me by my wrists, threw me over the couch and I landed on the floor on my back, pinned to the floor with him on top of me.

"There was force. He was on top of me. He tried to kiss me and held my hands tight." She was frightened, all too aware that he could easily overpower her.

"I felt like if I struggled, he probably wouldn't have let me up," she said.

"Whereas, if I treated him like a normal person, he might act like a normal person and let me up. So I said to him: 'Willie, you misunderstood something here. I think that you should let me up.' "

She told the D.A.'s Office that Willie replied: "What? There's nothing wrong with this. It's okay." She was terrified, certain that she was about to be raped.

"Well, after I asked him and acted as though it was a normal thing, he did let go of my arms and let me up," she said.

The struggle lasted about ten minutes. Afterward Smith tried to get her to go upstairs. But all she wanted was to get out of his apartment without any more trouble.

Willie walked her to the door, and let her out. She ran to her car and drove home. Shaken, she called a friend who also knew Smith and told him the story.

Ultimately, the judge did not allow these statements to be admitted at Smith's trial because an accused's past cannot be held against him.

In the wake of the Good Friday scandal, Joan was arrested for drunk driving in Quincy, her second arrest in Massachusetts in three years. A judge ordered her to spend the last two weeks of May 1992 in an alcoholic treatment center.

And it was revealed that Patrick had been treated for cocaine addiction in 1986, a fact that was news to voters in his Rhode Island district. Forced to explain the matter to his constituents, Patrick said, "As a teenager, I started down the wrong path in dealing with the pressures of growing up. I mistakenly believed that experimenting with drugs and alcohol would alleviate them."

TEDDY CHANGES HIS POSITION

Teddy had never needed a friend more than that summer 1991. Dragana Lickle had dumped him in April. He took time to heal on the French Riviera, where he had spent such happy times as a child. In St. Tropez he was photographed atop a twenty-two-year-old Marymount University graduate aboard a speedboat owned by game-show tycoon Chuck Barris. The photograph appeared in tabloids around the world. One admiring colleague in the Senate observed to Kennedy, "Well, I see you've changed your position on offshore drilling."

Still, Teddy yearned for a serious relationship. On June 17 he attended a party celebrating the fortieth wedding anniversary of Doris and Edmund Reggie at their summer home on Nantucket. Reggie, a former banker and retired judge of Lebanese extraction, hailed from Crowley, Louisiana, the heart of Cajun country. Long a power in Louisiana Democratic affairs, Reggie was currently under federal indictment for eleven counts of fraud in connection with the 1986 collapse of a Louisiana S&L and a bank. (He was convicted of bank fraud in October 1992.)

There Teddy encountered their daughter, beautiful, brown-eyed Victoria Reggie, thirty-eight, and took her to dinner the following week. Teddy had known Vicki casually since she was ten years old, but now he was looking at an elegant, mature woman.

Vicki Reggie was a whole new Kennedy woman with the kind of assets that impressed all Kennedy men: power and money. A graduate of Sophie Newcomb College, she went on to Tulane Law School where she edited the *Law Review* and graduated *summa cum laude*. Divorced since 1990 from Grier Raclin, a Washington lawyer specializing in telecommunications, she shared custody of their two children: Curran, nine, and Caroline, six.

Unlike the long-suffering Kennedy women, Vicki represented a new generation. During her hard-fought divorce settlement, she extracted annual child-support payments of $62,000, exclusive of school tuition, their $725,000 brick colonial house in Washington, their Nantucket vacation house, and all three automobiles. "Vicki has a lot more balls than Ted ever dreamed of having," said one admirer.

TEDDY EXAMINES CLARENCE

That fall, President George H. W. Bush nominated Clarence Thomas, a justice of the U.S. District of Columbia Court of Appeals, to a seat on the Supreme Court.

As Thomas was preparing for his Senate Judiciary Committee hearings, a former colleague, Anita Hill, was making a confidential statement to the Judiciary Committee, detailing what she claimed was Thomas's pattern of sexual harassment. Later the thirty-five-year-old University of Oklahoma law professor was interviewed by agents of the FBI. A staff member of the committee assured Professor Hill that her statement would be held in confidence and that when it was read to Judge Thomas he would immediately withdraw his name from consideration rather than risk public exposure. Professor Hill left confident that her name would not be mentioned at the hearings and that she would not be called on to testify.

But things did not go according to plan.

Someone leaked her statement to Nina Totenberg of the National Public Radio and to *New York Newsday*. Once Professor Hill's name was revealed, she had to testify.

On October 12–15, the Anita Hill-Clarence Thomas disputation was scheduled for televised hearings. Professor Hill appeared before the committee and charged that Thomas had made sexual advances to her when she was employed by him in two offices between 1981 and 1983. She had worked for him when he had been the supervisor in the Office of Civil Rights of the U.S. Department of Education, and afterward headed the Equal Employment Opportunity Commission.

Professor Hill, a graduate of Yale Law School, also charged that Thomas had discussed a pornographic movie featuring an actor called "Long Dong Silver," as well as films dealing with group sex and women having sex with animals; that he had boasted about the size of his own penis; that on one occasion "he told me graphically of his own sexual prowess"; that he once held up a can of Coca-Cola and demanded, "Who put pubic hair in my Coke?"

Although Senator Teddy was the chairman of the all-white, all-male Judiciary Committee, and a lifelong champion of women's rights, he was forced by his image problems to adopt the posture of near-mute bystander.

Teddy's former aide Richard Burke noted sadly that the Senator, forced into glum silence, was "a classic portrait of a man whose private conduct was forfeiting his public usefulness."

Nevertheless, after the committee voted to approve the nomination and send it to the full Senate for confirmation, Kennedy stirred. Rising to denounce the attacks on Professor Hill, he demanded:

"Are we an old-boys' club—insensitive at best, and perhaps something worse? Will we strain to concoct any excuse? To impose any burden? To tolerate any unsubstantiated attack on a woman in order to rationalize a vote for this nomination? Here in the Senate and in the nation we need to establish a different, better, higher standard."

The reaction was predictable and no one can say that Teddy didn't ask for it. "We do not need characterizations like 'shame' in this chamber from the Senator from Massachusetts," said Senator Arlen Specter (R., Pennsylvania).

Orrin Hatch, defending Republicans from charges that the harsh questioning of Professor Hill was orchestrated by the White House, declared, "The fact of the matter is, anybody who believes that, I know a bridge up in Massachusetts that I'll be happy to sell to them on behalf of the Senator from Massachusetts." (Later Hatch claimed he made an "unfortunate and insensitive mistake," and asked that his remarks be stricken from the record and that "a bridge in Brooklyn" be substituted.)

Millions of Americans watched the hearings on television, or listened to them on the radio. On Tuesday, October 22, the Senate voted to confirm Thomas by 54 to 48, the narrowest majority any Supreme Court justice had received since the turn of the century.

On October 24, after much conferring with advisors, Teddy chose an appearance before the Institute of Politics at the John F. Kennedy School of Government in Cambridge, on the twenty-fifth anniversary of its founding to read the following statement: "I am painfully aware that the criticism directed at me in recent months involved far more than honest disagreement with my positions or the usual criticisms from the far right. It also involved the disappointment of friends and many others who rely on me to fight the good fight.

"To them I say: I recognize my own shortcomings—the faults in the conduct of my private life. I realize that I alone am responsible for them, and I am the one who must confront them. I believe that each of us as individuals must not only struggle to make a better world, but to make ourselves better, too."

"It was a tantalizing tidbit," wrote Michael Putzel in the *Boston Globe*, "but there was little hint of what he thinks those faults are or of how he is working to confront them."

"He seemed to mention it in passing," wrote Curtis Wilkie, also of the *Globe*, "as if he were talking about the fact that he didn't brush after every meal, or failed to clean up his room."

New York columnist Jimmy Breslin chided the senator in a column that equated Teddy with "the classic town drunk" who promises his wife he will never leave her. "It was a speech most other drinkers make with a borrowed quarter," Breslin wrote.

A KENNEDY ON TRIAL

Senator Teddy's public apology was sincere and heartfelt and had nothing to do with any calculated effort to spruce up the image of Kennedy men before jury selection began on Halloween.

By December the case of *the State of Florida v. William Kennedy Smith* was ready to go before a West Palm Beach jury of four women and six men. Willie was charged with two counts of sexual battery (the equivalent of rape under Florida law). If convicted, he faced a maximum sentence of fifteen years. Almost a thousand journalists and broadcasters from all over the globe converged on the West Palm Beach courthouse, and the proceedings were telecast around the world.

Young Willie was represented by a defense team headed by

Roy E. Black, a Miami criminal lawyer considered one of the best in the country. He was paid $250,000 for his services. Cathy "Cat" Bennett, an expert in jury selection, was in a Houston hospital undergoing chemotherapy for breast cancer. She checked out, disregarding doctor's warnings that if she halted the treatment she might have only a month to live. Cat Bennett sat at the defense table throughout the sixteen days of jury selection. Six months after the trial ended, she died.

Things got off to a bad start for the prosecution when Judge Mary E. Lupo ruled that testimony by three previous veterans of the Willie Smith experience could not be admitted.

Ted returned to Palm Beach to testify on December 6. He looked thinner, healthy and sober in his blue suit, blue shirt and muted striped tie.

Unlike so many summer romances, Teddy's relationship with Vicki Reggie had continued after Labor Day. Since June he had been vigorously courting her with flowers, twice-daily phone calls, dates to the theater and Redskins games and, that summer, sailing vacations in the waters off Hyannis Port. He was said to be devoted to Victoria's two children and had even taken them trick-or-treating at Halloween. Vicki coached Ted on his testimony and was sitting in the front row when he took the witness stand. Observers noted that he occasionally caught her eye and smiled slightly.

Keeping to Kennedy tradition, Ted turned to the maudlin as prosecutor Moira Lasch allowed him to describe the sadness that came over him that night. "I lost a brother in the war," he said. "When Jean married Steve, we had another brother. When Steve was gone—something left all of us when we buried him."

"I think he was terrific," Willie commented after.

During the trial twenty-one Kennedys converged on West Palm Beach to show their support in court. Chief among them were Willie's brother, Stephen Smith, Jr., an instructor of international relations at Harvard. He had graduated from Harvard in 1979 and from Columbia Law School in 1983, and was considered something of an intellectual in the family. Stephen's interest in developing countries had been fueled by years of travel, including six months spent working in refugee camps in Thailand and a working stint in Costa Rica with his brother Willie.

Also present were Willie's adopted sisters, Amanda, twenty-five, who was enrolled in Harvard's Ph.D. program for special education, and Kym, twenty, a student at Brown. For the most part they refused comment, but Stephen exploded when his late father was cited in the usually Kennedy-friendly *People* magazine for his "notoriously indiscreet womanizing" and treating his wife "like dirt."

"My father never, ever treated my mother 'like dirt,' " Stephen, Jr., wrote to the magazine. "My recollection of my parents' marriage is of a warm and loving relationship which deepened over time." *People*'s response: "The story speaks for itself."

Jean Kennedy Smith attended her son's trial every day. John Kennedy, Jr., attended one session and denied reports that he had done so under family pressure, i.e., that his mother had been told that unless he appeared, there would be no family support if he ever decided to run for public office. "No one in my family ever pressured me to attend," he insisted. "I went to Florida because I wanted to go, and it wasn't to get a tan." Jackie remained conspicuous by her absence.

The trial took nine days. On December 11 the Kennedys and the Smiths and their attorneys had barely arrived at the mansion after the jury received the case, when they were summoned back. Deliberating only one hour and seventeen minutes, the jury acquitted Willie of all charges.

The Kennedys had won the case, but it remains to be seen whether they won the war. Certainly, the family's reputation took a major hit. Was this "The End of the Line" for Teddy, as *Esquire* suggested? Surely, only the most hard-core Kennedy loyalists could argue with *Time* magazine that the case "echoes an old pattern of recklessness, evasion and irresponsibility."

Willie Smith was not the only Kennedy man who had reason to celebrate that Christmas. Teddy's gift to Vicki Reggie that Christmas was the gift of the 1990s: a personal trainer. Clearly, things were getting serious.

Putting the trial behind him, young Willie went forward with his residency in internal medicine at the University of New Mexico Hospital in Albuquerque. A mystery blonde was a frequent visitor, telling nosy neighbors that she was his wife, Kelly Smith. The couple soon became so open about their relationship that when Willie ran in a marathon, she tagged along as his water girl.

The public got its first official sighting of Teddy and his new love in February 1992 at his sixtieth birthday party. It was a costume gala at his home in McLean, and the Senator dressed as Rhett Butler, Vicki as Scarlett O'Hara. (Willie Smith came as Elvis.) "They radiated happiness," said Washington Lee Fentress, an old friend of Ted. "He's in great shape, working very hard and very much in love."

Teddy had reportedly lost twenty-five pounds in the nine months he had been seeing Vicki. It was said that Vicki had even managed to get Teddy to cut his alcohol consumption down to two drinks a day, not counting white wine.

All this was covered in the media with the traditional positive spin. *People* magazine even reported that Teddy attended mass with Victoria and her children.

On March 16 Teddy announced their engagement with a simple but moving statement: "I love Victoria and her children very much, and she has brought enormous happiness into my life." Her engagement ring was a huge sapphire surrounded by diamonds.

In Boston, Joan was stunned. She, like most of the public, had known nothing about the romance. When a reporter from the *Boston Herald* called with the joyful news, her only comment was, "Oh? Is that true?"

When she was assured that it was, Joan replied, "I can't talk now," and hung up. After that she remained secluded in her apartment for weeks. Later a friend told *People:* "I know she wishes him the best."

The announcement also drew attention because both Teddy and Vicki were divorced Catholics with ex-spouses who were very much alive. Under canon law neither was free to remarry without church annulments of their previous marriages. As Cardinal Bernard Law of Boston explained that "in the eyes of the church," Teddy was still married to Joan.

Nevertheless, on Friday afternoon, July 3, thirty family members and friends of their families gathered at the Senator's McLean home for the wedding. They were married by Judge A. David Mazzone under a portrait of Old Joe. Teddy was in a dark suit and small-figured blue tie, Vicki in a short-sleeved, knee-length dress of handmade white lace over white silk and carrying three pink and white roses.

With typical Kennedy enthusiasm, Teddy rushed to kiss his new wife.

"Hey, I'm not finished," the judge said, then completed the ceremony and added, "You may kiss the bride." This time the couple kissed passionately while the gathered celebrants applauded.

After a dinner on the enclosed terrace, and a toast from Ted, Jr.: "I can't remember the last time I saw my dad so happy," he said. "And it is all due to Vicki." The couple left for a brief honeymoon in Stowe, Vermont.

When they returned, Vicki moved into the McLean house. Ted also purchased a two-bedroom condominium at 17 Marlborough Street in Boston, not far from Joan's apartment. Vicki's son and daughter were enrolled in the exclusive Maret School in Washington, where tuition is $10,500 a year.

And Vicki returned to her job with Keck, Mahin & Cate.

TEDDY'S THIRD PUBLIC CONFESSION

The marriage came in the nick of time, because Teddy's image was in the worst shape it had been since Chappaquiddick. An August 1991 telephone poll conducted by the *Boston Herald* and WCVB-TV, showed how dramatically his popularity had plummeted. In 1988 Ted had been swept back into office in a landslide, winning slightly more than two-thirds of the votes. The new survey reported that sixty-two percent of the voters believed that Ted should be replaced in the Senate. Only thirty-four percent said they favored his reelection.

By July 1992 a concerned Teddy was making himself and his new bride available for interviews on every outlet from the *Today* show to the *Cape Cod Times*. Attorney Vicki even posed in the kitchen for the *New York Times*.

Much of this effort was mounted to counteract publication of *The Senator: My Ten Years with Ted Kennedy* in which Teddy's former aide Richard E. Burke detailed a decade of womanizing and substance abuse. The book, highly promoted at the American Booksellers Association convention in Anaheim that June, was scheduled for fall publication by Putnam, a division of Hollywood leviathan MCA-Universal, which was in turn owned by the Japanese conglomerate Matsushita. Suddenly the book was yanked from that house's schedule. Kennedy allies characterized Burke, who had been the Senator's closest aide for a decade, as "a complete lunatic," who had resigned from his post in 1981 after he admitted that he had fabricated a series of hoaxes. Burke himself blamed his behavior on the stress of the job and the heavy drug use he indulged in with the Senator. The book was quickly picked up and published by St. Martin's Press, a small publishing house known for its independent spirit.

For all Teddy's past substance abuse and marital problems, his children seem to be on the right track now. Kara has been married since 1990 to Michael Allen. Skilled in audiovisual techniques, she has become a producer for Very Special Arts, her aunt Jean's non-profit organization to help the physically and emotionally challenged get into fine-arts institutes around the country.

In June, after obtaining a master's degree from the Yale University School of Forestry and Environmental Studies, where he majored in ecology, thirty-one-year-old Teddy, Jr., signed himself into the Institute for Living in Hartford, Connecticut, to deal with his alcohol problem. "At times, life has presented me with some difficult challenges, and I am doing my best to face up to them," he said in a prepared statement. "My decision to seek help was based on my belief that continued use of alcohol is imparing my ability to achieve the goals I care about." He remained active in his foundation, Facing the Challenge, which promotes self-help programs which encourage disabled persons to achieve their full potential in life.

Teddy, Jr., also became the director of community projects for the lead-detection program of Yale Medical School's pediatrics department.

His younger brother Patrick continued to pursue his political career with vigor. He won a second term in 1990 and a third in 1991.

With all the young Kennedy's interested in political careers, one former RFK aide has quipped: "In ten years, there could be a Kennedy caucus in Congress."

JOHN, JR., SAVES DARYL HANNAH FROM JACKSON BROWNE

In the fall a beautiful woman in distress turned to John, Jr., for help. Movie star Daryl Hannah had known John since the early 1980s when both were vacationing in St. Maarten in the Caribbean with their families. They ran into each other again at the 1988 wedding of his aunt Lee Radziwill to director Herbert Ross, who had worked with Daryl in *Steel Magnolias*. Though they were seen together after that, John also continued to date a string of others. And Daryl continued to live with her lover of nearly a decade, singer Jackson Browne, forty-two, whom she first met as a teenager when he pulled her onstage from the audience at a Chicago concert.

In September a domestic quarrel at the house Daryl and Browne shared in Santa Monica erupted in violence. "According to close friends of Hannah," *People* magazine reported, "she ended up with a black eye, a broken finger and numerous bruises, although she never pressed charges against Browne."

"I saw her shortly after the hospital," said her uncle, director Haskell Wexler, "I saw the damage that was done to her. The doctor was very concerned. Jackson was a very, very good friend of mine, but when I saw Daryl, I just felt betrayed."

John immediately flew to her side and brought her back to New York. Since then, Daryl has traveled with John to Providence for his tenth reunion at Brown, and he has visited her on the Los Angeles set of her HBO movie *Attack of the 50-Foot Woman*.

When John resigned from his $40,000-a-year job in the Manhattan District Attorney's Office in July, he threw a stag party for six of his colleagues at a New York steakhouse, the Old Homestead. Daryl joined them for dessert. He soon moved from his downtown penthouse and into her rambling Upper West Side apartment.

Newlywed Teddy showed up at his 1992 Christmas party for current and former staff members with his new bride. He traditionally arrived in costume (except for the year of Willie Smith's legal troubles). At one party during the Bush administration, bachelor Teddy had appeared as a scantily clad half of Milli Vanilli. When someone asked if he was Milli or Vanilli, he answered: "I must be Vanilli—Millie got fixed." This year the couple appeared as Beauty and the Beast, as if to underscore the fairy-tale aspects of their happy union.

SENATOR MIKULSKI: "TEDDY'S ONE OF THE GREAT GALAHADS OF THE U.S. SENATE."

On July 3, 1993, Tony Shriver married Cuban-born Alina Mojica, whom he had met at a Best Buddies cocktail party in 1991. She was already the mother of a three-year-old son, Teddy, by a previous marriage.

Gearing up for his 1994 Senate reelection, Teddy's campaign flew the nation's five Democratic women Senators to Boston for a thousand-dollar-a-plate luncheon for Teddy. "Their praise of Kennedy, given the simultaneous roles he had played on the Judiciary Committee and as a witness for a very aggressive defense in Palm Beach, seemed unintentionally ironic, if not ridiculous," commented *The New Yorker*, "especially [Barbara] Mikulski's assessment of Kennedy as 'one of the great Galahads of the United States Senate.' " That characterization prompted the Boston *Herald*'s Jeff Jacoby to remind readers, "Galahad was the *chaste* knight of the Round Table."

Several Kennedy partisans admitted that running against a woman would create special problems for Teddy. "There's no question that a woman presents some challenges," acknowledged campaign advisor John Sasso.

Joan, shattered by her ex-husband's remarriage, had started drinking again. Observers whispered about her condition after a February TV interview that was filmed during intermission at a Boston Symphony gala. "People gossiped about how she looked," said one insider. "She seemed pretty drunk." No one was surprised when she secretly checked herself into another detox clinic, Proctor House—part of the exclusive McLean Hospital in Belmont, Massachusetts, near Boston, after a major drinking binge. On her release from the $1,400-a-day haven for alcoholics and drug addicts, she returned to a low-profile life at her home on Cape Cod. "It's so nice to be sober again," she said.

Joan was still on probation for a drunk-driving offense. "Joan wasn't looking too good when she got here. But the staff seemed to know her from previous visits and she settled in quickly," said a fellow patient. "She's been here four times now—this last time for forty-five days."

Proctor House was considered one of the world's finest rehab centers, where each of its twenty-two patients received personalized treatment.

"I'd always held out some slim hope he'd come back to me," a tearful Joan, fifty-six, told fellow patients as she recalled the day when she learned that the senator would soon make Victoria Reggie his second wife.

"When I heard about the engagement, it was just too much," Joan sighed. "It made me realize how alone I was and seeing Ted with this young woman, who has a career and a family ahead of her, made me think how little I had to look forward to. It sounds pathetic, but alcohol was all I had."

In July the Kennedy's gathered in Hyannis Port for Rose's 103rd birthday. To celebrate the event, more than seventy-five family and friends sported Rose T-shirts, white shirts with the legend "Happy 103rd Birthday ROSE Fitzgerald Kennedy." In place of her name was the picture of a big red rose. Ted, her last surviving son, gave his mother 103 pink roses, a huge cake and a poem he had written just for her.

Sadly, a series of strokes had left Rose confined to a wheelchair and nearly comatose, but the family maintained that she was still "reasonably alert."

Soon after, John and Daryl took off for what was supposed to be an idyllic trip to the South Seas, a six-week trek across the Caroline Islands in Micronesia. During the four-hour flight from Los Angeles to Honolulu, John and Daryl necked, oblivious to the stares of their fellow passengers in first class. From Honolulu they flew on to Guam, and then to Palau Island in Micronesia. After eight days of swimming, walking and kayaking, they took off to tour the Philippines, Hong Kong, Vietnam and Bali, before they returned to the United States in September. Rumors flew that they were married or planning to marry, but nothing happened.

1993 was certainly a marrying year for the Kennedy family. On October 10 they gathered on Block Island to celebrate the wedding of law student Teddy, Jr., to Katherine "Kiki" Gershman, a psychiatrist and assistant professor at Yale.

The celebration marked the first time that the Senator's first and second wives had crossed paths, and friends were concerned that sparks would fly. Both women behaved with dignity and grace. "Vicki and Joan are very cordial with each other, and worked very hard together," said a Kennedy spokeswoman. "Joan and Ted's divorce was very civilized and was done with class. Joan even gave the Senator and Vicki a special toast during the rehearsal dinner."

During the festivities Max Kennedy, twenty-eight, and his wife, Vicki, introduced their twenty-day-old son Max, Jr. "Meet the youngest Kennedy," boasted Max, an assistant district attorney in Philadelphia. Even Willie Smith turned up, but the most notable guests were John Kennedy, Jr., and Daryl Hannah. His mother and sister were conspicuous by their absences. But if they wanted to indicate that they disapproved of the relationship, they needn't have bothered. It was clear to all that Daryl was not going to last much longer.

Only a week before, John had kept the movie star waiting for a half hour at a New York City rock concert. When he finally showed up, Daryl screamed: "That's the last time I'm waiting for you! You're so inconsiderate! I've been standing here forever." She and the clearly mortified John went inside, but didn't speak throughout the concert. He privately complained to friends that Daryl was possessive and jealous. The couple attended the wedding, but Daryl only stayed for an hour at the reception before John took her to a waiting private plane. It was with obvious relief that he turned back to having a good time with his cousins.

William Kennedy Smith also continued to make news. In July he cut short his residency in New Mexico, just as the first of twenty-one victims of the mysterious Hanta virus began arriving at a specially sealed wing of his Albuquerque hospital. He told his family that he was very depressed and frustrated treating patients with the deadly viral disease and was switching to the Northwestern Rehabilitation Institute in Chicago where he would treat patients recovering from strokes, spinal cord damage and other injuries.

"Dr. Smith completed one year of his internal medicine residency, and although it's a three-year program, he opted to go elsewhere," said a spokesperson at the University of New Mexico Medical Center.

The blond mystery woman who had sat silently offering her support during his rape trial was finally identified by television's *Hard Copy* as Kelly Squier, the stunning wife of Washington, D.C., lobbyist Mark Squier. They met after twenty-eight-year-old Kelly went to work for Senator Kennedy.

It was reported that she had dated JFK, Jr., first, until she was drawn to Willie. Romance blossomed during his trial.

According to *Hard Copy*, now that Willie was doing his residency in Chicago, Kelly often visited him at his town house there, while her husband stayed in Bethesda, Maryland.

JOE II'S EX CHARGES: "HE'S BRANDING OUR KIDS ILLEGITIMATE."

Yet another Kennedy scandal hit the fan on Easter weekend when Sheila Rauch Kennedy, Joe II's former wife, got a letter from the Boston diocese informing her that he was asking for an annulment. She feared that would make their two sons, now twelve, illegitimate. Even more painful, the congressman had not approached her in person.

"He didn't come to me. He had the Catholic Church send me a notice in the mail," she said. "It was devastating, but subtlety's never been one of Joe's strong points."

It was no secret that Joe sought the annulment so that he could marry Anne Elizabeth "Beth" Kelly, thirty-six, a longtime member of his staff.

An Episcopalian, Sheila had married Joe in the Catholic Church and promised to raise their children in the Catholic faith. If Joe succeeded in getting his annulment, in the eyes of the Church, his marriage to Sheila would never have existed.

"I will continue to defend the bond that brought my children into the world," Sheila maintained. "I know of few mothers who would do any less. I'm not going to lie in front of God so Joe can have a big Catholic wedding. I feel it would be wrong.

"I don't blame Joe for wanting to get on with his life," Sheila told Bob Michals of the *Globe*. "But you can't just say: 'There was never anything there to begin with—it just took me more than 20 years to figure it out.' "

The whole matter seemed ridiculous to Sheila.

"If I give Joe what he wants, I would be lying before God about the birth and conception of our children," she said, confident that justice was on her side. "The people at the Archdiocese of Boston have been very helpful and friendly to me, so I don't have any ax to grind with them."

For the first time Sheila spoke publicly about the breakup of her marriage and blamed it squarely on politics. "The more he got into being the standard-bearer of the Kennedy legacy, the less interested he was in a woman who had her own opinion about things."

Although Joe II was part of the baby-boomer generation, in private life he turned out to be just as much the sexual Neanderthal that his grandfather, father and uncles were. "He preferred women who were part of the 'team,' " said Sheila. "And who basically did what he told them to do. That wasn't me."

WILLIE'S BARROOM BRAWL:
"HE WAS OUT OF CONTROL."

Kelly Squier was with Willie when he was arrested on October 22, after a barroom brawl in Arlington, Virginia.

"He came in with a redheaded woman after midnight," said an eyewitness at the Bardo Rodeo Brew Pub, where a cornerstone of the decor is a car smashing through a glass window.

He was recognized as he ordered a beer, and word soon spread. Another patron yelled: "Hey, it's Willie the rapist!"

Willie tried to walk away, but the inebriated gentleman followed him yelling, "Look out, girls, it's Willie the rapist!" and "You got lucky, Willie!"

Willie and the redhead sat down in a booth, and the heckler joined them, uninvited, and whispered something.

There was shoving and Willie asked the man if he wanted to step outside.

"I felt bad for Willie because he was minding his own business," the bar's manager later told the *Star*. "He wasn't at all drunk, but the guy who insulted him certainly was.

"We could see there could be trouble, so I pulled the guy over to one side and another bouncer, 6' 6" Hank Cochran, took Willie outside through the glass front door.

"As Hank followed him out, Willie just swung out of nowhere—a huge, blind roundhouse punch right to Hank's nose.

"There was no provocation," added the manager. "We were just trying to help him. Hank's nose started pouring blood and he was totally stunned, lying on the floor."

Another witness marveled at the way Smith—who had spent the first part of the night in a nearby Italian restaurant, laughing it up with his stunning date—went from mild-mannered to manic in the twinkling of an eye.

"He suddenly turned from a human being into an animal," said Cochran.

"Then Hank got up and jumped on Willie and they started going at it. Willie just went crazy. He just couldn't let it go. He wanted a fight. It took four of us to hold him down," added the employee. "He was like a madman. We decided we'd had enough and called the cops.

"Then the enraged bouncer punched Willie a couple of times and slammed him up against the brick wall.

"Both their faces were covered with blood by the time the cops arrived."

Eyewitnesses said that before police arrived, Smith twice tried to escape bar staff who were holding him. He was arrested and charged with assault and battery. "He was totally out of control!" bartender Peter Evans told the *Enquirer*.

Hauled off to jail in Arlington, Virginia, Willie missed his cousin Joe II's wedding later that day. He faced a year in jail and $2,500 in fines if convicted on assault, battery and misdemeanor charges.

Willie and Cochran, who had a suspected broken nose, refused medical aid and were driven two blocks to the police station to appear before night-duty judge Edd Wilson.

"Smith was very apologetic and said he was sorry," said Wilson. "He wasn't drunk and was very polite."

Others disagreed. Joe Mullins of the *Enquirer* revealed that Willie had actually been drinking for hours before the fight broke out. And bartender Evans flatly declared: "Smith was drunk."

Willie pleaded no contest to assault and battery charges. He was sentenced to a year's probation and one hundred hours of community service at a Chicago health clinic. Cochran filed a $500,000 civil suit against Smith, but the case was finally settled out of court on July 27, 1994, a day before it was scheduled to go to trial.

In a statement released by his attorney, Gregory B. Craig, Willie said: "My friends and I were hassled, baited and insulted by people who wanted to pick a fight with me. It was a difficult situation, and I wanted to defend myself. I regret what happened."

Never known for his patience, Joe II soon grew tired of waiting for his Catholic annulment and finally wed his longtime personal assistant Beth Kelly in a twenty-minute civil ceremony. A justice of the peace united the two in the foyer of Joe's rambling Victorian home. Among the 140 guests were at least two priests, however: Father Michael Kennedy, a distant cousin, and exiled Haitian president Father Jean Bertrand Aristide, who read from the Bible and later toasted the newlyweds. Also present were Ethel, and Joe's brothers Robert, Jr., Michael, Max, Christopher and Douglas, and his sisters Kathleen Townsend, Kerry Kennedy Cuomo, Rory and Courtney with her husband Paul Hill. Aunt Patricia Lawford and cousin Patrick Kennedy were there along with his uncle Ted, without his new wife Vicki. But John F. Kennedy, Jr., and his girlfriend Daryl Hannah stayed away, possibly spooked by the hordes of paparazzi that had stalked them at Teddy, Jr.'s, Block Island wedding two weeks earlier.

Joe was "the talk of the day," said Chris Walker, who sang "I Am the Bread of Life" for the couple. "He was cracking jokes and making everybody laugh."

After the ceremony the newlyweds joined their guests in the backyard for a sumptuous buffet that included, at the special request of the bride and groom, Triscuits with peanut butter and bacon bits.

Kennedy pocket historian and political advisor Doris Kearns Goodwin summed it up best: "Everyone had the feeling that this was the right thing for them."

A KENNEDY WEDS AN ACCUSED ASSASSIN

In 1993 Kennedy men made news for controversial second trips to the altar and barroom brawls, but it was a Kennedy woman who made perhaps the most sensational news of all. If Bobby's sons, Joe II, Bobby, Jr., and the late David, made news because they continued the patterns of Kennedy men, it was Bobby's daughter Courtney who broke whole new ground in independence, first, by dissolving her marriage to Jeffrey Ruhe in 1991, and in 1993 by adding a convicted murderer to the family.

On June 26 Courtney and Paul Hill (out on bail appealing his murder conviction) were married in the Aegean Sea on a yacht owned by Greek TV magnate Vardis Vardinoyannis—who performed the ceremony himself. They planned to build a house in County Clare.

TEDDY: "THEY DON'T CALL ME TYRANNOSAURUS SEX FOR NOTHING!"

The Senator ended the year 1993 on a gay note. He showed up in a giant purple Barney costume, he entertained guests at his annual Christmas bash. His wife Vicki came dressed as a little girl, complete with blond braids, baby-doll dress and singing the Barney theme song. The couple performed in a skit in which Teddy got to quip, "They don't call me 'Tyrannosaurus Sex' for nothing." Mrs. Kennedy described how the astronauts tried to screw new parts into the Hubble Space Telescope and Teddy remarked: "Floating screw—that's what people used to call me."

"It was dirtier than usual," one eyewitness told the *New York Post*.

The revelers packed into the Senate Labor Committee meeting

room. Grown-ups loved it, but one toddler screamed when Teddy ripped off his Barney mask to reveal his own face.

In February 1994 Courtney Kennedy Ruhe Hill paraded through the fortified streets of Belfast in a motorcade with her husband on the way to the courthouse. The success of the film *In the Name of the Father*, which purported to tell how Hill and three companions were framed by British prosecutors for the 1974 pub bombing in Guildford, England, had focused new attention on Hill's murder conviction. Hill argued that physical and psychological abuse by English police led him to confess to helping kidnap and kill a former British soldier in Belfast in 1974. A flock of Kennedy relatives, including Ethel, joined Courtney as she sat with Hill in the Belfast courtroom.

Their presence reflected the Kennedy family's increasingly active role in the volatile issue of Northern Ireland. For years militant American supporters of a unified Ireland had criticized Teddy for not taking a more forthright nationalist stance. Now the family was taking the lead. The Senator and his sister Jean Kennedy Smith, the new U.S. Ambassador to Ireland, had both played critical roles in persuading President Clinton to grant Sinn Féin president Gerry Adams a visa to enter the United States. And Jean had created an international incident just months earlier when she crossed into Northern Ireland to observe the traditional juryless trial of seven teenage boys charged with a three-year-old Belfast bombing. American activists had long criticized such trials because of the absence of a jury, and they took her visit as a clear signal of the family's support.

In April the appeals court overturned Hill's murder conviction. The judge declared that "a confession obtained by improper means must still be excluded even if the court may consider it true." As the ruling was read, Hill sat between Courtney and Ethel. He clasped hands with each in turn when the verdict was announced. Afterward he announced that he was suing the British authorities for malicious prosecution.

Another Kennedy marriage collapsed when Robert F. Kennedy, Jr., secretly flew to the Dominican Republic on the morning of March 24 for a nine A.M. divorce hearing in Santo Domingo, then left the following day. Under Dominican law, foreigners can obtain divorces in a matter of hours, and thousands of people go there each year for that purpose.

Bobby, Jr., and Emily Black had been separated since 1992 and had two children, Robert III (1984) and Kathleen Alexandra (1988).

On September 19 Rory's first film, a documentary she produced and directed with Robin Smith about the struggles of drug-addicted women during pregnancy and motherhood, had its premiere at the Time & Life Building in New York. The film focused on three women. "Personal stories are the most compelling way to make a point," said Rory at an August press conference to promote interest in the film. "I felt that if their voices and stories could be brought directly to the public, we might have a better chance to improve opportunities for the women."

Rory became interested in the plight of drug-addicted mothers while she majored in women's studies at Brown University. "I learned that pregnant addicts have great difficulty getting into treatment," she said. "There is a tendency to moralize and blame the addicts, yet we're not providing them with services to recover."

As the younger generation of Kennedy's moved in directions that Joe and Rose could never have imagined, one of the most beloved figures of the Kennedy era was near death. In February 1994 the intensely private Jacqueline Onassis announced that she had been diagnosed with non-Hodgkin's lymphoma, a cancer of the lymphatic system, but was in remission. By March the cancer was back and had spread to her brain. She was weak, confused and complained of pains in her legs. Yet as late as April, she was going to her office at Doubleday.

Jackie's longtime companion, Maurice Tempelsman, stood by her as the disease ravaged her body. "He would help her into the examining room, help her walk to the ladies' room," said one hospital staffer. "He was always holding her hand or caressing her cheek."

By May the cancer had spread to her liver, and on May 18 she was discharged from the hospital and allowed to go home in accordance with the living will she had signed in February, which asked that no extraordinary measures be taken if her illness was grave. Visited by a stream of relatives and friends, she died the following night, May 19.

The next morning, John, Jr., faced the hundreds of reporters and spectators who lined the street outside his mother's apartment building and read a brief statement. "Last night, at around 10:15, my mother passed on," he said. "She was surrounded by her friends and family and her books and the people and the things that she loved. And she did it in her own way, and we all feel lucky for that, and now she's in God's hands."

John and Caroline planned their mother's May 23 funeral with her attention to detail, ordering white peonies to adorn the altar at St. Ignatius Loyala on Park Avenue, where Jackie had been baptized and confirmed. They personally called or sent hand-delivered invitations to some seven hundred family members, politicians and friends.

John read from the book of Isaiah. Caroline recited one of her mother's favorite Edna St. Vincent Millay poems. After reading "Ithaka" by the Greek poet C.P. Cavafy, Tempelsman bid Jackie a sad farewell. "And now the journey is over," he said, "too short, alas, too short." Lee's daughter, Tina Radziwill, gave a reading, and her son, Anthony Radziwill, was an honorary pallbearer. (The following August, Anthony would marry an ABC Network colleague, Carole Ann DiFalco, and dedicate the nuptial mass at Most Holy Trinity Church in East Hampton to his aunt and his father.)

After the service her body was transported on a chartered 737 Boeing jet from New York to Washington, where a motorcade of motorcycles, buses and limousines escorted Jackie through the black iron gates of Arlington National Cemetery.

Jackie, in a mahogany casket covered with ferns and a cross of white lillies-of-the-valley, was laid to rest between her husband Jack and her stillborn daughter. Her son Patrick, who died two days after his birth in 1963, lay on the former president's other side.

Among those present at Arlington was President Bill Clinton who said: "God gave her very great gifts and imposed upon her great burdens. She bore them all with dignity and grace and uncommon common sense."

As Jackie's friends and family knelt to touch her coffin one last time, filing past the eternal flame that she herself first lit three decades earlier, sixty-four bells rang out from the Washington National Cathedral across the Potomac, one for each year of her extraordinary life. Then the black limousines drove out of the gates, and the crowds began slowly to scatter.

Her will contained a few surprises. Her sister Lee was cut out completely, but Anthony and Tina Radziwill would continue to receive income from $500,000 trust funds Jackie had set up for them.

Casting grief aside that summer, the Kennedys had their traditional summer reunion at Hyannis Port. Among the throng was the newest arrival, Teddy's granddaughter Kiley Elizabeth, born August 6, to Teddy, Jr., and Kiki. Teddy, Jr., was currently attending Yale Law School. Even seventy-six-year-old Rosemary was allowed to visit for a month with her nurse. She spent hours sitting in the sun with her comatose mother.

TED CLASHES WITH POPE: DEMANDS FEMALE PRIESTS

Senator Teddy was in for the toughest race of his Senate career, as he faced the first serious challenger since he beat Ed McCormack in his first primary. Although it has been said that Teddy would "have to hit the pope and pee on the Irish flag to lose his Senate seat," it was his unfortunate luck that the campaign was happening during the twenty-fifth anniversary of Chappaquiddick. And this time his opponent was Mitt Romney, a fresh-faced Mormon family man and self-made millionaire, son of George Romney, the former governor of Michigan and onetime presidential candidate.

But Teddy was ready: his face puffy and flushed, his blue eyes rheumy and red-rimmed, his hands shaking more noticeably than ever, like an old warhorse, he stirred for one last race. Since late 1993 he had been traveling the country to raise campaign funds. Seven months before the election he had already raised $5 million, more than any other Senator running for reelection, and more than he had spent on his last campaign.

Teddy was buoyed by his new bride. "It's obvious that Vicki's made an enormous difference in my life," he told Peter J. Boyer of *The New Yorker*. She had "brought a great sense of happiness, inner kinds of serenity, and a sense of joy and optimism and hope. And that's obviously affected me very deeply personally, and, I think, my own relationship with family and friends, and I'm sure in terms of my effectiveness as a member of the Senate." To Boyer, Vicki Reggie was "a direct answer to the character issue, living evidence that Kennedy's raucous bachelorhood is over."

In family tradition Teddy had chosen a member of the family as his campaign manager. Michael, considered one of the steadiest of Ethel and Bobby's children, displayed a gift for politics. In April he managed to persuade star Alec Baldwin to appear on Teddy's behalf at several Boston college campuses, an effort that yielded fourteen hundred campaign volunteers.

"You know, there aren't too many people in this state without an opinion on my uncle," said Michael. "And that's both positive and negative."

Teddy was so desperate that shortly after Labor Day he came out in open opposition to Pope John Paul II. Only three months after the Pope declared that Catholics must accept that the priesthood was open only to men, Teddy announced that he supported allowing women to become priests.

"I count myself among the growing number of Catholics who support the ordination of women as priests," Senator Kennedy said in a brief statement issued by his Boston campaign headquarters.

Many Kennedy loyalists were no doubt heartened by Teddy's affirmation of faith. In the years of his philandering, his divorce and remarriage outside the Church and his assistance in covering up abuse of women from Chappaquiddick to Palm Beach, some of them might have occasionaly questioned their faith in this prominent Catholic layman. Now they could rest easy, for he had publicly taken a courageous stand on a matter of Catholic dogma. There is no reason to suppose that this stand had anything to do with the fact that his Republican opponent Mitt Romney was a member of the Church of Jesus Christ of Latter-day Saints that did not ordain women to its lay priesthood.

Lest anyone label Teddy a Catholic-basher, his brief three-paragraph statement included some praise for the Catholic Church's improved treatment of women. "I am heartened by the increasingly prominent official role that Catholic women are being given in the Church," he said. "I am also proud of their growing leadership in other important activities of the Church, such as health, education and social welfare."

Not everyone welcomed Teddy's praise. Helen Hull Hitchcock, executive director of Women for Faith and Family, which supported the Vatican's position on women's ordination, took a dim view of Teddy's statement. "What does being a Catholic mean if it doesn't mean you accept the teachings of that particular religion?" she asked. "I think it will have no effect on anybody," she said.

In the toughest race of his career, Teddy found himself under attack as an advocate of an outdated liberal philosophy which Romney blamed for soaring out-of-wedlock births, illegal immigration and violent crime. He was even forced to take part in a series of televised debates. During the first, Teddy became indignant when Romney suggested he had gotten a sweetheart deal in a Washington real estate investment. He turned to his challenger and declared: "Mr. Romney, the Kennedys are not in public service to make money. We have paid too high a price."

Teddy's references to his family's sacrifices also touched a chord with his opponents, who acknowledge that they were not only running against him, but against the entire Kennedy history. Republican Joe Malone observed that "I think the most difficult part of it is the legacy of Bobby and Jack and the love for Rose Kennedy." He recalled a 1988 fund-raising event, where he was working the room for money to pay off the debt he'd incurred in his losing cause, when someone told him to take a look at a documentary that was playing on one of the local television stations. "It was a half-hour show that covered everything from Jack's war record to his funeral, and everything else," Malone said. "I don't know if the timing was just a coincidence, but at the time I felt, here I am, killing myself to get a thirty-second ad on, and the ad costs five thousand dollars, and here he's got a thirty-minute ad, in effect, for free. So that comes to mind when I think about running against Teddy Kennedy."

JOAN TO TED: "I NEED MORE MONEY!"

To make the struggle worse, Joan chose September to press the Senator for more money. Joan had already met twice with Ted to discuss a more equitable agreement, but nothing came of it. Joan realized that she would have to go to court. She retained high-profile divorce attorney Monroe Inker to determine whether she had been shortchanged in her 1982 divorce settlement. "I want to get all the data from the lawyers involved in the original case and then determine if there was a substantial injustice," said Inker.

Joan was reportedly still seething at Teddy's attempt to seek an annulment of their marriage so that his second marriage to Victoria Reggie, who was twenty years younger than Joan, would be recognized by the Catholic church.

It was said that Joan was trying to force Ted to give her more money because she had gone through the $5 million he paid her when they divorced. And Ted, facing the toughest election of his career, was furious, fearing the negative publicity could end his career.

"He believes Joan wants to publicly embarrass him in the middle of a tough campaign so he'll throw more money at her to shut her up," said one insider.

Privately the sixty-two-year-old Senator complained to friends that Joan was using political blackmail.

Immediately after the divorce, Joan had spent nearly $1 million renovating the Beacon Hill condo. Since then she had been spending money like water.

According to journalist Patricia Towle, some of the money had gone to pay for Joan's stays in detox, but there had been luxuries, too. "Joan spends around $100,000 a year on clothing," one source told Towle. "She wears mostly designer clothes and uses a designer whose creations can cost $10,000 a dress. She also spends close to $200,000 a year on staff salaries and the maintenance of her two properties. And her travels run another $100,000 a year. She loves trips to exotic places and always goes first class.

"In the winter, she goes skiing in Aspen. During the summer, she flies to Austria for the Salzburg Music Festival. She also tries to go to Italy at least once a year. She recently visited Turin, Flor-

ence, Rome and Venice. She jets to London frequently. She spends
several weeks each year at her favorite spa, which costs as much
as $10,000 a week."

And then there was "entertainment." "Joan spends at least another $100,000 a year on entertainment," said Towle's source.
"She frequently goes back and forth between Boston and New
York City for plays and concerts. If she continues spending at her
current rate, she'll go broke."

Friends had noticed that for the last two summers Joan had
rented out the Squaw Island house for most of the season. And
even if she sold the summer place and the Boston condo, it
wouldn't be nearly enough to cover her forever.

This was coming at a time when Teddy was being forced to
fight harder than ever to hang on to his Senate seat. In one Massachusetts poll, a staggering sixty-two percent of the people said it
was time for a change.

Joan's lawyer had already gained access to the sealed divorce
settlement files and he was trying to get jurisdiction transferred
from Cape Cod, where TV cameras are not allowed in court, to
Boston, where TV crews could broadcast hearings.

Teddy finally succeeded in getting Joan to hold off on demanding more money until after the November election. Days after declaring that she was reexamining the divorce settlement, Joan
announced that she would postpone the court proceedings until
after the November 8 election.

"Ted must have been sweating bullets at the very thought of it
all," said Margery Eagan, a political columnist for the *Boston Herald*. "Can you imagine the headlines? 'Joan Claims: Ted Cheated
Me!' or 'Joan Charges: Kennedys Bought Me Out!' "

All her attorney would say was that Joan had sworn him to secrecy about the reason for her change of mind.

It's possible that Joan had not realized how hard up Teddy was.
He even had to borrow $2 million against his McLean home to
finance a last-minute flurry of campaign ads trumpeting his record. It was money well spent, however, for he swept to victory in
the November election.

Following Ted's reelection, it was revealed that he spent the
third-most money among the winning Senate candidates. According to a data analysis by the Associated Press of federal election
filings, Kennedy trailed only Texas Republican Kay Bailey Hutch-

inson, who spent $11.5 million, and California Democrat Dianne Feinstein of California.

Other Kennedys emerged victorious from the 1994 elections. Kathleen Kennedy Townsend, forty-three, was finally elected lieutenant governor of Maryland. Mark Shriver, the fourth of Eunice's five children, won a seat in the Maryland House of Delegates.

CHAPTER EIGHTEEN

FINAL CURTAIN

The true end of the Kennedy dynasty came in January 1995, with the passing of the former Rose Elizabeth Fitzgerald.

Crowds gathered around Old St. Stephen's Church on Tuesday, January 25, for her funeral. It was the same church were she had been baptized 104 years earlier.

Until disabled by her 1984 stroke, she had attended daily mass, usually alone, always dropping a single dollar into the collection plate.

Observers at the televised funeral mass were surprised to note Senator Kennedy receiving Communion from Cardinal Law. The question of whether his marriage to Joan had been annulled was raised, since normally only a Catholic in good standing could receive the sacrament of Holy Communion.

A spokesman for the Senator, with characteristic Kennedy candor, told the *Boston Globe* that Teddy's 1994 civil marriage to Victoria Reggie had since been "blessed by the Church." This only set off a flurry of inquiries into the Church's policy, since Catholic teaching does not allow remarriage after divorce unless a spouse has died or the earlier marriage has been annulled, meaning that it was found to have been invalid from the beginning.

Two priests interviewed by the *New York Times* explained that it was not the Church's practice to refuse the sacrament of the Holy Eucharist publicly to Catholics who approach the altar. Reverend Patrick Cogan, executive coordinator of the Canon Law Society of America, the professional body of Church officials who deal with such questions, acknowledged that many Catholics like Teddy whose marital status was irregular in the eyes of the Church sought Communion. Priests might speak to them before or after, he said, but many felt that publicly refusing them the sacrament would "cause further alienation from the Church."

A spokesman for the Archdiocese of Boston said Church officials were not free to comment on the question of whether or not any individual had obtained an annulment, "whether it's a famous person or an ordinary one."

Outraged Catholics throughout the country wanted to know if Teddy had received an annulment.

Officials of the Archdiocese of Boston and the Diocese of Arlington, Virginia, refused to answer any inquiries on the senator's marital status, other than to say it was "private." Pam Hughes, Teddy's Washington press secretary, would say only that Teddy's marriage was "blessed by a priest."

One of the country's foremost canon lawyers, who requested anonymity due to this sensitive position, told the Catholic weekly *The Wanderer* that Cardinal Law was "bound by his very office of bishop to publicly declare what Kennedy's marital status was."

Furthermore, "Lay people have the right to demand that the bishop explain Kennedy's marital status, because, by his receiving Communion, many Catholics were (and are) scandalized."

Journalist Paul Likoudis was concerned about "the impression given that a wealthy and powerful Catholic can flagrantly disregard the Church's moral teachings and still present himself as a Catholic by receiving communion."

And, of course, there was the matter of Teddy's long-standing support for abortion rights. "If Cardinal Law cannot see that Teddy Kennedy's manifest support for abortion is grave sin, then he has lost his conscience," said *The Wanderer*'s canon lawyer.

"If Kennedy and his wife had received their annulments and Kennedy had repented of his pro-abortion votes to the cardinal, then the cardinal could say, 'It's nobody's business,' " acknowledged the *Wanderer*'s canon lawyer. "But without such a statement from Kennedy, the faithful are scandalized. It seems to me that a wise and prudent Churchman would have determined Kennedy's status before Kennedy stepped forward for Communion."

Another theologian, Father Charles Fiore, concluded that

Teddy's reception of Holy Communion violated the rights of the faithful to "sound catechesis."

"When things are done that are clearly in violation of the teaching of the Church, it is the duty of the ordinary to state the facts and what is and what isn't the truth," said Fiore. "Now, if the reason that the bishops of Boston and Arlington didn't speak out is the argument that they want to avoid the greater scandal of telling the truth because Kennedy's marriage was not annulled, then the bishops should tell the truth and let the chips fall where they may—because the faithful are already suspecting that there is no annulment."

Father Fiore was adamant: "The reception of Communion, for any Catholic, is a matter of divine law, not Church law. One must be in a state of grace to receive Communion."

Poor Teddy, in his determination to pay homage to his beloved mother, once again inadvertently stirred up a controversy and raised up all his old scandals.

KENNEDY KID CHECKS INTO REHAB

Sadly, one of Rose's grandchildren did not make it to her funeral. Although Michael Kennedy, thirty-six, Robert's fourth son, was listed as an usher on the January 24 funeral program, he was unable to be present. Michael had checked into an alcohol-rehabilitation facility, Father Martin's Ashley Center in Havre de Grace, Maryland, near Baltimore, on January 22, the day before his grandmother died.

"He was so sick he was just in no state to make it back to Massachusetts for the service," said one friend. "It broke his heart to know that he had got to such a state that he could not even say goodbye to the woman who meant so much to him."

"I've come to recognize I had a dependence on alcohol," he said in a statement issued by the Citizen's Energy Corp. "I am currently participating in a program and I am committed to completing it this month." He had the full support of his wife, Vicki, and their children, Michael, Jr., eleven, Kyle, nine, and Rory, seven.

EUNICE KENNEDY SHRIVER CHARGES PALM BEACH COMMITTEE WITH HARASSMENT

With the departure of the matriarch, the Kennedy family became embroiled in its third and final legal battle with the Palm Beach Landmarks Preservation Committee. This time the committee was arguing that the oceanfront estate should be designated a landmark because of its historic importance and its architectural significance. Since 1980 the family had twice blocked the committee's efforts to make the mansion a landmark, but when the town tried again in February 1995 a fed-up Eunice sued, claiming that since the matter had been turned back twice in the past fifteen years, the new attempt was "nothing but harassment."

Eunice charged that "after two bites at the apple, respondents are not entitled to a third."

What was at stake was the market value of the mansion, which the family had been trying to unload for fifteen months at $7 million. It needed extensive repairs, and the family feared that a preservation order would scare off buyers.

Ned Monell, the broker handling the sale for Sotheby's International Realty, declined to comment on the preservation issue. "But there is tremendous interest in this wonderful property," he insisted. "The dispute hasn't curbed that excitement."

Less than a month after his Dominican Republic divorce, Bobby Kennedy, Jr., married Mary Richardson, an architect, aboard a boat on the Hudson River. Their son Conor was born later that year. Almost exactly a year later, on August 22, Mary gave birth to their second child, Kyra LeMoyne in Mt. Kisco.

Bobby, Jr., had become a zealous advocate for the protection of the upstate reservoirs that provided New York City with its drinking water. He freely exploited his access and charisma to get what he wanted and was quite willing to resort to radical tactics to state his case. In the fall of 1993 he oversaw the creation of a public service campaign that speculated about how much of Amy Fisher's urine was seeping into a city reservoir from the sewage of the nearby Bedford Hills Correctional Facility, where she was an inmate. At the urging of the Dinkins administration, which was in the midst of a reelection campaign, Bobby never ran the ads. But the incident had caught Dinkins's attention and won him a two-hour talk with the mayor.

Not all his upstate neighbors admired his activism. "I charcterize him as a carpetbagger," said Orville A. Slutzky, a member of the family that operated the Hunter Mountain ski resort.

Although many believed that he had forfeited the chance at a political career after his admitted heroin addiction, Bobby had still not ruled out a run for public office some day.

As for Eunice's children, Maria Shriver remained the most well-known, especially since her marriage to Arnold Schwarzenegger. The former muscle man was still a proponent of rigorous physical fitness and already had their three children, Katherine, five, Christina, four, and Patrick, two, working out.

"I have the kids working on monkey bars and doing little kinds of strength training," said Schwarzenegger, forty-eight. He and forty-year-old Maria regularly took the children with them when they worked out at the World Gym.

Schwarzenegger told television's *Inside Edition*, "They are doing the stationary bike, the treadmill." Although Maria said she would prefer that their children eventually play team sports, Schwarzenegger said he wanted them to bodybuild, which he credited for everything good that had happened to him.

Maria had twice been felled by meningitis. During the last bout she discovered she was pregnant with Patrick. "She kept gaining weight, then losing it, and seemed to be under spiraling stress," a friend told the *Star*. "People still ask her how on earth she continued to work flat-out throughout all her pregnancies. The truth is, Maria drove herself to the edge."

Now, Schwarzenegger was said to be pressuring his wife to slow down and have some more babies, but she feared losing ground in the highly competitive world of network television.

"I only have myself to blame," Maria acknowledged. "In the early part of our marriage, I let Arnold take the dominant role. Now, maybe it's coming back to haunt me! He wants to be sole breadwinner now. 'Another son, another daughter—with me stuck at home playing the great matriarch.' " But Maria has no desire to play the role her grandmother Rose once accepted.

Timothy Perry Shriver, thirty-six, who once considered becoming a priest, received his master's degree in spirituality and education at Catholic University. Since then he has worked with abused children in the New Haven, Connecticut, school system and taught high-school equivalency classes at the Lorton Prison near Washington. Married to attorney Linda Potter since 1986, they have three children: Sophia Rose (1987), Timothy, Jr., (1988), and Samuel Kennedy Potter (1992).

Bobby Shriver, thirty-two, a venture capitalist and part-owner of the Baltimore Orioles, lives quietly.

Mark Kennedy Shriver, thirty-one, is currently developing programs for Baltimore's inner-city children and is a member of the Maryland House of Delegates.

Tony Kennedy Shriver, now twenty-nine, focuses his attention on integrating the mentally disabled into mainstream society through one-on-one friendships with others. Since 1987 his volunteer organization Best Buddies has grown to include more than 6,500 participants in thirty-seven states as well as in Canada, Greece and India, and now includes Best Buddies High Schools, Best Buddies Citizens (for volunteers from corporations and churches) and Best Buddies Jobs (which helps the retarded find work). Headquartered in Miami, the organization has a budget of $2 million, $250,000 of which comes from a grant from the state of Florida.

"Part of our mission is to make it so people won't stare," says Shriver. "So when you go downtown or into church, they're used to having people with mental retardation there."

Tony shares a renovated Mediterranean-style, three-bedroom house in Miami with his wife since July 3, 1993, Cuban-born Alina, a student at Barry University, her son, Teddy, now seven, and their daughters, Eunice, two, and Francesca Maria, twenty-six months.

Speaking like a true Kennedy wife, Alina told a reporter: "We have to go to a lot of functions when I think we'd be better off at home with the kids. But what Anthony does is great." And, of course, he does not rule out an eventual move to politics.

People magazine ran a two-page story on Tony and his organization in February. Of course, it addressed the family's own experience with Rosemary and her disastrous 1941 lobotomy, but in an interesting bit of Kennedy-style revisionism, the story stated that

"Rosemary survived the operation partially paralyzed and was later institutionalized, although she was usually present at family gatherings."

Ambassador Jean Kennedy Smith was making plans for the August wedding of her adopted daughter, Kym, to Alfie Tucker, bar manager of Lillie's Bordello in Dublin. The Ambassador was said to be less than pleased that Kym had begun to search for her Vietnamese biological mother.

With the death of Rose, her surviving children were finally free to unload the Palm Beach mansion they had grown to despise. Tuesday, May 24, 1995, the Kennedy family handed over the deed to new owners. The family's fifteen-year feud with the landmark committee had finally been settled.

The house would become a historic landmark under an unusual deal struck by the Kennedys, the Palm Beach Town Council and the New York banker who bought the house and its furnishings, John K. Castle. The asking price had been $7 million, but none of the parties involved would say what Castle and his wife had paid.

In the years immediately after Joe acquired the property in 1933, he had taught his sons to swim there and it was beside the pool that President-elect Jack Kennedy selected his cabinet. But since Good Friday, 1991, the mansion had been associated with tales of Ted's drinking and his nephew's rape trial.

"Palm Beach is not a place where the youngest generation of Kennedys finds sustenance," intoned Arthur M. Schlesinger, Jr., another pocket historian who had been on hand to chronicle so many key events in the rise and fall of the dynasty. "They're all off involved in good works of sorts, and Palm Beach is dedicated to frivolity."

As part of the deal, the new owners would allow the town of Palm Beach to make the house a landmark within five years. In exchange, they would have those five years to make improvements, subject to town approval, that would otherwise be prohibited for a building with landmark protection.

As for contemplated renovations, the architect retained by the new owner was low-key. "We're just to bring it up to the lifestyle of the 1990s," he said. "The Kennedys have kept up the plumbing and electric and stuff, but it hasn't really been renovated in any manner since 1928."

In February, Caroline was named as honorary chairwoman of the board for the American Ballet Theater's 1995 season, and honorary chairwoman of the company's spring gala, which would be held May 1 at the Metropolitan Opera House. Her mother had been a trustee of the company for twenty-five years, and honorary chairman at the time of her death.

Since his mother's death, John Kennedy, Jr., had spent much of his time with Caroline sorting through Jacqueline Onassis's possessions, deciding what they wanted to keep and what they wanted to donate to the John F. Kennedy Library. He had a fling at local television, hosting a six-part series on deprived neighborhoods of New York City.

As 1995 drew to a close, John seemed to have finally found a project he could commit to. He and cofounder Michael Berman were immersed in plans for the September launch of their long-awaited political magazine *George.* John had been searching for a project ever since leaving the Manhattan prosecutor's office. Berman and John had been hanging around together one day, wondering about the next step in their lives, when they decided to start a magazine. The idea, according to Berman, was to advance a publication with absolutely no political affiliation, a magazine that would treat politics as pop culture, covering politics the way *Sports Illustrated* covered sports. While publicizing the magazine at a luncheon in Detroit in April, John told a gathering of advertising executives that his childhood idols had been "Mick Jagger and Muhammad Ali."

"We want to make politics sort of entertaining," he told another interviewer. "If it is entertaining, people are going to be interested in it, they might think more about it and maybe involve themselves in some way down the line." In line with that philosophy, they had commissioned articles by Roseanne ("If I Were President") and James Carville (a review of Al Pacino's *City Hall*).

John had also found a replacement for Daryl Hannah. Days after he moved his belongings out of Daryl's Upper West Side apartment, John was being seen in public with Carolyn Bessette. It was said that the couple met when John visited the Calvin Klein offices for a private showing of the designer's new men's collection. As P.R. director, it was Carolyn's job to show John the collection, and he was immediately taken with her. The couple was spotted kissing and necking in Central Park, and Carolyn Bessette was even seen walking his German shepherd, Sam. But John was still not ready for a permanent relationship and only allowed her to stay at his new downtown loft three nights at a time.

It may be one of Robert's brood who has moved the farthest from the Ambassador's dynastic master plan. For in January 1995 twin daughters were born to Kerry Kennedy and her husband, Andrew Cuomo. Both mother and father are dedicated to good causes in the Kennedy tradition: Kerry is executive director of the Robert F. Kennedy Memorial. Andrew is an assistant deputy secretary with the Department of Housing and Urban Development. But the most interesting thing about them was how they chose to name their daughters: Cara Ethel KennedyCuomo [sic] and Mariah Matilda KennedyCuomo [sic], joining two important names in the Democratic party, one old and one new. The name made a feminist statement as well: Clearly, Kerry and her twins were three Kennedy women who were not going to take their traditional background role in the family.

It is sad to note that the emergence of powerful women in the Kennedy clan comes too late for Joe and Rose's oldest surviving child. Rosemary, now 77, continues to spend her days in luxurious isolation in a small cottage on the grounds of St. Coletta's school in Jefferson, Wisconsin.

In 1941 she was a pretty, vivacious but not very bright twenty-three-year-old. Unable to cope with her ripening sexuality and her rebellious nature, her father ordered dramatic and highly questionable brain surgery. The results were disastrous, leaving Rosemary partially paralyzed, incontinent and mentally disabled. Joe sent her away and never saw her again. Ironically, it did not curtail her wanderlust, and she has still been known to elude her keepers on the occasional day trip. In October 1975 Rosemary disappeared in Chicago for four hours after wandering away from her sister Eunice.

Joe died in 1969, but it was not until 1974 that her mother allowed Rosemary to come home to Hyannis Port. Since then, she has spent a month each summer there and several weeks each winter at the Palm Beach mansion.

Eunice has been a very regular visitor and has also brought her daughter Maria and son Tony to visit. There are other visitors, too, sometimes not so successful.

"Once when Teddy was visiting, they were all sitting around, and Teddy said something," an observer told the *National Enquirer*. "Rosemary started shouting at Teddy sort of incoherently. Teddy and the others calmed her down, but it was a bad scene for a while."

APPENDIX

WHAT'S IT LIKE TO LIVE LIKE A KENNEDY?

None of the family had any idea how much money they had or
what anything cost.

—A family friend

To be a Kennedy means never having to ask "how much?"

A Kennedy never carries cash and rarely pays for anything. As
President, Jack Kennedy often attended mass with his great friend
Lem Billings and would borrow $10 from him for the collection
plate. When Teddy Kennedy realized he was in dangerous waters
on Chappaquiddick and placed an urgent call to a female friend,
he had to borrow the dime to call her collect. An Aspen caterer
had to sue Ethel Kennedy to collect on a bill. Noelle Fell, who
worked for Ethel for six years, recalls stepping out to help her boss
carry her bags from a taxi—just in time to see Ethel let the cabbie
have it across the face with a stinging blow. "She roared: 'That
fare is outrageous! You people are always trying to take advantage of the Kennedys. I refuse to pay!' It was only $12 or $13—the
standard fare from the airport."

If you are Congressman Joe II, a designated aide holds your
wallet and pays your dinner check. Once Joe II tried to write a
check in a bakery and wound up yelling at the cashier, "Don't you

know who I am?" And when he lived on New York's Upper West Side, John, Jr., was said to be habitually late with his rent checks.

According to Barbara Gibson, Rose's longtime personal assistant, it was nothing for the younger generation to borrow money from the chauffeur and the nanny, but it somehow slipped their minds to pay it back.

"The Kennedys were not giving people," says Noelle Fell. "They paid the staff just above minimum wage and were miserly with raises. Ethel kept promising me a raise but I never got it.

"When she went on trips, she'd always tell me she brought me a gift. But I'd never see it. It was always a new excuse, like her suitcase was missing, the gift was being shipped, or she left it with someone else. It was funny to see what thin excuse she'd come up with next."

Eunice was known to arrive in Palm Beach for the weekend needing a new dress to wear to a cocktail party. She would then go to Martha's, an exclusive Worth Avenue dress shop, buying an expensive dress which she proceeded to wear to the party. Then, on Monday morning, on her way to the airport, Eunice would drop off the dress at her assistant's office, telling her to return it for full credit.

Kennedys also try to save on help. Rose Kennedy's homes were notoriously understaffed, even when she had nine children at home. Eunice, well-known for her good work with the Special Olympics, was said to occasionally use the retarded in her home as unpaid domestics. "She either did not pay them, or else she paid them far less than she would have to pay for someone else to do the identical work. She justified it as some sort of on-the-job training. Everyone else just saw her using cheap labor."

If you are Teddy Kennedy, your staff prepares a set of 3" × 5" cards for you every morning. You carry them in an inside jacket pocket and they tell you where you must be, minute by minute, hour by hour.

Although Joe offered his sons $2,000 if they did not take up smoking until they finished college, Bobby was the only one who collected. The others all liked a good cigar. These days, Teddy favors Davidoffs.

Some Kennedys, like Eunice, are indifferent to fashion, but others are not. John, Jr., wears $179 Persol sunglasses.

Although they insist that their women sign a prenuptial agreement, Kennedy men can be generous to their wives and mistresses. When Rose gave birth to her eighth child, Jean, in 1928, Joe was in Palm Beach pursuing Gloria Swanson, and didn't make it up to Boston to visit immediately. But when he did arrive, he brought a lovely diamond bracelet. When John F. Kennedy became engaged to Jacqueline Bouvier, he gave her an emerald-and-diamond ring from Van Cleef & Arpels, the exclusive Fifth Avenue jewelry store. At their wedding rehearsal dinner, he casually dropped a diamond bracelet in her lap. During his affair with Judith Campbell, Jack presented her with a diamond-and-ruby brooch. And he marked his tenth anniversary with Jackie by letting her pick her own present: She selected a coiled serpent antique bracelet.

When Bobby and Ethel became engaged in 1949, he sent a man from Cartier with a whole tray of rings for his fiancée to review. She chose a tremendous marquise diamond that a friend said you could land a plane on. Teddy continued the generous tradition: Victoria Reggie's engagement ring was a huge sapphire surrounded by diamonds.

No Kennedy woman has to cook. An aide recalls that in the 1970s Joan Kennedy was such a stranger in her McLean, Virginia, kitchen that she did not know how to boil water on a gas range.

But when the marriage is over, Kennedy men can be ruthless, seeking to remove all traces of it. Joan Kennedy and Sheila Rauch were both shocked when their ex-husbands sought Catholic annulments so that they could remarry in the Church. And Joan was so disappointed in her 1982 settlement that in 1994 she retained a high-profile attorney to reexamine the records.

The Kennedys have certainly had their share of headaches with their children, but they have access to the best counseling money can buy. Ethel, for example, often telephoned Dr. Robert Coles, Harvard's resident authority on child psychology, for advice.

Even when a Kennedy goes into rehab, he/she goes first class. In 1995 Michael Kennedy became the latest Kennedy to acknowledge a problem and seek help when he entered a program at Father Martin's Ashley Center. The Center is housed in a huge nineteenth century mansion in picturesque Havre de Grace, Maryland, near Baltimore. A standard thirty-day program there costs $15,435. David Kennedy's stints in other clinics were said to cost $20,000 at a time. And Rosemary's long-term care at St.

Coletta's bills at $50,000 a year, plus the $1 million donation the family made to the school in 1983.

Being a Kennedy means never being overdrawn or worrying about your checking account balance. If you're overdrawn, the bank has only to call the Park Agency, and the overdraft will be covered immediately. The same goes for a credit card balance. At the Park Agency a staff of fifteen, including eight accountants and two former IRS agents, produces comprehensive monthly statements for family members, prepares tax returns, insures the family valuables and occasionally even renews a driver's license.

Since the death of Stephen Smith in 1990, the deceptively austere Park Agency has been overseen by Egyptian-born Joseph Hakim. President of Kennedy Enterprises since 1980, Hakim introduced such modern techniques as computers. Until then, the office was using handwritten ledgers.

But to live like a Kennedy also means to live with the constant threat of violence. A few months after Caroline met Ed Schlossberg, she received John Hinckley-like letters from a California law school graduate who wanted to marry her. The man was later arrested. Three years later a thirty-two-year-old drifter tried to break into her office at the Met, determined to propose marriage.

WHAT WILL HAPPEN TO THE KENNEDY MILLIONS?

Most Kennedys take little interest in how their money is invested, or even how much they are worth. Their bills are all paid by the Park Agency. Even their income tax returns are prepared and filed by the Agency, which also buys and sells their houses and cars, and pays their tuition, clothing and travel bills, even their servants.

That was just the way the founding father wanted it. He did not want his children involved in business at all. "We never discussed money in the house because, well, money isn't important," he told one of Jack's biographers. And his children listened. None of his nine children and almost none of their children has shown any interest in business. In 1991 *Forbes* magazine estimated that the Kennedy fortune amounted to $350 million. "As family fortunes go, that isn't a great deal," wrote Laura Jereski. "And most of it is in a single, illiquid real estate property with no great future." She concluded that "although the aura of the name may linger for a generation or two, the day is probably past when the family can buy its way into politics."

Jereski also revealed that the Kennedy fortune has never been as big as was reported. "The Joe Kennedy estate finances luxurious lifestyles and several political careers on principal that is worth less than half of what many—including *Forbes*—have long supposed it to be," she wrote. According to Jereski, the miscalculations began with a 1957 *Fortune* article that pegged the family's wealth at $250 million. In reality, Joe's fortune was probably half that, and it has not been invested wisely. Moreover, according to Jereski, "The Kennedys have been consuming capital at such a rate that the fortune will not last far into the next century."

On the deaths of Joe's two youngest children, Ambassador Jean Kennedy Smith and Senator Teddy, the trusts terminate and the principal will be distributed among their heirs.

Since the death of Stephen Smith, however, there has been no one adding to the fortune. With his job at the Merchandise Mart, Christopher Kennedy seems to be the only heir interested in business at all.

If the family continues to spend at the present rate, and nothing is added to the principal, the Kennedy fortune will run dry early in the next century.

NONPROFIT ORGANIZATIONS ASSOCIATED WITH THE KENNEDY FAMILY

In 1987, three years before his death, Stephen Smith and the trustees of the Joseph P. Kennedy, Jr., Foundation established the Associate Trustees System budgeted at $2.5 million to fund the special philanthropies of the third generation. The Kennedy cousins draw on this for seed money for their myriad projects, some of which are listed below:

• **Best Buddies:** Anthony Shriver, Founder and President, 1987.
• **Choice:** Mark Shriver used some of his Kennedy trust fund to

found this Baltimore-based social-service program for inner-city teenagers and juvenile offenders in 1986. He is president.
- **Citizens Energy Corporation:** A nonprofit corporation founded in 1979 by Joe II to provide low-cost fuel oil to poor families in Massachusetts. 1985 president, Michael Kennedy.
- **Facing The Challenge:** organization for handicapped and disabled, founding director, Edward M. Kennedy, Jr.
- **John F. Kennedy Library**
- **Joseph P. Kennedy, Jr., Foundation**
- **Robert F. Kennedy Memorial Foundation:** helps disadvantaged teenagers.
- **Robert F. Kennedy Memorial Center For Human Rights:** supports the work of political activists around the world. Founder and executive director, Kerry Kennedy Cuomo.
- **Park Foundation**
- **Special Olympics**
- **Very Special Arts:** nonprofit organization which helps physically and emotionally handicapped people get into fine-arts institutes around the country. Employs Kara Kennedy as a producer.

ARRESTS, CONVICTIONS AND NOTABLE FINES

What other American family as illustrious as the Kennedys has compiled quite their record of conflict with the law? In the mid-1930s Joe, Jr., and Jack spent a night in the Edgartown jail after an overly boisterous celebration in an Edgartown hotel of their regatta victory. When a local police officer discovered that Caroline Kennedy was growing marijuana in the backyard of her mother's home in Hyannis Port, he merely informed her mother. When Sydney Lawford was caught with drugs while speeding in her grandmother's car in Florida, she was let off with a warning. It seems safe to assume that for many reasons a softhearted lawman might choose not to mar the records of young Kennedys with arrests and citations, which makes the infractions they have compiled all the more interesting.

SENATOR EDWARD M. KENNEDY

7/25/69: District Court in Edgartown. Senator Kennedy pleaded guilty to the single charge against him: leaving the scene of a motor-vehicle accident. He was sentenced to the minimum jail term of two months in the house of correction at Barnstable and sentence was suspended. His driver's license was suspended for a year.

Although the judge who presided at the inquest for Mary Jo Kopechne concluded "that there is probable cause to believe that Edward M. Kennedy operated his motor vehicle negligently . . . and that such operation appears to have contributed to the death of Mary Jo Kopechne," he did not make any recommendation for criminal prosecution and has chosen not to comment on the matter since. The day after releasing his report, he retired from the bench.

JOAN BENNETT KENNEDY

After the scandal of the Good Friday rape, Joan was arrested for drunk driving in Quincy, Massachusetts. Because it was her second arrest in that state in three years, the judge ordered her to spend the last two weeks of May 1992 in an alcohol treatment center.

By 1994 she had been arrested three times for driving under the influence.

EDWARD M. KENNEDY, JR.

December 18, 1982, young Ted, Jr., was arrested on his way home from Wesleyan University. He was stopped by a New Jersey state trooper and charged with driving his Jeep sixty-four miles-per-hour in a fifty miles-per-hour zone. The trooper noticed an open box of pot in the car and he was arrested and charged with possession of marijuana. Young Ted was released in time to spend Christmas with the family in Aspen. He eventually paid $30 in fines and court costs.

ETHEL SKAKEL KENNEDY

On December 14, 1960, she was fined $40 in absentia by an Arlington County, Virginia, court judge for going seventy in a forty-mile-per-hour zone of the dangerous George Washington Memorial Parkway. She was also charged with not having a Virginia permit. Her attorney appeared in court and paid the fine because she was in Palm Beach.

ROBERT F. KENNEDY, JR.

In July 1970 he was arrested in a Hyannis Port drug raid, charged with smoking marijuana and placed on thirteen months' probation.

In August 1983 he was cited by the Coast Guard for operating a sixteen-foot Boston Whaler without registration, life jackets and distress signals. The small boat had been adrift for some twenty hours about a mile off the coast of Hyannis.

In September 1983 he was arrested in Rapid City, South Dakota, and charged with possession of heroin, a felony punishable by two years in jail and a $2,000 fine. Convicted March 1984, he was given a suspended sentence and put on two years' probation for heroin possession.

DAVID A. KENNEDY

In 1979 he was beaten and robbed while buying heroin in Harlem on September 5, but he was listed as the victim of a crime. Police chose not to charge him with driving with an expired Virginia driver's license, a glove compartment full of parking tickets, and lying to them at first about the circumstances of the robbery.

In 1982, on his release from a year of treatment at the Aquarium Effort in Sacramento, he was arrested for drunk driving, pleaded guilty and paid a $380 fine.

DOUGLAS HARRIMAN KENNEDY AND RORY KENNEDY

Circa 1984, at sixteen, Rory and her brother were arrested for protesting apartheid in front of the South African embassy. The charges were later dropped.

JOHN F. KENNEDY, JR.

After graduating from New York University Law School and before taking up his first full-time job, as an assistant district attorney in Manhattan, John paid $2,300 in outstanding parking tickets.

CHRISTOPHER KENNEDY LAWFORD

In 1980, at twenty-five, he was arrested for impersonating a physician in order to buy Darvon, a prescription painkiller from an Aspen, Colorado, pharmacy. The suspicious pharmacist called the police. Charges were later dropped. In December of the same year, he was arrested trying to buy heroin outside a bar in Boston, and again received probation.

ROBERT S. SHRIVER

He was busted for pot with cousin Bobby Kennedy in July 1970.

ANTHONY SHRIVER

Tony made headlines when he allegedly displayed "erratic" (i.e. drunken) driving in Palm Beach, Florida, after a party at Donald Trump's Mar-A-Lago estate.

WILLIAM KENNEDY SMITH

Willie was acquitted of rape charges.

On October 23, 1993, he was arrested after punching a bouncer in the nose at the Bardo Rodeo Brew Pub in Arlington, Virginia, and charged with assault and battery. He pleaded no contest in November and was sentenced to a year's probation and one hundred hours of community service at a Chicago health clinic.

REHABILITATION FACILITIES
ASSOCIATED WITH THE KENNEDYS

JOAN
- McLean (spring 1979, once earlier)
- Silver Hill Foundation (spring 1974, twice)
- Dried out in a small hospital in Capistrano, California
- Switzerland 1973
- Last two weeks of May 1992, alcohol treatment
- March 1993: Proctor House, McLean

BOBBY, JR.
- McLean Hospital
- Fair Oaks Hospital, Summit, New Jersey

DAVID
- McLean Hospital
- Aquarian Effort, Sacramento, California
- Sussex, England, Margaret Patterson, "neuro-electric" therapy, 1979
- 1979, Massachusetts General, Methadone program
- St. Mary's Rehabilitation Center, Minneapolis. Registered as "David Kilroy," March 19–April 19, 1984

TED, JR.
- Institute for Living, Hartford, Connecticut, for alcohol problems

PATRICK
- Spofford Hall, a drug rehabilitation center, Spofford, New Hampshire, 1986, for cocaine addiction

MICHAEL
- Father Martin's Ashley Center in Havre de Grace, Maryland

CHRISTOPHER LAWFORD
- McLean, treatment for heroin addiction, 1978
- Cambridge Hospital, Massachusetts, Addictive Behavior Course, 1985

NOTES AND SOURCES

The files of Ambassador Joseph P. Kennedy, including his unpublished memoir, are at the John F. Kennedy Library, where they are sealed.

The medical records of John F. Kennedy are currently classified "closed."

The financial records of Joseph P. Kennedy, John F. Kennedy and Robert F. Kennedy at the Kennedy Library in Boston are all classified "closed."

Judith Campbell Exner's 1975 testimony before the Senate Select Committee on Intelligence was immediately sealed and will not be made public until 2025.

One thousand pages of the Florida State Medical Examiner's report into the death of David Kennedy, including the toxicologist's report, remain sealed.

Of the events immediately following the assassination of John F. Kennedy, no verbatim transcript of the questioning of Lee Harvey Oswald by the police, FBI or the Secret Service exists. The chief autopsy surgeon, Commander James Humes, burned his preliminary draft notes of the autopsy, and on November 24, 1963, wrote a second draft which was subsequently revised and submitted to Admiral Burkley in the White House. It has since disappeared.

Although John F. Kennedy taped all activities in the Oval Office, these tapes were edited and all "sensitive" material erased before they were donated to the John F. Kennedy Library. One eyewitness claims that the material deleted included intimate conversations with Marilyn Monroe and Judith Campbell.

NOTES

CHAPTER ONE

128 votes. James MacGregor Burns, JOHN KENNEDY: A POLITICAL PROFILE (New York: Harcourt, Brace & World, Inc. 1961), p. 17

Baseball. Richard J. Whalen, THE FOUNDING FATHER: *The Story of Joseph P. Kennedy*, (Washington, D.C.: Regnery Gateway, 1993), p. 27, others

Rose's diploma. *People*, 2/6/95

Rose's coming out. Barbara Gibson and Ted Schwarz, ROSE KENNEDY: *A Life of Faith, Family, & Tragedy* (New York: Birch Lane Press, 1995) p. 65

Joe's smile. Doris Kearns Goodwin, THE FITZGERALDS AND THE KENNEDYS: *An American Saga*, (New York: Simon & Schuster, 1987), p. 124

Fitzgerald dynasty. Goodwin, ibid, p. 129

Curley announcement. John Henry Cutler, "HONEY FITZ": *Three Steps to the White House* (Indianapolis and New York: The Bobbs-Merrill Company, Inc., 1962) pp 215–216

"The Kennedys are a self-contained unit." Jerome Beatty, "Nine Kennedys and How They Grew," *Readers Digest*, April, 1939. Betty Compson. Charles Higham, ROSE KENNEDY, p. 78

"I always felt . . ." Joseph F. Dineen, THE KENNEDY FAMILY (Boston: Little, Brown, 1959) p. 37

Joe Jr.'s bullying. Goodwin, p. 348

"couldn't pass a hat" Leo Damore, THE CAPE COD YEARS OF JOHN FITZGERALD KENNEDY (Prentice-Hall, Englewood Cliffs, 1967), p. 26

Joe's attempts to dominate. Clinch, p. 75

"cross as a billy goat" Hank Searls, THE LOST PRINCE: *Young Joe, the Forgotten Kennedy*. (New York: New American Library, 1969), 96

Nigel Hamilton. *People* 12/21/92

Joe at Galen Stone. Victor Lasky, JFK: THE MAN AND THE MYTH, (New York: Macmillan, 1963) p. 40

"It came ashore . . ." Whalen, p. 58

Frank Costello. NYT interview with Peter Maas 1973

Sam Giancana. Sam and Chuck Giancana, DOUBLE CROSS: *The Explosive Inside Story of the Mobster Who Controlled America* (New York: Warner Books, 1992)

"Gee you're a great mother" Goodwin, p. 353

"take it in stride" ibid.

"How Long . . ." Lasky

Patricia Kennedy. Lawrence Leamer, THE KENNEDY WOMEN, p. 162

CHAPTER TWO: Joe Heads for Hollywood

Epigraph: Buck, Pearl, THE KENNEDY WOMEN: *A Personal Appraisal* (New York: Cowles, 1970), p. 186

Trust funds. Whalen, p. 74; *Forbes*, October 21, 1991

"He was speculating . . ." Ralph G. Martin and Ed Plaut, FRONT RUNNER, DARK HOURSE (Garden City, New York: Doubleday & Company, Inc., 1960) p. 121

Magic moment. Gloria Swanson, SWANSON ON SWANSON, (New York: Random House, 1980)

First real affair. Goodwin, p. 393

Board of Overseers.

"When are the nice people . . ." Ralph Blagden, "Cabot Lodge's Toughest Fight," *The Reporter*, September 30, 1952

"hell to pay." Clinch, p. 32

Pornographic magazines. *People*, December 21, 1992

Jack aboard *Rose Elizabeth*. Lester David, GOOD TED/BAD TED, *The Two Faces of Edward M. Kennedy*, (New York: Birch Lane Press, 1993) p. 61

John E. Schowalter: *McCall's*, August 1991

Swanson. Goodwin, p. 415

Joseph Swanson: Swanson's son Joseph, an electrical engineer, died suddenly in 1975 in Danvers Massachusetts of an internal hemmorhage, leaving a widow and two daughters. (Who's Who in Hollywood 1900–1976, David Ragan, Arlington House Publishers, New Rochelle, N.Y. 1977)

Pantages. Kenneth Anger, HOLLYWOOD BABYLON II

CHAPTER THREE: Joe Kennedy Discovers Franklin D. Roosevelt

Epigraph: Dineen, p. 69.

"I wanted him in the White House." Joseph P. McCarthy, THE REMARKABLE KENNEDYS (Dial Press: New York, 1960) p. 58

Lem Billings. Clay Blair, Jr. and Joan Blair, THE SEARCH FOR J.F.K. (Putnam: New York, 1976) pp 26–27; Peter Collier and David Horowitz, THE KENNEDYS: *An American Drama* (New York: Warner Books, 1985), p. 65

Losing virginity. ibid, p. 465

George Washington. Richard E. Burke, THE SENATOR: *My Ten Years with Ted Kennedy*, p. 30

Rose's travels. Clinch, p. 77

Rose and women's lib. Gibson, ROSE KENNEDY, p. 175

Joe used young Roosevelt. *Forbes*, October 21, 1991

"Maybe Jimmy thought . . ." Joseph McCarthy, THE REMARKABLE KENNE-DYS, p. 60

Palm Beach. *New York Times*, May 24, 1995

Rose's carbons. Collier and Horowitz, p. 148

Joe's correspondence. Goodwin, p. 351

"praiseworthy and smoldering side." Clinch, p. 74

Harold Laski. Clinch, p. 79; Goodwin, p. 467

"He has often sat . . ." Goodwin, p. 468

"a tough, minute disciplinarian . . ." ibid, p. 353

cigars. Clinch, p. 73, 267

Joe and Arthur Krock. Collier and Horowitz, p. 80

Joe, Jr. at Harvard. Clinch, p. 82

Jack on Joe. ibid, p. 97

Jack's health. Goodwin, p. 491

Jack's biography in Who's Who. Davis, p. 141

Jack and Joe, Jr. at Harvard. Clinch, p. 83

Arthur Krock. Collier and Horowitz, p. 84

"I have no political ambitions . . ." Joseph P. Kennedy, I'M FOR ROOSEVELT (New York: Reynal and Hitchcock, 1936), p. 3

Jack and Lem Billings abroad. Collier and Horowitz, p. 86

FDR "laughed . . ." Collier and Horowitz, p. 86

CHAPTER FOUR: The Kennedys in the Court of St. James

Epigraph: Whalen, p. 461

Joe's press agent. Gibson, ROSE KENNEDY, p. 222; Goodwin, p. 514

Joe at Harvard. Clinch, p. 84

Ambassador Kennedy. Davis, p. 100

Barbara Hutton. C. David Heymann, POOR LITTLE RICH GIRL: THE LIFE AND LEGEND OF BARBARA HUTTON

Pamela Digby. Truman Capote's roman a clef, "Answered Prayers," caused a sensation when it was published in *Esquire* in November 1975. The story was to be part of a long-promised novel, *Answered Prayers*, whose central character was inspired, at least in part, by Pamela Churchill. The character claims the Ambassador forced his attentions on her.
"The book was fiction and Truman sometimes made things up, so he may just have elaborated a good story," acknowledged his biographer, Gerald Clarke. "But I did find out that while Truman occasionally exaggerated, and although he had a reputation as a tremendous liar, really most of the things were true."

Christopher Ogden, THE LIFE OF THE PARTY: *The Biography of Pamela Digby Churchill Hayward Harriman*, p. 308

Marlene Dietrich at Eden Roc. Steven Bach, MARLENE DIETRICH: HER LIFE AND LOVES p. 241

Dietrich and the Kennedy men. Higham, p. 186

Athenia. Collier and Horowitz, p. 115

S.S. Washington. ibid, p. 115

Bombing raids. Ogden, p. 72

After Chamberlain. Collier and Horowitz, p. 119

Krock's trial balloon. ibid, p. 121

Rosemary problem. Goodwin, p. 640

Why England Slept. Collier and Horowitz, p. 121

Gonorrhea. *New York Review of Books*, January 14, 1993

Somerset. Lasky, p. 28

CHAPTER FIVE: The Kennedys Go To War

Epigraph: Chicago Daily News, Dec. 6, 1945

"Kennedys . . . feeling of being heightened . . ." Collier and Horowitz, p. 131

Inga Arvad. William G. Cahan, NO STRANGER TO TEARS: *A Surgeon's Story*, p. 88

Jack and Inga. Sommers, 265

Rosemary's trip with Eunice. ibid, p. 106

Teddy and Rosemary. Higham, p. 238

"Jews and radicals . . ." Collier and Horowitz, p. 136

Jack and Inga in Charleston. Sommers, 265

Inga's marriage. Collier and Horowitz, p. 145 Inga and Tim McCoy would have two sons. She died of breast cancer in 1973. Cahan, p. 88

"You son of a bitch." Cahan, p. 88

Joe Jr. and Jack competition. Searls

PT-109. Davis, p. 117; *People*, December 21, 1992

Toast to Joe, Jr. Higham, 247; Searls, p. 202; Davis, p. 83

Jack returned. Higham, p. 249

"Heartbroken . . ." Goodwin, p. 677

"It's a horrible thing." Collier and Horowitz, p. 161

Joe's last mission. Ralph G. Martin, SEEDS OF DESTRUCTION: Joe Kennedy and His Sons, p. 118

Death of Joe. Jr., Davis, p. 128

John J. Reynolds. *Forbes*

Merchandise Mart. ibid

Bobby in the Navy. Clinch, p. 263

CHAPTER SIX: The First Kennedy Campaign

"We're all in this together." Collier and Horowitz, p. 180

Jack's spending. *Forbes*, October 21, 1991

Joe on Eunice. Collier and Horowitz, p. 159

Jack romanced. Goodwin, p. 723

Gene Tierney. Jane Ellen Wayne, MARILYN'S MEN, p. 168

"tendency to prowl." Collier and Horowitz, p. 211; David, p. 59

Edie. ibid, p. 211

"My mother is a nothing." ibid, p. 212

Kennedys on the prowl. Goodwin, p. 724

Jack and pursuit. Collier and Horowitz, p. 214

William O. Douglas. Davis, p. 168

Jack in Ireland. Ogden, p. 195

Jack's condition. ibid, p. 196

Addison's disease. ibid, p. 195

Jack and Rosemary. Goodwin, p. 734

Family lied. Two principal pathologists who performed the autopsy on the president at Parkland Memorial Hospital published an article in the October 7, 1992 issue of the *Journal of the American Medical Association,* with George D. Lundberg, the *Journal's* editor. In an editorial accompanying the article, Lundberg wrote: "Based on published and verified clinical information and verified autopsy findings, we may now make a firm diagnosis of chronic Addison's disease, probably ideopathic [arising from an unknown source] in John F. Kennedy." [David 114]

"slow motion leukemia." Goodwin, p. 743

Cortisone. Goodwin, p. 745

Cortisone side-effects. *Vogue,* October 1993

Earl of Fitzwilliam. Ogden, p. 194

Flight to Cannes. Davis, p. 130

Jack and Kick's death. Collier, p. 206

Lem on Jack. Goodwin, p. 744

Repeat third grade. Jerry Oppenheimer, THE OTHER MRS. KENNEDY: *Ethel Skakel Kennedy: An American Drama of Power, Privilege and Politics,* p. 232

Bobby at University of Virginia Law School. Higham, p. 374

Law School Forum. ibid

Bobby at Justice Department. ibid, p. 271

"white hats." ibid

Jack's card file. Davis, p. 173

Bobby campaign manager. Collier and Horowitz, p. 225–7

Joe's tie. Lasky, p. 29

"queer." Higham, p. 296

CHAPTER SEVEN: Jack Aims for Vice President and Takes a Bride

Auchincloss children. Heymann, p. 45

Black Jack at Silver Hill. ibid, p. 55

Auchincloss pornography. ibid, p. 65

Jackie's education. *People,* June 6, 1994; *McCall's,* July 1989

Eunice toast. Collier and Horowitz, p. 264

Smathers on Jackie. New York Post, July 25, 1994

Engagement ring. *Star,* November 29, 1994

Janet's opinion. Davis, p. 255

Torbert Macdonald. ibid, p. 257

"Wish you were here." ibid, p. 260

French clinic. Dubois, p. 71

Peter Lawford. Spada, p. 206

Jack's operation. Goodwin, p. 776

Contributors to PROFILES IN COURAGE. Davis, p. 273

Jack in Mediterranean. Davis, p. 273; Goodwin, p. 785

Priscilla McMillan. *Globe*, March 28, 1995

Peter Ward. DuBois, p. 82

Evelyn Lincoln. *Globe*, March 28, 1995

Stephen Smith. Martin, p. 230

Caroline christening. Davis, p. 277

Robert's career. Clinch, p. 273

"Jack is the greatest attraction . . ." Clinch, p. 39

Aristotle Onassis. *Redbook*, July 1986

Rosemary. Dineen, via Gibson, ROSE KENNEDY, p. 100

PART THREE: Living on the New Frontier

Epigraphs: Cholly Knickerbocker, New York Journal-American, January 22, 1961; George E. Reedy

CHAPTER EIGHT: Jack's Presidential Campaign

"It's time . . ." Lasky, p. 471

Max Jacobson. Michael Gross, MODEL: *The Ugly Business of Beautiful Women*, p. 233; Richard Reeves, PRESIDENT KENNEDY, p. 36

Cortisone. Davis, p. 282

Eunice. Lasky, p. 457

Caroline. Davis, p. 284

Giancana. Spada, p. 233

West Virginia. ibid, p. 255

Giancana and White House, Davis, p. 289

Beverly Hilton. Wayne, p. 166; Spada, p. 256

Truman and Eleanor Roosevelt. Davis, p. 292

Joe and Luce. David Halberstam, THE POWERS THAT BE, p. 78; Clinch, p. 38

Angie Dickinson. *Star*, November 20, 1993; *Tatler*, undated, 1993

Marilyn and Jeanne Carmen. *Globe*, January 17, 1995

Nixon's skin. Lasky, p. 475

Kennedy's secret weapon. Reeves, p. 36

Palimony payment. Davis, pp. 426, 626, 744

Ambassador. David, p. 51

Nixon infiltrator. Lasky, p. 493

Addison's disease. Clinch, p. 259

Electoral college. Reeves, p. 18

Cook County votes. David E. Scheim, CONTRACT ON AMERICA: *The Mafia Murder of President John F. Kennedy*, p. 88

Mickey Cohen. Cohen, p. 236

Addison's disease. Reeves, p. 24; *Time*, November 21, 1960

Cook County votes. Reeves, p. 25

CHAPTER NINE: Days of Heaven: Life in the Kennedy White House

Epigraphs: Nancy Dickerson and Jacqueline Kennedy: McCall's 7/89

Eunice. Davis, p. 335

"blood brother." David, p. 54

"balls." Oppenheimer, p. 197

Peter Maas. New York Times, 5/7/61

Doug Kiker. Oppenheimer, p. 221

Sophie Burnham. ibid

Statler Hilton, Judith Campbell. Davis, p. 327

Angie Dickinson. *Star*, November 30, 1993

Peter Lawford. Oppenheimer, p. 203

Glenys Roberts. *Tatler*, undated, 1995

Benno Gaziani. *New York Post*, July 25, 1994

Joseph McCarthy. David

J.F.K. Lasky, p. 503

Lem Billings. Gibson, ROSE KENNEDY, p. 273

Restless temperment. Lasky, p. 502

Fiddle and Faddle. Spada, p. 278

Bay of Pigs. Oppenheimer, p. 210

Failure. Oppenheimer, p. 212; Spada, p. 316

Johnny Roselli. Spada, p. 317

Judy Campbell. Spada, p. 318; *People*

Max Jacobson. Gross, p. 233

"We have to confront them." *Vogue,* October 1993

BLAUVELT FAMILY GENEOLOGY. Benjamin Bradlee, CONVERSATIONS WITH KENNEDY, p. 45; LC #56-10936

Salinger. Bradlee, p. 46

Sam Giancana. Tatler, n.d., 1995

Mrs. Frank Appleton. *Globe,* 1992

Sam Giancana. Davis, p. 385

White House school. *Ladies Home Journal,* March, 1989

Smoked pot. *American Spectator,* December, 1993

Mary Meyer. Ron Rosenbaum, TRAVELS WITH DR. DEATH *And Other Unusual Investigations,* p. 131

Diary. ibid, p. 126

Lem Billings. Reeves, p. 89

Joe Kennedy. Clinch, p. 39

Joe's stroke. ibid, p. 40; Spada, p. 313

Frank Saunders. Spada, p. 313

"Now it's Ted's turn." David, p. 68

Fulfill his father's dream. ibid, p. 71

Edward L. McCormack. ibid, p. 17

Ted's statement. ibid, p. 73

Teddy's campaign. ibid, p. 74–79

Ted's enlistment. ibid, p. 38–40

CHAPTER TEN: Dark Clouds Gather

Phil Graham: Deborah Davis, KATHARINE THE GREAT: *Katharine Graham and the Washington Post* (Bethesda, Maryland: National Press, 1987), p. 158

Graham demise: Deborah Davis, p. 165–70

Jelly donut: C. David Heymann, A WOMAN NAMED JACKIE (New York: New American Library, 1989) p. 395

Death of Patrick: Ralph G. Martin, SEEDS OF DESTRUCTION; Kitty p. 438–39; Kelley, JACKIE O! p. 109

Theodore H. White and Camelot: Thomas Griffith, HARRY AND TEDDY: *The Turbulent Friendship of Press Lord Henry R. Luce and His Favorite Reporter Theodore H. White* (New York: Random House, 1995) p. 276

Assassination rehearsal: Martin, p. 450

"It's Bobby's turn." John H. Davis, p. 543

Camelot: L. Fletcher Prouty, JFK: *The CIA, Vietnam, and the Plot to Assassinate John F. Kennedy* (New York: Birch Lane Press, 1992), p. 140–141

Mickey Cohen: p. 237

CHAPTER ELEVEN: Bobby's Brief Moment

Epigraph: Kathleen Kennedy Townsend, "My Father, Robert F. Kennedy," with Lester David, *McCall's*, May 1988

"I was the seventh . . ." Goodwin, p. 364

"I know of no credible evidence . . ." *Vogue*, October 1993

Bobby and Herodotus: Collier and Horowitz, p. 399

"We could talk in the way a girl and a man can talk . . .", Oppenheimer, p. 399

"Stop seeing my sister . . ." Oppenheimer, p. 612; *New York Post*, August 1, 1994; Higham, p. 389

"I do not lightly dismiss the dangers . . ." *Life*, June 1988

Stephen Smith at Arlington: Arthur M. Schlesinger, Jr., ROBERT F. KENNEDY AND HIS TIMES, Ballantine Books, New York: 1978, p. 983

Roger Edens: Spada, p. 396, 428

Joan Braden: *People*, June 6, 1994

PART FIVE: The Rise and Fall of Cadillac Eddie

Epigraphs: Teddy Kennedy, 1969, Martin, p. 590; *Time*, January 10, 1969.

CHAPTER TWELVE: Teddy's Turn

Epigraph: E. M. Byro, "Joan and Ted Separate," *Photo Screen*, December 1969, p. 55

Peter Lawford. Collier and Horowitz, p. 266

"How's my girl?" ibid, p. 358

"the gay illiterate." Hamilton, p. 683

Ted's enlistment. *National Enquirer*, September 21, 1969

Ted at rugby. *National Enquirer*, September 13, 1969

Dick Tuck. *Gentlemen's Quarterly*, February 1990

"It wasn't my personality to make a lot of noise . . ." Marcia Chellis, THE JOAN KENNEDY STORY: *Living with the Kennedys*, Simon and Schuster, New York: 1985, p. 43

"Car's stuck . . ." Frank Saunders with James Southwood, TORN LACE CURTAIN: *My Life with the Kennedys*, 1982, p. 336

"I told him ten times, 'Ted, you'reacting like a fool . . ." Martin, p. 591

CHAPTER THIRTEEN: Chappaquiddick

Epigraphs: Teddy Kennedy 1969, statement; Gordon N. Walker, *Time*, August 15, 1969; Michael Kennedy, *GQ*, February 1990; Teddy Kennedy 1973, statement.

Russell Peachey: Joe McGinnis, "The End of Camelot," *Vanity Fair*, September 1993

Helga Wagner. At the time she and Senator Teddy met in 1967 she was married to Robert Wagner, vice president of Amrican Eastern Company. They divorced in 1970. Burke, p. 112; *Ladies Home Journal*, March 1983.

Ed Joyce. Ed Joyce, PRIME TIMES, BAD TIMES, Doubleday, New York, 1988, p. 262

"I could hear Ted talking to Helga . . ." Chellis, p. 86

Countess Llana Campbell. Burke, p. 293

"It was a coverup . . ." *People*, July 26, 1989

Gwen Kopechne. *Ladies Home Journal*, July 1989

CHAPTER FOURTEEN: Teddy's Power Fades

Epigraph: Burke, p. 128

"Make-up 'theatrically thick' . . . ," Burke, p. 41; "dragged through a rathole," David, p. 100

"I tried to talk about it . . ." Chellis, p. 48

Candice Bergen. *National Star*, May 31, 1994

H.R. Haldeman. ibid

John Culver. David, p. 243

"Like all Kennedy men, he thought he was irresistable . . ." *People*, April 1991

"I saw the Senator . . . lying atop the sexy Greek singer . . ." Burke, p. 42

". . . penchant for three-ways . . . ," Burke, p. 131, 135

". . . what an incredible asshole Teddy was . . . ," Oppenheimer, p. 373

Bobby Shriver and Bobby Kennedy, Jr. 1970 arrests, Oppenheimer, p. 381

Erasing Oval Office tapes. Burke, p. 50, 108; *National Star*, March 22, 1994

Pamela Kelley accident. Burke, p. 38, *US* magazine, June 23, 1981

Joan Kennedy 1974 alcohol treatment. Burke, p. 58; Chellis, p. 49, David, p. 168

". . . captive to their father's sexual flings . . ." Burke, p. 72

Page Lee Hufty. Burke, p. 54; David, p. 106

Ted with Joe II and Christopher Lawford in Palm Beach. Gibson, ROSE KENNEDY, p. 472

Amyl nitrate and cocaine. Burke, p. 98

Judith Exner: "The Kennedy men were morally bankrupt. . . ." David, p. 65

Joan Kennedy 1976 alcohol treatment. Burke, p. 90; Chellis, p. 51

Taki story. Taki, PRINCES, PLAYBOYS AND HIGH-CLASS TARTS, p. 103; Ted and cocaine. Burke, p. 112

Helga Wagner. ibid.

Joan Kennedy 1977 alcohol problems. Burke, p. 120

"My uncle's as bad as I am . . ." Oppenheimer, p. 458

Smith deal with *Enquirer*. Burke, p. 151; Chellis, p. 166

Joan's 1978 alcohol problems. Chellis, p. 65

Joan's 1979 alcohol treatment. ibid, p. 66

David's drug problems. Oppenheimer, p. 458; Taki, p. 38; Burke, p. 166

David at McLean Hospital. Burke, p. 167

Aquarian Effort. Oppenheimer, p. 464

"Teddy's Woman Problem/Women's Teddy Problem," *Washington Monthly*, December 1979

CHAPTER FIFTEEN

Epigraphs. Edward M. Kennedy campaign speech, 1980

Coke, booze and women and venereal disease scare. Burke, pp. 262–65

Christopher Lawford 1980 drug arrest and beyond. *People*, March 11, 1991

Joan and Jackie. Chellis, p. 213

Teddy linked to Louise Steel, Angela Wepper, Amanda Burden, Suzee Chaffee and Helga Wagner. David, p. 176

Teddy strolls naked. *GQ*, February 1990; Barbara Gibson, THE KENNEDYS, p. 205

Lacy Neuhaus. David, p. 106; Lally Weymouth, "Kennedy on the Sidelines," *New York Magazine*, June 27, 1983, p. 53; Taki, p. 103

Ted, Jr. arrest. Burke, p 298, 302

"I think he's got to put his private house in order . . ." Weymouth, p. 53

"Everyone knew Lem was queer . . ." Oppenheimer, p. 461

Robert F. Kennedy, Jr. 1983 drug arrest. *Time*, September 26, 1983; *Newsweek*, September 26, 1983; *New York Times*, February 13, 1995; *People*, February 27, 1995 and October 3, 1983.

David Kennedy, April 1984 drug treatment. Oppenheimer, p. 46

"20/20" 1985 Marilyn Monroe segment. *New York Post*, October 20, 1994

Teddy at *La Colline*, *GQ*, February 1990

"Tabletop consummation." *The New Yorker*, May 23, 1994

Teddy at *La Brasserie* 1985, *GQ*, February 1990; David, p. 106; *Globe*, May 7, 1991

Patrick Kennedy 1986 drug treatment. David, p. 205; *Cosmopolitan*, undated, 1992; *People*, November 7, 1994

Sheila and Joe II. Maureen Orth, "Sheila and Joe Kennedy," *Vogue*, February 1987, p. 363

Christopher and Jeannie Lawford drug treatment 1985. *People*, March 11, 1991

Teddy at *La Brasserie* 1987. *GQ*, February 1990; *Globe*, May 7, 1991

Teddy's youth outreach 1988. David, p. 107; *GQ*, February 1990

CHAPTER SIXTEEN: A New Generation in the Spotlight

Epigraph: "Neither Joe nor Jack was punished . . ." Michael Kelly, *GQ*, February 1990

"Blond-of-the-Month Club." David, p. 182

CHAPTER SEVENTEEN: Palm Beach Scandal

Epigraphs: Orrin Hatch. *GQ*, February 1990; "In the long downward slope . . ." *People*, April 1991; Palm Beach socialite, *People*, April 1991

Lisa Lattes statement. *Globe*, August 13, 1991

Lynn Gulledge statement. *Globe*, August 13, 1991

Joan Kennedy driving arrest 1992. David, p. 179

Edmund Reggie bank fraud conviction. *New Yorker* May 23, 1994

Willie Smith and Kelly Smith. *Globe*, February 22, 1994

Joan Kennedy alcohol treatment, 1993. *Star*, June 8, 1993; *National Enquirer*, July 13, 1993

Willie Smith and Kelly Squier. *Globe*, February 22, 1994

Willie Smith barroom brawl. *National Enquirer*, November 9, 1993; *Globe*, November 9, 1993; *New York Post*, July 28, 1994, *Star*, November 9, 1993.

Sheila Rausch. *Globe*, September 21, 1993

Joan Kennedy 1994 divorce action. *Star*, October 25, 1994; *Enquirer*, September 27, 1994

CHAPTER EIGHTEEN: Final Curtain

Michael Kennedy alcohol treatment, 1995. *New York Post*, February 13, 1995; *Star*, February 21, 1995; *People*, February 27, 1995.

Robert F. Kennedy marries Mary Richardson. Oppenheimer, p. 487, *New York Post*, August 23, 1995

BIBLIOGRAPHY

Anger, Kenneth, *Hollywood Babylon II*, Dutton, 1984: New York

Austen, Ian, "All in a Boston Family," *MacLean's*, September 8, 1986

Avery, Caryl S., "Jackie: A Mother's Journey," *Ladies' Home Journal*, March 1989

Bach, Steven, *Marlene Dietrich: Her Life and Loves*, William Morrow, New York: 1992

Blair, Joan and Clay, *The Search for JFK*, Putnam, New York: 1976

Boyer, Peter J., "We're Not in Camelot Anymore," *The New Yorker*, May 23, 1994

Brown, Peter Harry, and Patte B. Barham, *Marilyn: The Last Take*, Dutton, New York: 1992

Buck, Pearl S., *The Kennedy Women: A Personal Appraisal*, Cowles, New York: 1970

Burke, Richard E., *The Senator: My Ten Years With Ted Kennedy*, with William and Marilyn Hoffer, St. Martin's Press, New York: 1992

Cahan, William G., *No Stranger to Tears: A Surgeon's Story*, Random House, New York: 1992

Carmen, Jeanne, "True Confessions of a Hollywood Party Girl," *Globe*, January 17, 1995

Carpozi, George S., "The Ted Kennedy Story," *National Enquirer*, September 7, 1969

Cassini, Igor, *I'd Do It All Over Again*, G.P. Putnam's Sons, New York: 1977

Chellis, Marcia, *The Joan Kennedy Story: Living with the Kennedys*, Simon and Schuster, New York: 1985

Chin, Paula, William Sonzski and Katy Kelly, "Facing Divorce, Joe Kennedy Says No to Higher Office—For Now," *People*, March 27, 1989

Churcher, Sharon, and Ellen Hawkes, "The Weddings of the Summer," *Ladies' Home Journal*, August 1986

Clinch, Nancy Gager, *The Kennedy Neurosis: A Psychological Portrait of an American Dynasty*, Grosset & Dunlap, New York: 1973

Cohen, Mickey, *Mickey Cohen: In My Own Words as Told to John Peer Nugent*, Prentice-Hall, Englewood Cliffs, N.J.: 1975

Collier, Peter, and David Horowitz, *The Kennedys: An American Drama*, Warner Books, New York: 1985

Cook, Anthony, "The Man Who Bugged Marilyn Monroe," *Gentleman's Quarterly*, October 1990

Damore, Leo, *The Cape Cod Years of John Fitzgerald Kennedy*, Prentice-Hall, Englewood Cliffs, N.J.: 1967

David, Lester, *Good Ted/Bad Ted: The Two Faces of Edward M. Kennedy*, Birch Lane Press, 1993

David, Lester, "My Father, Robert Kennedy," *McCall's*, May 1988

David, Lester, "Caroline Kennedy at 30," *McCall's*, September 1987

David, Lester, "A Girl for Caroline," *McCall's*, September 1988

Davis, Deborah, *Katharine the Great: Katharine Graham and the Washington Post*, National Press, Bethesda: 1987

Dineen, Joseph F., *The Kennedy Family*, Little, Brown, New York: 1959

DuBois, Diana, *In Her Sister's Shadow: An Intimate Biography of Lee Radziwill*, Little, Brown and Company, Boston: 1995

Evans, Peter, "Our Most Famous First Lady's Second Marriage," *Redbook*, July 1986

Farrell, Jane, "Memories of Mary Jo," *Ladies' Home Journal*, July 1989

Feldman, Jill, "The Next Kennedy: Bobby Kennedy's Son Joe Carries the Torch into the Next Generation," *Gentleman's Quarterly*, September 1988 [cover story]

Gaines, Richard and Scot Lehigh, "The Littlest Kennedy," *The New Republic*, December 30, 1985

Gelman, David, et al., "The Kennedys: A New Generation Moves Up," *Newsweek*, September 8, 1986

Giancana, Sam and Chuck, *Double Cross: The Explosive Inside Story of the Mobster Who Controlled America*, Warner Books, New York: 1992

Gibson, Barbara, and Ted Schwarz, Rose Kennedy: *A Life of Faith, Family & Tragedy*, Birch Lane Press, New York, 1995

Goodwin, Doris Kearns, *The Fitzgeralds and the Kennedys: An American Saga*, Simon & Schuster, New York: 1987

Gould, Martin, "Bobby Kennedy Kid Checks Into Booze Clinic," *Star*, February 2, 1995

Gray, Kevin, and Cindy Dampier, "Best of Buddies," *People*, February 7, 1995

Griffith, Thomas, *Harry and Teddy: The Turbulent Friendship of Press Lord Henry R. Luce and His Favorite Reporter, Theodore H. White*, Random House, New York: 1995

Grogan, David, with S. Avery Brown, "Another Kennedy, Another Victory: Young Patrick Takes Providence," *People*, October 3, 1988

Gross, Michael, *Model: The Ugly Business of Beautiful Women*, Morrow, New York: 1995

Halberstam, David, *The Powers that Be*, Dell, New York: 1979

Harper's Bazaar, "New Talents: Patrick J. Kennedy," March 1989

Heymann, C. David, *Poor Little Rich Girl: The Life and Legend of Barbara Hutton*, Random House, New York: 1983

Heymann, C. David, *A Woman Named Jackie*, New York: New American Library, 1989

Higham, Charles, *Rose: The Life and Times of Rose Fitzgerald Kennedy*, Pocket Books: New York 1995

Jereski, Laura, "Shirtsleeves to Shirtsleeves," *Forbes*, October 21, 1991

Joyce, Ed, *Prime Times, Bad Times*, Doubleday, New York: 1988

Kappel, Kenneth, *Chappaquiddick Revealed: What Really Happened*, St. Martin's Paperback, New York: 1991

Kelly, Michael, "Ted Kennedy on the Rocks," *Gentleman's Quarterly*, February 1990

Kessler, Ronald, *Inside the White House: The Hidden Lives of the Modern Presidents and the Secrets of the World's Most Powerful Institution*, Pocket Books, New York: 1995

Kramer, Carol, "Those Spunky Kennedy Women," *McCall's*, October 1987

Kramer, David, "The Kennedy Complex: Why They Womanize," *McCall's*, August 1991

Kunen, James S., et al., "Frustrated Grand Jurors Say It Was No Accident Ted Kennedy Got Off Easy," *People*, July 26, 1989

Lacey, Robert, *Grace*, G.P. Putnam's Sons, New York: 1994

Lasky, Victor, *JFK: The Man and the Myth*, Arlington House, New Rochelle: 1966

Lessard, Suzanne, "Teddy's Women Problem/Women's Teddy Problem," *Washington Monthly*, December 1979

Likoudas, Paul, "Canonists and Theologians Say Faithful Have a Right to Know about Kennedy," *The Wanderer*, February 9, 1995

Madamoiselle, "The K-List: A Single Woman's Guide to the Kennedys," February 1992, p. 102

Martin, Ralph G., *Seeds of Destruction: Joe Kennedy and His Sons,* G.P. Putnam's Sons, New York: 1995

McCarthy, Joseph P., *The Remarkable Kennedys*

McGinnis, Joe, "The End of Camelot," *Vanity Fair,* based on *Senatorial Privilege: The Chappaquiddick Coverup* by Leo Damore, September 1993

Michals, Bob, "True Confessions of a Hollywood Party Girl," *Globe* January 17, 1995

National Star, "Exclusive: Marilyn Monroe Love Tapes," March 22, 1994

Ogden, Christopher, *Life of the Party: The Biography of Pamela Digby Churchill Hayward Harriman,* Little, Brown and Company, Boston: 1994

Oppenheimer, Jerry, *The Other Mrs. Kennedy: Ethel Skakel Kennedy: An American Drama of Power, Privilege and Politics,* St. Martin's Press, New York: 1994

Orth, Maureen, "Sheila and Joe Kennedy," *Vogue,* February 1987

Rainie, Harrison, "How Jackie Became Her Own Strong Woman, *Ladies' Home Journal,* September 1984

Rainie, Harrison, "Why Bobby Kennedy's Sons Went Wrong," *McCall's,* January 1984

Reeves, Richard, *President Kennedy: Profile of Power,* Simon & Schuster, New York: 1993

Rosenbaum, Ron, *Travels With Dr. Death and Other Unusual Investigations,* Penguin Books, New York: 1991

Safire, William, "The Kennedy Tapes," *The New York Times,* December 26, 1994

Scheim, David E., *Contract on America: The Mafia Murder of President John F. Kennedy,* Zebra Books, New York: 1988

Schlesinger, Arthur M., Jr., "Kerry On," *Vanity Fair,* June 1993

Schlesinger, Arthur M., *Robert F. Kennedy and His Times,* Ballantine Books, New York: 1978

Spada, James, *Peter Lawford: The Man Who Kept the Secrets,* Bantam, New York: 1991

Steinfels, Peter, "Kennedy Blessing Raises Questions for Catholics," *New York Times,* January 28, 1995

Swanson, Gloria, *Swanson on Swanson: An Autobiography,* Random House, New York: 1980

Taki, *Princes, Playboys and High-Class Tarts,* Karz-Cohl Publishing Co., New York: 1984

Thomas, Bill, *Club Fed: Power, Money, Sex and Violence on Capitol Hill,"* 199?

Towle, Patricia, "Big-Spending Joan Kennedy Hitting Ted for More Money," *National Enquirer,* September 27, 1994

Warhol, Andy, *The Andy Warhol Diaries,* edited by Pat Hackett, Warner Books, New York: 1989

Wayne, Jane Ellen, *Marilyn's Men,* St. Martin's Press, New York: 1992

Weymouth, Lally, "Kennedy on the Sidelines," *New York Magazine,* June 27, 1983

Whalen, Richard J., *The Founding Father: The Story of Joseph P. Kennedy,* New American Library, New York: 1964

Wilentz, Amy, "Can 'Daddy's Team' Be Beaten?" *Time,* September 8, 1986

Wilentz, Amy, "Meet the Newest Kennedy," *Time,* November 17, 1986

INDEX